Shakespeare's storms

Manchester University Press

Shakespeare's storms

GWILYM JONES

Manchester University Press

Published by Manchester University Press
Altrincham Street, Manchester M1 7JA, UK
www.manchesteruniversitypress.co.uk

British Library Cataloguing-in-Publication Data
A catalogue record for this book is available from the British Library

Library of Congress Cataloging-in-Publication Data applied for

ISBN   978 0 7190 8938 1 *hardback*

First published 2015

Typeset in Levato by
Koinonia, Manchester
Printed and Bound in Great Britain by
Lightning Source

For my parents

Contents

Acknowledgements

I am grateful to everyone at MUP for their help and understanding. The anonymous readers who provided comments on various stages of this book did so with enviable insight and I am very thankful.

Nicholas Royle's encouragement has left a great impression on my work. I do hope it shows. Nick has been one in a long line of noteworthy teachers through my life: without Catherine Withers and M. Wynn Thomas, I would not have come this far, and I remember them with gratitude and affection.

I am grateful to my former colleagues and students at Queen Mary, from whom I learned a great deal. In particular, I am indebted to Warren Boutcher, who provided invaluable support and advice throughout the project. I am grateful to William McEvoy and Mark Robson for their careful reading of the original thesis of this work, and for their judicious comments. I am also thankful to everyone at Shakespeare's Globe, in particular to Farah Karim-Cooper for her guidance.

A great many people have been generous with their time and intellects: Thomas Alexander, Eve Dirago, Mark Doman, Sarah Dustagheer, Maya Gabrielle, Jennifer Mae Hamilton, Natalie Lane, Sophie Leighton-Kelly, Mark Morgan, Ryan Nelson, Claire Rakich, Nicholas Robins, Will Rutter, Glyn Samways, Patrick Spottiswoode – I am obliged to them all. I am also grateful to my brother, Gareth, for being a good example, as well as putting his energy into transcendental number theory and giving me a free run at the easy stuff.

The warmth, hospitality and generosity of my parents-in-law, Bridget and Doug Morgan, has bordered on the miraculous, and Los Altos, Truckee and Kauai have all proved excellent places to forget Shakespeare.

My wife, Molly – the staff of my age, my yoke-fellow, with whose help I draw through the mire of this transitory world – puts up both with my arbitrary periods of tempestuousness and my unmerited periods of calm. And chuckles at my overblown quotations.

I owe the greatest debt to my parents, Celia and David, the first in that line of teachers, and to their parents also. Without them, all of this would be utterly unthinkable.

Earlier versions of Chapters 2 and 9 have been published elsewhere. Chapter 2 here is published with the permission of Cambridge Scholars Publishing, and Chapters 2 and 9 with the permission of Arden Shakespeare, as an imprint of Bloomsbury Publishing, PLC. I am grateful to these publishers for their permission, and to Pascale Drouet, Farah Karim-Cooper and Tiffany Stern, the editors of the collections in which the chapters appeared.

Textual note

Unless stated otherwise, all Shakespearean quotations are from *The Arden Shakespeare Complete Works*, ed. Richard Proudfoot, Ann Thompson and David Scott Kastan (London: Arden Shakespeare, 2001) and line references included in the text. All Biblical quotations, unless otherwise noted, are from the Geneva text of 1560, reprinted in facsimile as *The Geneva Bible: 1560 Edition* (Peabody, MA: Hendrickson, 2007).

When quoting directly from early modern texts I have altered *i, j, u, v* and *vv* where necessary, and included omitted letters where an elision is indicated, but otherwise preserved original spelling. So, for example, a phrase from II Kings 1:10 appears as 'let fyre come downe from the heaven' rather than 'let fyre come downe frō the heaue'.

Introduction

It is 1 May 2008, around 2:40 in the afternoon. I am standing in the yard of the reconstructed Globe playhouse in Southwark, watching the matinee performance of *King Lear*. For most of the first two acts, as the cast have been delivering a comic interpretation, the weather has been pleasant – a mild spring day. Now, though, as Goneril and Regan begin to trim their father's retinue – 'What, fifty followers? ... What should you need of more?' (2.2.429–30) – the skies above the open roof begin to darken. Some twenty-five lines later, when Lear's company has been whittled away entirely – 'What need one?' (455) – some fine raindrops begin to fall. As Lear delivers his impassioned but impotent reply, the rain grows faster and steadier. There is a rustling flurry in the yard, as the standees pull on their water-proof clothing. At Lear's exit, Cornwall's line is greeted with a warm laugh: 'Let us withdraw; 'twill be a storm' (476). The daughters and Gloucester debate Lear's destiny briefly as the rain gets heavier still. As they exit, the slam of the door prompts the first burst of staged thunder, and an almighty deluge falls. As Kent appears – 'Who's there besides foul weather?' (3.1.1) – the yardlings divide, some pressing towards the stage, and some towards the seating bays, all trying to try to squeeze under the slim overhangs of thatch. A wide strip of concrete in the yard is exposed, the thick down-pour skipping on its surface. The actors are virtually inaudible; Lear really is contending with the fretful element. I am heavily soaked, and pressed against the wooden divide between the yard and the front row of the seated audience. Behind me are two elderly ladies, leaning forward incredulously. As I pull my drenched hair away from my ears, I hear one say to the other, 'how are they *doing* this?'

I was, and am, delighted by this question. How better to illustrate the irreducible difference between performance conditions for early modern audiences and for our own? But though it may seem innocent, it is also a reminder that Shakespeare's storms have so far been misread, if not ignored. Taking this as my cue, I ask similar questions of those storms. What did Shakespeare understand weather to be? How do the storms affect current critical discourses, and change the way we experience early modern theatre? And yes, how *did* they do it?

Storms of separation and spectatorship

We split, we split, we split!
The Tempest 1.1.62

Shakespeare was remarkably fond of storms, not only in the stage effects he so often calls for, but in the metaphors and similes he gives to his characters. Indeed, if such images are included, there is some instance of storm in every Shakespearean play. Moreover, the storm is a trope that has carried across literature from ancient epic to twenty-first-century narrative non-fiction, from *Aenied* to *Zeitoun*. Although there is scope for a study of Shakespeare's storms that locates them in this literary tradition, my main emphasis is on the ways that the storm scenes can be read in the contexts of early modern theatrical practice, meteorological understanding and contemporary theory. This approach is inevitably exclusive and I have had to be selective. But whilst the details of individual plays are my focus, there is one panoramic view worth glimpsing.

If the storm in Shakespearean drama is to be thought of as functional, then its primary function is to separate characters. Most obviously, this separation is achieved with a shipwreck, as in *The Comedy of Errors, Twelfth Night, Pericles* and *The Tempest*. In *Othello*, a storm splits the Venetian fleet without splitting the ships themselves, with the effect that characters are divided briefly. The sea is not necessary for a storm to separate – in *King Lear*, the weather divides characters into indoor and outdoor groups – but it is tempting to view the shipwreck storms as motifs. This temptation is amplified if we concentrate on *The Comedy of Errors, Twelfth Night* and *The Tempest*, and the chronological detail that these plays date from the beginning, middle and end of Shakespeare's playwriting career. But these storms cannot be dismissed so neatly. Shakespeare, rather than re-use the same storm for each play, approaches each play with distinct requirements and concerns, made manifest in the texts and the storms themselves. What is ostensibly a recurring motif, then, reveals a progression from topos to topography, and concerns from the classical to the contemporary.

Within this progression, too, is a pattern. If Shakespeare's sea-storms are approached in chronological order then we see an increasing interest in bringing the storm into a more immediate, and thereby dramatic and threatening, presentation. In the development of Shakespeare's storms, there is, indeed, a calm before the storm. To illustrate this, here are those storms in the order in which they were written.[1]

In Egeon's narration in *The Comedy of Errors*, the storm is long in the past. It is digested and given narrative structure with a definite beginning, middle and end. Thus, Egeon starts his story: 'In Syracusa was I born', before eventually devoting thirty lines to the storm and subsequent shipwreck (1.1.36; 61–91). Compelling though Egeon's story may be, he has over four fifths of the lines in the scene. It is perhaps unsurprising that Shakespeare presents the next storm of separation differently. In *Twelfth Night* the fallout of the shipwreck is still happening: it is staged. The narrative is fragmented and the narrators unsure: 'Perchance he is not drown'd: what think you sailors?' (1.2.5). Rather than discover the characters' situations before they appear, as in *The Comedy of Errors*, we see them in the immediate aftermath, washed ashore and separated. Indeed, so great is the emphasis on the present as presented, that we are not told what caused the shipwreck: we tend to assume it is a storm, I suspect because of those in other plays, but an assumption it remains. Instead we have the lived experience of the survivor. In *Othello*, this immediacy is taken one step further: The sea-storm is happening, off stage. Again the narrative is fragmented, but is now also unfinished. For the first time, the sea-storm has spectators, both in the characters and in the audience themselves. Next comes *Pericles*, and the process of bringing the storm closer to the dramatic action continues. In Act 2, Scene 1, we have spectators in the Fishermen, and Pericles enters 'wet' (2.1.0sd). In Act 3, Scene 1, the sea-storm is staged. Here, the audience experiences the storm, and the separation of characters, along with the characters involved. When we come to *The Winter's Tale*, we find the sea-storm happening, off stage. The increasing immediacy peaked with *Pericles*, but this is partly the point. The separation of characters in the play is not a consequence of the storm, but rather is figuratively reinforced by the storm: 'In my conscience, | The heavens with that we have in hand are angry | And frown upon's' (3.3.4–6). The separation has already happened – the audience have seen it unravel in detail – the storm is a staged consolidation of it. In any case, the storm is quite immediate: although the shipwreck is not staged, it is foreseen from dry land, which is a novelty (3.3.3; 8–11). Again, there is a spectator, the Clown, who provides the story of the death of those on the ship. In his phrases, the immediacy is emphasised: 'Now, now: I have not winked since I saw these sights: the men are not yet cold under water' (102–3). Finally, in *The Tempest* is the conflation of everything we have seen so far. The sea-storm is staged, the mariners wet. The ship is wrecked before our eyes: 'We split, we split, we split!' Afterwards, several narrators give slightly different versions of the wreck, and each in turn different from the version seen by the audience. There are survivors, of course, who are separated. The play's opening storm consolidates each element of Shakespeare's earlier storms of separation. In Chapter 9, I argue that *The Tempest* goes further still. Ariel acts as a personification of theatrical storms, a move that has profound implications for the play's representation of environment.

Shakespeare, then, is not simply deploying the storm functionally, but is, rather, invested in developing its dramatic immediacy. From the earliest, though, the device also contains the symbolic possibility of separation from oneself. In *The Comedy of Errors*, once Egeon has narrated the story of the storm, Antipholus of Syracuse is introduced:

> I to the world am like a drop of water
> That in the ocean seeks another drop,
> Who, falling there to find his fellow forth,
> Unseen, inquisitive, confounds himself.
> So I, to find a mother and a brother,
> In quest of them unhappy, lose myself.
>
> (1.2.35–40)

The divisions that Antipholus notes here are the result of the storm which the audience learns of in the first scene, so it is particularly apt that his imagery is focused on the ocean. The sea, having been complicit in the separation of Antipholus from his 'fellows' is now the only medium for imagining the scale of that separation. And yet the argument is not related to the sense of division from others, but from himself: 'a drop ... confounds himself. So I ... lose myself'. It is especially touching that a twin emphasises his loss of self by constructing his identity as ultimately inseparable from countless identical others. Moreover, his speech, a soliloquy, is delivered after Antipholus has parted company with a merchant with the phrase 'Farewell till then. I will go lose myself' (30). From the outset, then, before any literal confusion of identity, the concept of individuality is troubled and elusive.

Whilst Antipholus of Ephesus appears self-assured and sociable in comparison with his brother, he has a similar sense of insecurity thrust upon him by his wife Adriana:

> O how comes it
> That thou art then estranged from thyself? –
> Thy 'self' I call it, being strange to me
> That, undividable, incorporate,
> Am better than thy dear self's better part.
> Ah do not tear away thyself from me;
> For know, my love, as easy mayst thou fall
> A drop of water in the breaking gulf,
> And take unmingled thence that drop again
> Without addition or diminishing,
> As take from me thyself, and not me too.
>
> (2.2.128–32)

As Adriana here mistakes her brother-in-law for her husband, the sense of self-loss is compounded for Antipholus of Syracuse, whose own simile is reconstructed for him. In his own terms, he is 'confounded'; his identity lost because of his proximity to an unknown other. The sense of confusion on Antipholus' part is evident. He is:

> As strange unto your town as to your talk,
> Who, every word by all my wit being scanned,
> Wants wit in all one word to understand.
>
> (151–3)

A loss of identity, then, which is so severe that it cannot comprehend the same construction of self which its speaker narrated 'but two hours' ago. The echo of simile is, in this respect, an auditory and linguistic confusion of identity to parallel the visual elements on which the farcical comedy of the play relies.[2]

The storm, then, continues to carry its work out after it has passed. In *The Winter's Tale*, this figurative power is more important than the practicalities of separating characters. In the play, we encounter the storm through the experience of the participants – Antigonus and the Mariner – but the shipwreck through the account of the spectator, the Clown. The Clown characterises the storm with classical paradigm: 'I have seen two such sights, by sea and by land! But I am not to say it is a sea, for it is now the sky: betwixt the firmament and it you cannot thrust a bodkin's point'[3] (3.3.82–5). The confusion of sea and sky in a storm is a poetic device as old as poetry itself.[4] In expanding on this, however, the Clown incorporates something that is quite new in Shakespeare's plays and worth quoting at length:

I would you did but see how it chafes, how it rages, how it takes up the shore! But that's not to the point. O, the most piteous cry of the poor souls! sometimes to see 'em, and not to see 'em: now the ship boring the moon with her main-mast, and anon swallowed with yest and froth, as you 'd thrust a cork into a hogs-head. And then for the land-service, to see how the bear tore out his shoulder-bone, how he cried to me for help and said his name was Antigonus, a nobleman. But to make an end of the ship, to see how the sea flap-dragoned it: but first, how the poor souls roared, and the sea mocked them: and how the poor gentleman roared, and the bear mocked him, both roaring louder than the sea or weather. (87–100)

The spectator of the shipwreck, although not as familiar as the sea/sky confusion, is also a classical commonplace. Compare this passage, for example, with the opening of Lucretius' second book of *De Rerum Natura*:

> What joy it is, when out at sea the stormwinds are lashing the waters, to gaze from the shore at the heavy stress some man is enduring! Not that anyone's afflictions are in themselves a source of delight; but to realise from what troubles you yourself are free is joy indeed.[5]

It is likely that Shakespeare would have encountered at least this passage from *De Rerum*: the first two lines (of the original poetic form) are quoted by Montaigne, whose essays are a key source of the playwright's imagery, phrasing and philosophical development at the time of *The Winter's Tale*. Florio's translation of Lucretius (via Montaigne) differs somewhat from the modern one quoted above: "Tis sweet on graund seas, when windes waves turmoyle, | From land to see an others greevous toyle'.[6] The context in which Montaigne quotes Lucretius is an apposite one for the first half of Shakespeare's play:

> Our essence is symented with crased qualities; ambition, jealosie, envy, revenge, superstition, dispaire, lodge in us, with so naturall a possession, as their image is also discerned in beasts: yea and cruelty, so unnaturall a vice: for in the middest of compassion, we inwardly feele a kinde of bitter-sweet-pricking of malicious delight, to see others suffer.[7]

Regardless of how much familiarity Shakespeare had with Lucretius's ideas, the passage from *The Winter's Tale* embodies the principles of the philosopher poet. The qualification of Antigonus as 'a nobleman' is indicative of the distance the Clown feels from him: not only physical and emotional but social too. The scene marks the transition in the play from tragedy to comedy; the abandonment of Perdita is a curse for Antigonus, a blessing for the family. The quotation also expresses the shift from courtly tension

to the Epicurean fulfilment that characterises the fourth act and is also the
defining feature of Lucretius' poetic philosophy. As Hans Blumenberg puts
it, 'the advantage gained through Epicurean philosophy is solid ground'.[8]
Each of these shifts, then, is embodied by the movement from shipwreck to
spectator – most fundamentally differentiated in the modulations of focus
from pain to pleasure, from winter to spring and from death to life.

By extension, we might read the metaphorical values of this scene into
the play's finale, as Leontes finds redemption in an act of spectatorship.
Just as the Clown is aware of his own inability to transcend his position
of spectator ('I would you had been by the ship side, to have helped her:
there your charity would have lacked footing' betrays that understanding as
much as a comic touch. 3.3.7–9) so Leontes revels in it: 'What you can make
her do, | I am content to look on' (5.3.91–2). Equally, the king is conscious of
the state which his experience of the 'statue' leaves him in, and a dialogue
of spectatorship is imagined: 'does not the stone rebuke me | For being
more stone than it?' (37–8) It is this realisation, of the effect of the power
of his beholding, that prompts his own inward looking: 'There's magic in
thy majesty, which has | My evils conjur'd to remembrance' (39–40). The
influence of spectatorship is also encapsulated by Perdita, in her final
words: 'So long could I | Stand by, a looker on' (85). In considering such
language here, it should be remembered, of course, that the very action of
the play depends entirely on the spectatorship of Leontes in the opening
act. From the outset, the king is invested in and affected by the processes
of spectating:

> But to be paddling palms, and pinching fingers,
> As now they are, and making practis'd smiles
> As in a looking-glass; and then to sigh, as 'twere
> The mort o'th'deer – O, that is entertainment
> My bosom likes not, nor my brows.
>
> (1.2.115–19)

Here, Leontes builds up his jealous rage; he conflates the emotional and
the bodily both in the object of his vision and his own subjectivity. This is
the same empathetic vision he experiences in the finale ('being more stone
than it'). *The Winter's Tale*, then, may be seen as punctuated by crucial acts
of spectating. The conversation between the three Gentlemen in Act 5 is
another notable example. The First Gentleman notes the limits of spectatorship: 'the wisest beholder, that knew no more but seeing, could not say
if th' importance were joy or sorrow' (5.2.17–19). The debate on spectating is
maintained when the two other Gentlemen appear: 'Did you see the meeting

of the two kings?' asks one (40–1). Upon the reply, he follows with 'Then you have lost a sight which was to be seen, cannot be spoken of', before spending over one hundred words speaking of it (43–59). In his speech, the issue of spectatorship and report is implicitly linked to the limitations of theatre, for which a compromising line must inevitably be drawn between what can be staged and what must be related through exposition. The figure of shipwreck with spectator in the midst of the storm is an integral part of the same structure.

It is the approach to issues of spectatorship that allows the play to develop themes found in *Pericles*. As I have mentioned, the first shipwreck of that work also receives comment from witnesses, albeit in a scene attributed to George Wilkins. As in *The Winter's Tale*, there is a notable comedic vein attributed to the role of spectator, as the fishermen joke and pontificate whilst discussing the storm: 'I am thinking of the poor men that were cast away before us even now' moves seamlessly to 'I marvel how the fishes live in the sea' ... 'as men do a-land: the great ones eat up the little ones' (2.1.18–24). The shipwreck spectators of both plays speak in calculatedly rustic prose. Similar instances of the use of opposites and moral platitudes characterise their conversation. They are, in short, quite alike, although the Clown is somewhat more energetic and moved by what he has seen. Where *Winter's Tale* builds on *Pericles'* foundations of spectatorship is in the respective resurrections of heroines. Thaisa is revived almost immediately following her 'death', whilst Hermione's reintroduction is saved for the finale of the play. In the case of *Pericles*, then, the audience's spectatorship is removed from that of Pericles and Diana themselves when their reconciliation finally occurs; the work of dramatic irony is to alter the position of spectatorship. In contrast, the audience of *The Winter's Tale* is emotionally aligned with Leontes in the witnessing of his wife's revival. Just as Leontes is a spectator, so are the audience – both of Hermione's reappearance and Leontes' observation. The development made in the later play, is, therefore, that the representation of spectatorship is more closely aligned with the aesthetic experience of drama itself. As Blumenberg has remarked, the conflation of the nautical and the theatrical 'is entirely plausible if the interiorized double role of the single subject – on the one hand tossed about by storms and threatened by death, on the other, reflecting on his situation – is to be presented'.[9] In *The Winter's Tale*, we have the case of this 'double role of the single subject' in the figures in the storm. We also find the figure of Leontes presenting a complementary kind of interiorised spectating as the revival of his wife becomes the platform for his reflection: 'No settled senses of the world can match | The pleasure of that madness' (5.3.72–3). It is the very maddening pleasure of spectating which the experience of *The Winter's Tale* relies upon; indeed, the very maddening pleasure of theatre itself. It is, perhaps, for this reason that Shakespeare's sea-storms tend towards increasing immediacy: the audience are made spectators of the storm, rather than listeners, as in *The Comedy of Errors*, or late witnesses, as in *Twelfth Night*. Spectatorship is the achievement of the storm of separation. But as we will see throughout this book, ideas of spectatorship are constantly probed and reworked in Shakespeare's storms. Indeed, the storms are dependent on Shakespeare's understanding of the expectations of his audience, and the ways in which those expectations can be avoided, subverted or exceeded.

Shakespeare's storms in theatrical context

The anecdote with which I began this book illustrates an important point about the storms of Shakespeare and his contemporaries. Performances at the Globe – whether in seventeenth-century or twenty-first-century Southwark – are open to a particular kind of dramatic irony: that of the environment. All performances take place on a stage, and for an audience, subjected to the elements.[10] When an actor delivers lines that prompt the audience to imagine the elements of the play-world, an automatic ironic relationship with the elements of the real world is established. In the case of that particular performance of *Lear*, the rain, remarkably, stopped at the interval at the end of Act 3, and the sun persisted for the second half. Almost every reference to the weather in Acts 4 and 5, however separate from the action or tone of the scene itself, was met with laughter and applause (in particular the Gentleman's lines describing Lear's halting convalescence, 'You have seen | Sunshine and rain at once', 4.3.17–18). The play's treatment of weather need not be as exhaustive as that of *King Lear*, of course. The damp summer months of 2012 saw the opening of the Globe's *Richard III*, in which Richard asks 'who saw the sun today' to which Ratcliffe replies 'Not I, my Lord' (5.3.78).[11] Of course, the real weather need not match the play's weather for this environmental irony to be available. Francisco's ''Tis bitter cold' can generate laughter in a heatwave, just as it can on a chilly day (*Hamlet*, 1.1.7). Obviously, there is no way of ascertaining whether or not Elizabethan and Jacobean audiences recognised or responded to environmental irony in the same way as modern theatregoers do. What we can say, though, is that Shakespeare and his fellow playwrights wrote for a form of playhouse in which environmental irony was conceivable and it is instructive to read plays of the period in light of this. Shakespeare's storms are always in a flux in performance, for no two sets of performance conditions are the same.

This environmental irony notwithstanding, however, it is possible to trace certain trends in the dramatic context of Shakespeare's writing life. Of all the critics who have written on storms in early modern drama, only Leslie Thomson has attempted a comprehensive study stretching across playwrights, in her essay, 'The Meaning of *Thunder and Lightning*: Stage Directions and Audience Expectations'. Thomson's argument is that "*thunder and lightning*" was the conventional stage language – or code – for the production of effects in or from the tiring house that would establish or confirm a specifically supernatural context in the minds of the audience'.[12] Given that the essay's focus is 'Elizabethan and Jacobean plays', the argument is, broadly, well founded, and supported by several examples. And yet if this 'specifically supernatural context' was indeed convention, then it was a convention subject to many variations and some subversions. There are numerous examples of Elizabethan and Jacobean playwrights teasing nuances out of this basic expectation. The examples of Shakespeare suggest that, faced with the effects of the staged storm, the audience should rarely have been confident in expecting anything conventional.

Thomson's argument relies, in part, on the assumption that rather than being 'theatrical in origin', 'the [thunder and lightning] effects were a theatrical representation of unnatural disruptions generally believed to accompany the appearance and actions of figures such as witches, devils, and conjurers in the real world of the audience'.[13] Moreover, the widespread belief in such figures 'meant less disbelief to be willingly suspended'.[14] The connection between the paranormal and storms is, of course, well established: Thomson cites Reginald Scot's *The Discoverie of Witchcraft* to support the claim, but there are several other sources with which it may be reinforced.[15] Less clear is whether the tradition of using storm effects to create a supernatural context can be ascribed to this popular belief, or whether it grew from a similar theatrical practice. Both angels and devils were directed to use fire effects, similar to those used for lightning, in mystery cycles and earlier Tudor secular plays.[16] Although the connection of witches and magi with violent weather can be traced to superstition, then, the similar connection of the forces of heaven and hell with storm has deep theatrical roots by the late sixteenth century. Of the examples cited by Thomson and others alluded to in her essay, there are just as many instances of thunder accompanying the descents of gods and ascents of devils as there are which accompany the specific act of conjuring. This would indicate, then, that whilst Elizabethan and Jacobean stage thunder panders to or reflects popular belief, it also operates as the successor to a more specific tradition of the theatre in which thunder and lightning is conflated with heavenly or hellish figures rather than the earthly beings who conjure them.

Thomson's essay supports its assertions with examples from several early modern plays in which the stage effects of thunder and lightning serve to establish a supernatural context, and there are many more examples that can be added. *The Devil's Charter*, by Barnabe Barnes, is a work that tells a fantastical version of the life of Pope Alexander VI and, in so doing, revels in the connection between storm effects and the supernatural. First performed *c*. 1606, the play embodies all of Thomson's arguments, several times over in spectacular detail. In a preludic dumb-show, a Monk draws circles on the stage, *'into which (after semblance of reading with exorcismes) appeare exhalations of lightning and sulphurous smoke in midst whereof a divil in most ugly shape'*.[17] This direction alone is enough to establish the familiar idea, but the dumb-show is emphatic in this point. Roderigo, who wants a particular quality of spirit, turns his face from the devil,

> *hee beeing conjured downe after* **more** *thunder and fire, ascends another divill like a Sargeant with a mace under his girdle: Roderigo disliketh. Hee discendeth: after* **more** *thunder and fearefull fire, ascend in robes pontificall with a triple Crowne on his head, and Crosse keyes in his hand: a divill him ensuing in blacke robes.*[18]

The repetition of the special effects reinforces the conflation beyond doubt. When the dumb-show is finishing, there is one final direction, *'this donne with thunder and lightning the divills descend'*.[19] In the dumb-show, then, the thunder, lightning and fire function as a symbolic definition of the liminal points between worlds. This function is re-employed later in the play to spectacular effect: 'Fiery exhalations lightning thunder ascend a King, with a red face crowned imperiall riding upon a Lyon, or dragon'; 'The divell descendeth with thunder and lightning and after more exhalations ascends another all in armor'; 'Devill desendeth with thunder &c.'; 'Thunder and lightning with fearefull noise the divells thrust him downe and goe Triumphing'.[20]

Barnes's play was performed by the King's Men. This company – for whom Shakespeare acted and wrote – were in an enviably secure position by this point. It is tempting to imagine that their properties really did include both a lion and a dragon, and that the King's ascent could thereby vary with each performance. But Barnes's use of the effects goes beyond those mighty set pieces. In addition to being used in the entrance and exits of the spirits, the effects are also recalled in the language of the play:

> With golden majesty like *Saturnes* sonne
> To darte downe fire and thunder on their foes.[21]

Or later:

> For beare your violence in the name of God:
> Fearing the scourge, and thunder from above,
> Our offers are both just and reasonable[22]

When the stage effects are as insistent as in *The Devil's Charter*, then these verbal reminders are resonant, particularly when 'the name of God' is juxtaposed for contrast, and a dialectic of good and evil established. Perhaps the most significant verbal instance in the play comes at its finale:

> Dead, and in such a fashion,
> As much affrights my spirits to remember,
> Thunder and fearfull lightning at his death,
> Out cries of horror and extremity.[23]

The death in question – that of Alexander at the hands of the devils – is the self-stated subject of the play, and this quotation follows the last incident of thunder and lighting, which it describes. There is, then, a definite closure of the play that echoes the way in which it began: with the thunder and lightning related to otherworldly characters. Moreover, the double meaning of 'spirits' here has the effect of adding human emotion to the fusion of storm and the supernatural, thus further, and finally, consolidating the notion of thunder and lightning as the sound of a boundary between mortal and immortal dimensions. Although Barnes's play is mostly known for its elaborate stage directions, it establishes a poetics of storm to complement its fiery effects.

Further examples of storm effects accompanying the supernatural abound. We might thinks of Robert Greene's *Friar Bacon and Friar Bungay* (c. 1589).[24] The brazen head, created by the magician Bacon, '*speaks and a lightning flasheth forth*'.[25] Perhaps the same effect is required earlier, as '*Bungay conjures, and the tree appears with the dragon shooting fire*'.[26] In any case, the notion that lightning is linked with conjuration is explicit. But there are also more subtle employments of the effect. In *The Puritan*, which was first performed in 1606, there is a definite ironic tone.[27] In this play when thunder is signalled Idle uses the convenient sound to reinforce the effect of his fraudulent conjuring of a devil. The sound effect is enough to convince the onlookers, one of whom comments: 'Oh admirable Conjurer! has fetcht Thunder already', shortly before another says 'O brother, brother, what a Tempest's ith'Garden, sure there's some Conjuration abroad'.[28] Thus the correlation of storm and the supernatural is staged and used metatheatrically: the gulls are, in effect, a naïve audience, operating on a basic level of understanding. Thomson notes the irony on which this episode relies, but does not examine it in detail.[29] Crucially, the characters' error is an aural one – they only see Idle through a keyhole, and the 'devil' is 'conjured' with a fake voice – for it is the sound of thunder even more than the flash of lightning which seems to establish the theatrical context of the supernatural. It is also a demonstration of the dramatically ironic reifying of theatrical effect: the audience understand that the staged sound is 'real' because the gulls understand it as supernatural. Hence layers of irony cover any possible deficiency in stage mechanics. As with my account of the performance of *King Lear*, all performances are open to environmental irony. As plays such as *The Puritan* demonstrate, the differentiated levels of weather can be stratified beyond a simple real/theatrical binary.

Other plays of the period also employ storm effects subtly. In Robert Armin's *The Valiant Welshman* (c. 1612), there is no sound directed to accompany the entrance of Fortune at the beginning of the play: '*Fortune descends downe from heaven to the Stage, and then shee cals foorth foure Harpers, that by the sound of their Musicke they might awake the ancient Bardh*'.[30] Although thunder and lightning often occurs simultaneously to descents from the heavens, then, Fortune here apparently enters in silence, especially if '*and then*' is taken literally. Despite the obvious supernatural context of the scene, it is the music that seems to cue the magic: '*The Harpers play, and the Bardh riseth from his Tombe*'.[31] Later in the play, however, as the Witch, her son and the evil Gloster plot the latter's revenge, the son conjures a spirit to 'havocke all the borderers of Wales'.[32] As he casts the spell, off stage, '*Thunders and Lightning*' is directed, which the Witch comments on:

> Now whirle the angry heavens about the Pole,
> And in their fuming choler dart forth fires,
> Like burning *Aetna*, being thus inraged
> At this imperious Necromantike arte.[33]

Thunder also sounds when the spirit enters, in the form of a serpent, both in this scene and later in the play.[34] Evident in the play, therefore, is the connection between storm and evil magic, to the extent that the latter is distinguished by stage effects whereas other supernatural events are staged in silence or with music. Similarly, Thomas Dekker's *If it Be not Good, the Devil is in it* (c. 1611), begins with the entrance of Pluto and Charon, '*at the sound of hellish musick*', but the effect of '*Rayne, Thunder and lightning*' is saved for Lucifer's entrance, with devils.[35] Again, the storm effects' correlation is with the specifically evil, rather than more broadly supernatural. The shifts between thunder and music are also evident in John Fletcher's play *The Mad Lover* (1617). Thunder is directed shortly before Venus descends. However, three lines after the direction for thunder comes the following: '*Musicke. Venus descends*'.[36] It is possible that there is a scribal error in the Quarto text, and that only one sound effect was meant for performance. If, however, the transcription is accurate, then the thunder acts as a signal of the supernatural rather than as its accompaniment. Chilax responds to the visit of Venus, 'I'le no more Oracles, nor Miracles |...| Am not I torne a pieces with the thunder?' Later in the scene, the same character has the line 'No more of that, I feare another Thunder', to which the response, 'We are not i'th' Temple man' reinforces the notion that thunder is only possible in the rarefied and magical setting of invocation.[37] As with Armin and Dekker's plays, the expectations of what thunder and lightning portend are troubled.

The most sustained engagement with storm effects in the period probably belongs to Thomas Heywood, who uses thunder in four of the five plays of his sequence, *The Ages*.[38] In the first of these plays, *The Golden Age* (c. 1610), Jupiter is presented with '*his thunder-bolt*', yet the sound effects are reserved for Neptune, whose epithet, '*Hee can make Tempests, or the waves appease*', is carried through in the stage direction which follows: '*Sound, Thunder and Tempest*'.[39] The episode, although similar to other examples, has the attraction of staging the meteorological understanding of its audience. Thus, a thunderbolt is construed as quite distinct from a tempest, which in turn, is separate from wind: '*Enter at 4 severall corners the 4 winds: Neptune riseth disturbed: the Fates bring the 4 winds in a chaine, and present them to Æolus, as their King*'.[40] Whilst the scene might be said merely to depict the attributes of the classical gods, the delineation of those attributes speaks to a meteorological model which had remained largely unaltered since the classical period. The sound effects of the storm, then, are still linked with the supernatural, but in a way that also enacts an allegorical template for the natural philosophy-based understanding of the Jacobean audience. At the beginning of the next play in the sequence, *The Silver Age* (c. 1611), the familiar formula is again revisited, free from any meteorological overtones: 'Thunder and lightning. Jupiter descends in a cloude'.[41] The effect is repeated several times in similar contexts through the play, most notably as Jupiter burns Semerle to death. Most dramatically of all, however, *The Brazen Age* (c. 1611) stages the death of Hercules: '*Jupiter above strikes him with a thunder-bolt, his body sinkes, and from the heavens descends a hand in a cloud, that from the place where Hercules was burnt, brings up a starre, and fixeth it in the firmament*'.[42]

As with the other plays discussed, though, there is more to these examples than the spectacular. This becomes apparent if the plays are viewed as a cohesive sequence. The descending of gods through *The Ages* becomes increasingly less prominent, just as their influence on the drama decreases. It is no coincidence that the fourth play, *The Iron Age Part 1*, contains no directions for thunder, or that in Part 2, we find only the following: '*They both wound him, at which there is a greate thunder crack*'.[43] The victim here is Agamemnon, whose dying speech reminds the audience of the difference between this thunder and that in the plays which have gone before:

> This showes, we Princes are no more then men.
> Thankes *Jove* tis fit when Monarches fall by Treason,
> Thunder to all the world, would show some reason.[44]

Despite Thomson's claims, this passage cannot be held up as a supernatural scene.[45] There is no descent of god here, nor ascent of devil, no conjuration or invocation of spirits. It is surely more fitting to read the episode in light of there being no supernatural intervention, when the three plays quoted above all use thunder differently. Agamemnon's lines might allude to Jove, but their purpose is to draw attention to his lack of intervention on the stage. Heywood here subverts the storm/supernatural relationship he elsewhere maintains, and does so with the effect of highlighting the sheer lack of influence held by the mortal characters. The lines quoted might just as easily represent the willingness of the human to ascribe deep importance to random weather events, subverting the tradition in order to mark that randomness more starkly. The audience expectations of which Thomson writes are also staged in the aftermath of Agamemnon's death: 'Prodigious sure, | Since 'tis confirmed by Thunder'.[46] The idea in Pyrrhus's lines that the thunder invests the situation with a specific level of meaning is related to the way in which Thomson claims the contemporary audiences generally thought. As we have seen, however, this level of meaning is not manifested in the play; indeed, it gradually diminishes over the course of the sequence.

The examples I have given do not contradict the notion that a play-house audience would expect some sort of supernatural element when storm effects were staged. They do, though, show some of the ways in which the expectation itself was not the end point, but rather a platform on which to build dramatic subtleties, whether poetic, ironic, thematic or sonic. Far from being an awkward and limited cliché, the storm effects and their accompanying associations could be worked and reworked for many differing nuances. It is, perhaps, this quality of theirs which so attracted Shakespeare – for the storms in Shakespeare's plays constantly shift in the way that they present the supernatural, or its absence. From his earliest *thunder and lightning* – in the *Henry VI* plays, to his latest – in the romances and *Two Noble Kinsmen* – the audience could rarely have been long in a posi-tion to interpret what they saw and heard decisively. For there are orthodox descents of supernatural figures (Jupiter in *Cymbeline*, Ariel in *The Tempest*) but there are also gods who do not come down, no matter how loud the effects, or the invocation. There are witches who enter to, or conjure with, the sound of thunder (*2 Henry VI*, *Macbeth*) but there are also characters for whom the effects are all too visceral, all too real. If there is anything approaching a constant in Shakespeare's staged storms, it is variability.

The question of which of Shakespeare's storm effects is earliest would doubtless be a contentious one, were it prized as highly as other Shakes-pearean puzzles. It is not simply a matter of the difficulty of claiming with any certainty which of the two contending plays was written first, *1* or *2 Henry VI*, for it is generally agreed that Shakespeare is one of several autho-rial hands in each. Are any of the scenes in which the effects are staged actually by Shakespeare? Could it be that he wrote the scene in *Part 1* (5.2) in which Joan Puzel invokes the spirits to the sound of thunder, but not that in which Talbot swears vengeance (1.4)? Could it have been the other way around, or did he write both or neither? Was Act 4, Scene 1 of *Part 2*, if that is Shakespeare's, earlier in any case? I am content to let such questions rest, and to concentrate instead on the plays as we have them, for the sake of space if not of sanity. Because the episode in *Part 2* offers illuminating connections with *Macbeth*, I will discuss it in Chapter 6. The storm effects in *Part 1*, however, are best discussed in light of the examples from Shake-speare's contemporaries that I have given above.

After Salisbury and Gargrave are shot on the turrets, Talbot swears revenge:

> He beckons with his hand and smiles on me
> As who should say, 'When I am dead and gone,
> Remember to avenge me on the French'.

> Plantagenet, I will [...]
> Wretched shall France be only in my name.
> *Here an alarum and it thunders and lightens*
> What stir is this? What tumult's in the heavens?
> Whence cometh this alarum and the noise?
>
> (1.4.91–8)

Talbot's initial response is enough to allude to the notion that the weather is responding to his oaths, or to the death of Salisbury. Although there is a hint of a connection between the storm and some sort of cosmic justice, there is no theophany. Here, then, the human apprehension of weather may allow for the possibility of the supernatural, but an apprehension only it remains. Talbot is not, apparently, soliloquising; Glansdale is still on stage. But for his questions concerning the noise to be answered, there is an entrance. Rather than a god or a devil, though, it is a messenger. We can read or hear the Messenger's lines either as an answer to Talbot's questions, or as an unrelated communication:

> My lord, my lord, the French have gathered head.
> The Dolphin, with one Joan de Puzel joined –
> A holy prophetess, new risen up –
> Is come with a great power to raise the siege.
>
> (99–102)

Having had the opportunity to understand the storm effects in the context of Talbot's oaths the audience is immediately given a fresh perspective. If we hear the Messenger's lines as answers to Talbot's questions, then the *thunder and lightning* become signifiers of maleficent forces – a cosmic rumble to complement the French alarum – a holy prophetess with a great power. In the space of a few moments the play's weather seems to echo Talbot's call for revenge and then change sides. If the audience recall the sound of the shot that kills Salisbury and Gargrave, which is also a pyro-technic effect, then it too may retrospectively take on a sinister character. There is certainly nothing fixed here, and the audience is surely left in a state of doubt. As Edward Burns puts it, 'Is this gunfire, a natural storm of a presage of witchcraft? The ambiguity is particularly effective in the context of the English paranoia in the face of (historically) superior French firepower and what seems like magic'.[47] This paranoia is both represented and questioned from the start of the play, at Henry V's funeral, as Exeter asks 'shall we think the subtle-witted French | Conjurers and sorcerers, that afraid of him | By magic verses have contrived his end?' (1.1.25–7). Exeter's question is paralleled by that which the audience asks of the staged thunder and lightning – with all of its dramatic connotations – three scenes later. The climax of this process is at the end of the play. Joan Puzel's encounter with the '*fiends*' who join her on stage in Act 5, Scene 3 has been an uncomfortable one for critics, who see it as reductive.[48] Critical discussion tends to emphasise the frequent accusations of witchcraft levelled at Joan through the play. But whilst the scene does suggest 'that Talbot was right all along', it does so in a way more subtle than generally acknowledged.[49] For it is not simply the slanders of the English knights that Joan's invocations confirm: it is also the play's signification of thunder. By staging a generic pairing of thunder and fiends, the scene suggests that the storm has been supernaturally charged throughout. Joan is depicted as living up to expectations – expectations that have been augmented throughout the play. The thunder that accompanies Talbot's oaths is the same noise as that which brings Joan's spirits on to the stage. In this scene, we see the 'great power' the Messenger warns Talbot of. But we also see that power abandon Joan. The actions of the fiends mark their rejection: '*They hang their heads* [...] *They shake their heads* [...] *They depart*' (5.3.38–44sd). The scene reifies the superstitions hinted at by Exeter, but also indulges in the fantasy that any French victory was brought about by dark magic. The association of storm and the supernatural means that that dark magic can be heard throughout the play, but its presence confirmed only at the finale. For this, the storm effects are required not only to suggest the supernatural, but also to raise doubt.

It is doubt, indeed, that persists through Shakespeare's storms. There are unambiguous instances: in *2 Henry VI* and *Macbeth*, as we will see, and in *Cymbeline*, '*Jupiter descends in thunder and lightning, sitting upon an eagle: he throws a thunderbolt. The Ghosts fall on their knees*' (5.4.93).[50] But generally the storm effects in Shakespeare's plays that are far less straightforward, and even *Macbeth*, as I will show in Chapter 6, is not as direct as it may appear. Perhaps Ariel's descent in *The Tempest* seems similar to Jupiter's: '*Thunder and lightning. Enter Ariel, like a harpy*' is directed shortly after '*Solemn and strange music, and Prospero on the top, invisible. Enter several strange shapes*' (3.3.53; 19). But, as I will argue in Chapter 9, the scene is a culmination of the play's treatment of storm, a treatment which depends on the effects being able to suggest very different things. Rather than the direct correlation of storm and the supernatural, Shakespeare insists more habitually on staging the human interpretation of the weather. Take, for example, *Julius Caesar*. As in *1 Henry VI*, the meaning of the weather (in addition here to the other 'prodigies') is debated: 'let not men say | "These are their reasons, they are natural" | For I believe they are portentous', runs Casca's argument. Cicero's response is 'men may construe things after their fashion | Clean from the purpose of the things themselves' (29–30; 34–5). These lines are a rebuttal both of Casca's point and of the dramatic tradition with which Casca's position coincides. Whilst there is a definite custom of theatrical signification that would suggest concurrence with Casca's reaction, it is not the driving force of the scene. Shakespeare, rather, stages 'the things themselves' and allows for, or indeed encourages the variety of possible responses. Hence in, for example, *King Lear, Othello, Pericles* and *The Winter's Tale*, the emphasis is on the human experience of the storm, rather than on the effects as a flat background for supernatural entrances.[51] Moreover, even in plays which do conflate the storm and the supernatural – *Macbeth* and *The Tempest*, say – there are characters voicing responses to the weather that are at odds with that conflation.

As I have been demonstrating, Shakespeare's storms can be read alongside a wide range of storms written by his contemporaries. Several of these other playwrights engage with audience expectations just as Shakespeare does, and utilise them for aesthetic effect. The basic storm/supernatural axis is a formula which we will continue to see Shakespeare complicate throughout this book. For when it comes to Shakespeare's plays, any audience alive to what Thomson calls 'the specific meaning of the use of thunder', is surely left wondering what that meaning specifically is.

Shakespeare's storms and ecocriticism

I think that I have already failed the test. In the title of her essay, Sharon O'Dair asks 'Is it Shakespearean Ecocriticism if it isn't Presentist?', and soon enough we are told that the 'short answer ... is "no"'.[52] Readers will have noticed, I am sure, my privileging of Globe productions, as though forming a theatrical hierarchy based on performance conditions. My notes betray an even more suspicious tendency, full as they are with signatures and folios and the names of booksellers who traded on stalls and not online. I suspect that I may be accused of coding 'presentists ... as unscholarly' and will be eyed warily by self-proclaimed ecocritics as a result.[53]

I do, however, think we can get along. Partly this is because I value the Globe not for its putative historical authenticity (which, in any case, would quickly see me thrown out of the historicist club too) but for its capacity to illustrate that Shakespeare's plays are living artefacts, always subject to reimagining anew, often accidentally. Partly it is because the juxtaposition of the historical perspective and modern lived experience is illuminating. I'm not writing this book because the world is ending, but I do think that it has implications for those who want to read early modern drama in that way. For example, another important idea raised by that overheard question in the Globe – how are they doing this? – is the notion that the weather in theatres can be controlled. It is hardly so farfetched: audiences in indoor theatres will often see manufactured rain in *Lear*'s third act, or whenever else it is deemed appropriate, and thanks to modern sound technology will hear recordings of thunder too.[54] The question, then, was one that came from a familiarity with the theatre, however anachronistic it may have been at the Globe. The will to control, or fantasy of controlling, weather is surely of interest to many ecocritics, and can be read through performance studies just as it can in *Lear*'s lines. Similarly, by acknowledging the environmental irony of Shakespeare's plays, we can come to appreciate Timothy Morton's contention that 'A more honest ecological art, would linger in the shadowy world of irony and difference'.[55] Chapter 6 shows that *Macbeth* stages different concepts of the weather – natural and supernatural – and keeps them ironically separate. An activist might insist that this aesthetic move finds remarkable analogies in positions propounded by climate change deniers, and that Duncan notes the sweetness of the air up to the point that Macbeth, of the filthy air, kills him. But the play does not need to be brought into the present for its ecology to ring true to us: its 'shadowy world of irony and difference' is unavoidable once brought into the light.

Of chief importance, though, is the fact that ecocriticism can benefit from historicist perspectives. There is little in the way of advocacy or activism to be found in my arguments, and so I also fall foul of Simon C. Estok's criteria for 'Doing Ecocriticism with Shakespeare'.[56] However, Estok's work on theorising 'ecophobia' would be stronger for a little historical awareness. The knowledge, for example, that the actor playing Lear would be seeing real fire spitting when he said 'Spit fire' on the early modern stage is surely crucial to Estok's claims. The concept of ecophobia would thereby have to take on board the ways in which an audience could be excited, scared and alienated simultaneously by the stage effects of the playhouse as well as the poetry of the play. Indeed, as terror or phobias surely reside in the blurring of distinctions between real and imagined threats, the hyper-real representation of lightning on the early modern stage may be seen as a necessary adjunct to all that is terrifying or phobic about nature in *King Lear* or any other stormy play. A historically informed criticism – one that places at its centre the material context of production in the early modern playhouses

– is therefore necessary if presentist approaches are to develop their theories fully, just as present concerns shape the interests of historicist critics. Evidence and discussion of material practices of renaissance theatre can enrich ecocritical thinking, whether it 'counts' as 'doing ecocriticism' or not. Estok claims that 'It is the activist ambitions that have differentiated us [the ecocritics] and what we seek to do from the legions of staid thematicists who muse endlessly as the world smolders to an end'.[57] In so doing, he misses the intersections of thematic and activist criticism and, curiously, figures the former as the passive spectator. As we have seen, Shakespeare's storms amount to a career's worth of engagement with the idea of spectatorship. Thematic studies can teach us not only what to look at, but also how to look at ourselves looking. The greatest activist ambition that literary ecocritics can pursue is that of convincing readers to think more carefully about – and hence to be more careful with – the environment. But the environment is a sociocultural construction, as well as anything that it is in manifest reality or scientific evidence.[58] As such it is understood as forged by the circumstance of thought, belief, art. For Shakespeare, the environment is theatre, and theatre environment. Convincing Shakespearean readers and audiences to think more carefully about the environment, therefore, requires an exploration of its theatricality.

The understanding that our representations of weather are fundamentally affected by the real weather, and that our experience of the real weather is fundamentally aesthetisced by dramatic weather prompts us to remember that activism is about changing minds, not actions. We are allowed to consume carbon fuels, fill land with rubbish, factory farm other sentient beings and so forth, precisely because our understanding of our relationship with the environment is aestheticised. As Morton puts it, 'democracy is well served by irony, because irony insists that there are other points of view that we must acknowledge'.[59] Those points of view may even be our own. Any encounter with environmental irony, whether storms by Shakespeare, or, say, silence by John Cage, makes us briefly uncannily aware of our latent environmental attitudes. Understanding and exposing the means by which Shakespeare stages these uncanny moments requires an approach grounded in a thorough appreciation of early modern theatre. Any ecocritical thinking must be shaped by our understanding of the past, as well as the threat of any putative, punitive, future. Just as we cannot totally shake off present concerns when uncovering historical contexts, nor can we fully explicate our understanding of the present without examining its foundations, available to us in cultural, societal, religious or artistic artefacts. This examination must take into account the material circumstances of production if the subsequent understanding is to be informed. One thing environmental irony does is remind us that storms in the early modern playhouses are invariably open to the metatheatrical, and Shakespeare's storms in particular are always alive to this possibility. Again, for Shakespeare, theatre is environment, environment theatre. An awareness of this brings the two critical approaches of ecocriticism and theatre history together. Theatre history stands to gain an appreciation of the ways in which its discoveries of material practice can be brought to bear on current events or movements in theory. Scholars of performance must acknowledge the importance of special effects not only for the sake of drawing faithful reconstructions but also as evidence of early modern fears, desires, superstitions and expectations. Ecocriticism, meanwhile, stands to gain an understanding of the representations of the environment that are rooted in early modern theatrical practice.

Of the work that brings an ecological approach to early modern literature, still the most wide-ranging and ambitious is Robert N. Watson's *Back to Nature*.[60] Watson argues that the origins of the modern ideas of nature as sacrosanct are located in the 'Late Renaissance', and his book examines 'artistic responses to the nostalgia for unmediated contact with the world of nature'.[61] *Back to Nature* amounts to an anatomy of early modern epistemology, drawing on several areas of anxiety – theological, political, economic, scientific – to explain 'nostalgia for Eden, for the Golden Age, for an idealized collective agrarian feudal England, and for a prelinguistic access to reality'.[62] In not knowing themselves, then, the Late Renaissance subjects Watson pieces together provoke the idea of nature as a truthful and direct experience. The consequences of this idea have been outlined in great detail by Morton, whose *Ecology Without Nature* argues that any notion of 'nature' is essentialising and deeply troubling for the ecological: 'to contemplate deep green ideas deeply is to let go of the idea of Nature, the one thing that maintains an aesthetic distance between us and them, us and it, us and "over there"'.[63]

How to reconcile such approaches with a study of Shakespeare's storms? In staging thunder and lightning which is not an indication of supernature, but a representation of natural phenomena, Shakespeare's plays offer a critique of the relationship between human beings and their environment. Taking Leslie Thomson's conclusion, Gabriel Egan argues that the fact that the storm in *King Lear* 'is only a meteorological phenomenon, is a trap that the character and the playhouse audience are led into'.[64] Leaving aside the troubling notion that a character can be tricked by a device that operates on audience expectations, let us concentrate on what such a conclusion means. Firstly it surrenders the idea that the audience are familiar with plays such as *Julius Caesar* in which the origins and meanings of thunder and lightning are debated without supernatural figures. Secondly it assumes that, having listened to, for example, Lear's first two speeches in the storm, an audience would still expect a god to descend. In every example we have seen in which the storm and the supernatural are conflated, the amalgamation happens very quickly – within the space of a few lines – if not simultaneously. Thirdly, and perhaps most importantly, Egan's argument loses sight of the environmental question. *King Lear* need not rely upon theatrical traditions of thunder and lightning and spirits. Rather, Shakespeare stages the problems of constructions of nature as other. In the widespread juxtaposition of storm and the supernatural, is the implicit notion that weather is to be treated with suspicion and to be feared, or else revered. Also, and crucially, it conceives the weather as *to be controlled*. In Shakespeare's play, storm and the psyche are figured as interdependent in Lear's speech:

> Thou think'st 'tis much that this contentious storm
> Invades us to the skin. So 'tis to thee;
> But where the greater malady is fixed,
> The lesser is scarce felt. Thou'dst shun a beat,
> But if thy flight lay toward the roaring sea
> Thou'dst meet the bear i'th' mouth. When the mind's free,
> The body's delicate. This tempest in my mind
> Doth from my senses take all feeling else
> Save what beats there: filial ingratitude.

> (3.4.6–14)

Here, the separation of body and mind is remarkable for many reasons, though perhaps most importantly, for *not* being a separation of body and soul. The speech figures the mind as enabling the organs of awareness, 'my senses' to apprehend the weather: 'When the mind's free, | The body's delicate'. The weather, then, depends upon the human perception of it. The important storm in this respect, therefore, is not the one suggested by the stage effects, but the figurative one which interrupts that human perception: 'This tempest in my mind'. These different storms operate as an allegory of the human relationship to the environment. Watson's work is illuminating here: the 'prelinguistic access to reality' of the free mind which is the essentialising drive towards the experience of Nature is offered linguistic capability by that experience: the external storm allows for the creation of the internal. Nature remains as 'outside' here, therefore, even in the most extreme representation of its proximity. This is equally clear in the idea that Lear's speech creates the storm just as Lear responds to it. The weather in *Lear* exists only in the apprehension of those who are involved in it, just as we in the audience or as readers must surely realise that we are involved in climate change, just as we constantly refine and redefine our notions of what climate change is and how we are to deal with it. I return to the performativity of storms – their creation through language as well as through stage effect – in particular when dealing with *King Lear* and *Macbeth*. It should be remembered then that the questions I raise in such an approach are necessarily ecological as well as thematic. Chapter 4, on *King Lear*, speaks to ecocritical ideas about wilderness and shows that the play's representation of nature has been misunderstood. Chapter 6, on *Macbeth*, details the way in which early modern anxieties about the supernatural allow for, or prompt, a play with discrete weather systems. *Pericles*, too, is a divided play, and in Chapter 8, I show that its 'lasting storm' is a performance aesthetic that bridges the divisions and allows us to think more carefully about them.

This, then, is a book that uses the discourses of performance history and ecocritisim to argue that Shakespeare's storms have so far been misread or ignored. The storms represent changing theatrical and technical practices. These practices are the focus of Chapter 2, which argues that Shakespeare's investment in storm in *Julius Caesar* is a canny, financial one, for Shakespeare seriously considered the impact of the special effects of thunder and lightning when writing staged storms. In the case of *Julius Caesar*, this amounted to an attempt to create the sense of the new Globe as an exciting venue, where poetic eloquence is matched with spectacular display, one designed to generate an instant reputation for the playhouse. That playhouse, I argue, had a capacity for special effects that can be mapped onto the text of the play.

The storms also represent the evolving understanding of meteorological phenomena in late sixteenth- and early seventeenth-century England. I therefore include chapters on thunder, lightning, wind and rain. These phenomena are so familiar that we take for granted our understanding of them. In so doing, we lose sight of poetic nuances, some of which I hope I recover. Finally, in Chapter 9, I show that *The Tempest* has something to offer for each of the approaches I take throughout the book. Ultimately, Shakespeare's representation of storms is one of character, as Ariel becomes the storm he narrates. Ariel is the ultimate pathetic fallacy, the personification of the storm as a character. Fundamentally, *The Tempest* highlights the dramatic quality of its presentation of nature. In order to achieve this, the storm in the first scene must be rendered convincingly, for only then is the theatricality of the human apprehension of nature exposed. In order to make this move work, the play has to draw on highly unusual staging practices – practices that find their most lucid conceptualisation in current ecocriticism.

1

Thunder

Pyrrhus stood,
And like a neutral to his will and matter,
Did nothing.
But as we often see against some storm
A silence in the heavens, the rack stand still,
The bold winds speechless, and the orb below
As hush as death, anon the dreadful thunder
Doth rend the region; so, after Pyrrhus' pause
Aroused vengeance sets him new awork[.]

Hamlet 2.2.481–9.

The Player's speech seems to glorify delay. Pyrrhus's pause has a purpose: to arouse vengeance. That vengeance, thunder-like, contrasts, of course, with the inaction of Hamlet, who listens to this speech. Here the delay is a means to aggrandise the action: there is a kind of potential energy in the image throughout. It is apparently a coincidence that the *Oxford English Dictionary*'s first noted instance of the phrase 'the calm before the storm' is nearly contemporaneous with *Hamlet*.[1] The idea had been in currency for several years previously, and the phrase 'after a storm comes a calm' for decades before that.[2] In *Hamlet*, the idea resonates with the play's theme, and its fatal dénouement. I offer it here, though, as it is specifically concerned with thunder. In this brief chapter, I will outline the meteorological understanding of thunder in early modern England, before examining the ways in which such understanding helps us to read lines like the Player's.

Meteorological principles in early modern England were largely derived from the work of classical philosophers. Of these works, the first to attempt to unify a theory of the weather into one system was Aristotle's *Meteorologica*.[3] In the *Meteorologica*, Aristotle explains atmospheric phenomena in a way which is recognisable to any reader of similar texts from Elizabethan and Jacobean England: a system of 'exhalations' and 'vapours', which are together best understood as 'evaporations'.[4] Aristotle's theory states that the sun draws these evaporations upwards, potentially through three regions of the air, during which process, they account for all various types of weather. Vapours, warm and moist, are drawn from bodies of water, rivers, bogs and marshland. The exhalations, by contrast, are hot and dry, and drawn from the earth. As the evaporations rise, they change in temperature – caused by the air's different regions, proximity to the sun or the varying temperature of the sun itself – and this change is manifested in different types of weather, or meteor. Which meteor occurs depends on the mixture of evaporations and how their temperature is altered. From vapours come rain, snow, clouds, hail, frost and mist, whilst exhalations produce thunder and lightning, winds, comets and earthquakes as well as the occasional airborne fireball. Our modern notion of a storm, then, with rain, thunder, lightning and wind, requires several simultaneous evaporations producing discrete meteors. Many other atmospheric phenomena are accounted for by the reflection of sun, moon or stars, in configurations of airborne vapours. This group of phenomena, which includes rainbows and multiple suns, are known as 'reflections'.[5]

Although meteorological theory in early modern England was based on the principles outlined by Aristotle, it was more specifically derived from the Roman thinkers who translated the texts from the Greek. Within the works of Plutarch, Seneca and, in particular, Pliny the Elder, exhaustive summaries are available of Aristotle's system and the additions made by subsequent generations. As the Roman thinkers collected and commentated on meteorological theories, the empiricism of Aristotle was 'embellished with ... many elements of wonder and even superstition'.[6] Both of these elements, as we shall see, are found in many of the meteorological writings of Elizabethans and Jacobeans, whether scientific text or artwork.

Fortunately for our purposes, the Elizabethan and Jacobean meteorologists clearly found thunder and lightning fascinating. As S. K. Heninger writes, '[n]o phenomenon, in fact, was more carefully and variously explained – by the meteorologian, the astrologer, and the merely superstitious'.[7] Whilst Aristotle's model of the processes by which thunder and lightning are produced still held firm for such writers, the opportunity to expound it in fresh language was clearly appealing to, and popular with readers. A common feature of the weather phenomena I will be examining is that each was thought to come from clouds. A brief description of clouds is therefore an appropriate starting point:

> A Cloude is a *vapor* cold and moist, drawn out of the earth, or waters by the
> heate of the sunne, into the middle region of the ayre, where by colde it is so
> knit together, that it hangeth untill either y^c waight or some resolution cause
> it to fall downe.[8]

This description is taken from *A Goodly Gallery*, a work of meteorology by
William Fulke first published in 1563. Fulke's text was a great success, and
was reprinted in varying editions at least five more times in the following
eighty years. That success cannot be attributed to novelty: Fulke's theory
here is essentially the same as one of Pliny's, just as Pliny's is elicited from
Aristotle.[9] Yet what Fulke lacks in innovation, he makes up for in concision. Pliny is concerned with the height of clouds, and discusses the matter
in some detail.[10] Aristotle tries to solve the puzzle of why – if cold forms
clouds – there are no clouds in space.[11] Fulke, though, simply accounts for
the processes behind meteorological phenomena; his inquisitiveness is
directed at those processes, and no further. For Fulke, the cloud is vapour
held together by cold, and contains the potential energy to fall.

When the condensed vapour of a cloud traps an exhalation, then
thunder can result:

> Thonder is a sound, caused in ye cloudes by the breaking out of a whote
> & dry *Exhalation*, beating against the edges, of the cloude ... but when the
> whot *Exhalation* cannot agrée with the coldnes of ye place, by this strife being
> driven together, made stronger and kendled, it wil neades breake out which
> soden & violent eruption, causeth ye noyse which we cal thonder.[12]

As with his explanation of clouds, Fulke's account of lightning can be traced
back to Aristotle.[13] Although the Roman commentators do broadly accept
the same explanation, however, other, more fanciful theories are advanced
alongside. A falling star, for example, might cause thunder and lightning if it
strikes a cloud.[14] These theories are outlined but rejected by Fulke. However,
whilst Fulke's default position is Aristotelian, his method of reasoning is
not. He counters the theory of falling stars in an explicitly Christian way:
'it is evident that ye starres of the firmament can not fall, for God hath set
them fast for ever, he hath geven them a commaundement whiche they
shal not passe'.[15] This argument highlights a curious aspect of early modern
meteorology: God rarely features in explanations of the weather. Meteorological phenomena are generally explained as natural processes, with two
exceptions. Either God interferes directly or some dark supernatural power
subverts the natural order. There are examples of both of these exceptions in
Shakespeare's plays, and they are discussed below.[16] The grey area between

these exceptions and the natural processes is, of course, substantial and there are examples throughout this book of it being exploited. Thunder might be the result of an exhalation trapped in a cloud, but that same thunder could equally be interpreted as the voice of God[17] or the work of a witch, depending on the vested interest of the interpreter. Alongside this is the shifting body of superstitions to consider. In this wide opportunity of interpretation, perhaps, lies the appeal of weather as metaphor.

How does an understanding of the basic meteorology of thunder contextualise the reading of dramatic poetry? Fulke's description of thunder is typical in that it stresses the fierce nature of the phenomenon: *breaking, beating, strife, violent eruption*. That sort of evocative diction is found in all meteorological descriptions of thunder from the period. The storm is necessarily vicious before the effects are seen or heard. Although thunder is simply a noise, then, and the truly damaging potential of a storm lies in lightning, wind and heavy rain, thunder itself is conceived as violent.

Hence in the Player's speech, it is the thunder that is damaging: 'anon the dreadful thunder | Doth rend the region'. Rather than being a signal that destruction is about to occur, the thunder is itself part of that destruction. Similarly, Volumnia's call to Coriolanus 'To imitate the graces of the gods | To tear with thunder the wide cheeks o' the air' has implied devastation before the 'bolt | That should but rive an oak' (5.3.152–4). Such images are not based on thunder being a violent noise, but the received understanding that it is a destructive process.

Whilst the connotations of violence attached to those images stem from contemporary meteorology, thunder is also a commonplace metaphor for loud volume. Here, as with meteorology (perhaps even more so) it is difficult for the twenty-first-century reader to imagine fully the differences between our experience and that of an Elizabethan. Late sixteenth-century England was a much quieter place, without traffic and aircraft noises or cinema or volume controls. Hence, the loudness of thunder is often mentioned (Prospero's 'dread rattling thunder', for example (*The Tempest* 5.1.44). But also, the available metaphors for loud volumes are limited in number, and it is not surprising that thunder should occur so often in this context. Cleomenes's speech in *The Winter's Tale* is a good example:

> But of all, the burst
> And the ear-deaf'ning voice o'th'Oracle,
> Kin to Jove's thunder, so surpris'd my sense,
> That I was nothing.

> (3.1.8–11)

Here the loud noise of the oracle's voice is suited to the comparison with thunder, as it lends each a heavenly or otherworldly context. The same might be said of Pericles's exhortation to 'thank the holy gods as loud | As thunder threatens us' (5.1.199–200). But the metaphor is also found in more earthly contexts. Take, for example, the terrified question normally ascribed to Gertrude: 'Ay me, what act | That roars so loud, and thunders in the index?' (Hamlet 3.4.52–3). Other loud noises open to experience for Shakespeare's audience include artillery, trumpet alarums and drums, all of which could be encountered in the open-air playhouses of London. Indeed, as we shall see in Chapter 2, those battle noises were a constituent part of dramatised thunder and so perhaps it is unsurprising when the two noises are connected. This is the case, for example, in King John, as the Bastard boasts of a drum that 'shall | As loud as thine rattle the welkin's ear | And mock the deep-mouth'd thunder' (5.2.171–3). Frequently, images of thunder involve the conflation of violence and volume, as when Petruchio promises to tame Kate: 'For I will board her though she chide as loud | As thunder when the clouds in autumn crack' (The Taming of the Shrew 1.2.94–5). In this image, the loudness and the cracking belong to Kate, but Petruchio's threat is to overcome both. Elsewhere the volume level is enough to understand what type of prediction is meant: ''tis like to be loud weather', notes the Mariner in The Winter's Tale (3.3.11).

There is a great deal more to Shakespeare's engagement with thunder than I have outlined here. As well as the basic meteorology, there are superstitions; in addition to imagery, we find the sound effects of the stage. These will be addressed in the following chapter, on Julius Caesar. Even with the cursory sortie into thunder above, though, we can find points of contrast between early modern understanding and experience of thunder, and our own. Those distinctions show that thunder is not as familiar as we might casually think. Thunder is not simply loud, but is a touchstone of loudness. It is not just a metaphor for violence but is conceived as violent in and of itself. Such contrasts must be attended to when dealing with the storms of Shakespeare and his contemporaries.

2

Storm and the spectacular: *Julius Caesar*

Julius Caesar is a pivotal text, containing as it does Shakespeare's first staged storm.[1] In the time between the indelicate lightning of the *Henry VI* plays, the narrated sea-storm of *A Comedy of Errors* and this tragedy, the playwright has clearly developed a far more deft approach to the nuances of the device. It is in *Julius Caesar* that we find the underpinning of the later storms of *King Lear*, *Macbeth* and *The Winter's Tale*, in which the portent and significance of the weather are debated. The Roman play, however, goes far beyond simple groundwork and, as with each of Shakespeare's great storm plays, *Julius Caesar* emerges with a singular oragious identity. The chief characteristic of this identity, I will argue, is the play's engagement with the spectacular, in which the storm itself plays a major part. The first part of this chapter will be concerned with questions about the staging of the storm, exploring the opening of the Globe, the legacy of theatrical storm effects and the evidence for their use in the original production of 1599. This section will address the considerable question, 'why is Shakespeare's first staged storm in this play?' I will then look at the pertinent example of a noteworthy storm in London, 1599, and examine the ways in which it might have been interpreted. Finally, I will draw these two lines of inquiry together to investigate the ways in which Shakespeare depicts weather interpretation in the text of *Julius Caesar*.

To begin, then, with the spectacular. *Julius Caesar* contains several moments that encapsulate the importance of spectacle in gaining and consolidating power. Most obviously, perhaps, the corpse of the freshly dead Caesar becomes a contested prop; it is a battleground of interpretation for the conspirators and Antony. The conspirators 'bathe' their hands in Caesar's blood to reinforce their cries of 'Peace, Freedom and Liberty' to the citizens (3.1.105–11). The self-dramatisation of Cassius which accompanies this act reinforces the significance of the spectacle: 'How many ages hence | Shall this our lofty scene be acted over... ?' (111–12). For the conspirators, Caesar's blood is a sign that his physical body – and by implication his ambition – is 'No worthier than the dust' (120). Antony's employment of the corpse, in contrast, is the climax to a crescendo of props. He enters with the body (3.2.40sd) and refers to it throughout his eulogaic speeches. But before the body is revealed, the people are shown the will of Caesar (130) and his mantle (168). To each of these props is given an interpretation, a narrative. Through Antony's manipulation, the will of the people is driven by the production of display: 'If you have tears, prepare to shed them now...' (167), he says. But before removing the mantle from the corpse, Antony narrates the body's significance and its signification: it becomes a symbol of the betrayal to which he has succumbed – 'then burst his mighty heart' (184) denotes a grieving, metaphorical death, rather than a literal one. Antony's management of the stage spectacle outdoes the conspirators' interpretation, so that he may name their crime: 'bloody treason' (190). In this way, we see that the power rests not simply in those who theorise the role of theatre in history, as the conspirators have done, but in the recognition of the potential of hierarchical exhibition – that is, the corpse is a more effective display than the conspirators' 'red weapons' (3.1.109), especially when it follows the show of the will and the mantle. This efficacy is encapsulated by the First Plebian's response: 'O piteous spectacle' (3.2.196).

Even without the storm, then, here is a play concerned with the influence of display, its interpretation and its language. The political implications of this quality have already been explored.[2] This chapter however is more concerned with the ways in which the storm scenes fit into a wider reading of a further kind of display: the play's advertising and empowerment of the new Globe playhouse. For in considering the storm and the spectacular in *Julius Caesar*, it is crucial to bear in mind that it was one of the first plays to be performed at the original Globe theatre, when it opened in the early summer of 1599.[3] Whether it was indeed the playhouse's opening play or not, it is certainly a work invested in the new theatre. Because of this, I want to consider *Julius Caesar* as a prime example of theatrical bravado: it is the work of a playwright with the keys to a new playhouse; one with a fresh and eager audience; the work of a playwright, as we shall see, who is invested in, and reliant upon, spectacle.

The need for an impressive opening show at the Globe is obvious enough. This was to be the third theatre on Bankside alone, an area also accommodating other public 'entertainments', such as bear-baiting. Although the Swan had been forbidden a permanent company since 1597, it still produced plays, and likely hosted touring productions. Closer to the Globe was the residence of the Admiral's Men, the Rose; the two theatres, indeed, were around 50 yards apart. In addition, there were numerous emergent theatres, both around and within the City – some inns and others full-sized playhouses. Furthermore, as James Shapiro notes, 'troubling still was word that, after a decade's hiatus, the boys of St Paul's would shortly resume playing for public audiences at the Cathedral'.[4] Another company of boy players would soon be resident at the indoor venue Blackfriars. Nor was the Globe a tentative measure for the Chamberlain's Men, but a total commitment for the shareholders, the first group of actors to own their own permanent playing space. As Andrew Gurr makes clear, 1599 was, for those in the theatrical profession, 'a time of high investment and high risk'.[5] This was a period of great theatrical competition, especially for a budding venue, and there was no time for faltering starts.

In modern editions of *Julius Caesar*, little is made of the theatrical effect of the storm. Martin Spevack's gloss of the first incidence of thunder is fairly typical: 'Thunder was produced by rolling a cannon-ball down a wooden trough, the "thunder-run", by drums or cannon-fire; lightning, by some kind of fireworks'.[6] Often, mention is made of the prologue in Ben Jonson's *Every Man In His Humour*, in which the playwright dismisses the 'rolled bullet heard, | To say, it thunders, or tempestuous drum | Rumbles to tell you that the storm doth come'.[7] It seems to me that none of the current editions capture the potential force of a display of theatrical storm. The quotation from Jonson, which is found in at least one edition of every play glossing Shakespeare's thunder, does little to help this cause, as its tone is purposefully deprecatory and scornful of the practice of, it seems, anything which detracts from a playwright's words. The same applies to the Induction of *A Warning for Fair Women*, which the Oxford *Julius Caesar* also quotes: 'a little rosin flasheth forth, | Like ... | ... a boy's squib'.[8] This play was published anonymously in 1599, but we know from its title page that it was acted by the Chamberlain's Men. The same is true of Jonson's play, first published in quarto form in 1601, but likely first performed by the same company at the Curtain in 1598. Jonson's prologue, however, with its dismissive lines was added only in the 1616 Folio text; it is inviting to specu-late that both Jonson and the anonymous playwright of *A Warning for Fair Women* were mocking Shakespeare, their fellow Chamberlain's writer, and his fondness for fire and noise.[9] However, not every playwright wrote about fireworks in the same way, and, although it is a later play, the Prologue of the anonymous *Two Merry Milke-Maids* (1619) offers some context:

> How ere you understand't, 'Tis a fine Play:
> For we have in't a Conjurer, a Devill,
> And a Clowne too; but I feare the evill,
> In which perhaps unwisely we may faile,
> Of wanting Squibs and Crackers at their taile.
> But howsoever, Gentlemen I sweare,
> You shall have Good Words for your Money here.[10]

Here, it is acknowledged that 'Squibs and Crackers' guarantee a degree of audience satisfaction, and that their absence is 'unwise'. Indeed, the Red Bull playhouse, the venue for which this speech was written, had built a reputation around its penchant for the spectacular, of which the fire effects mentioned were a key component. The reasons that an audience being promised 'Good Words' instead might find the resulting drama deficient, or 'wanting', become obvious when the evidence for special effects is examined. For it must be made clear that thunder and lightning in an Elizabethan theatre had the potential to be a hugely impressive and noisy affair, with rockets, fireworks, drums and squibs providing noise and spectacle. It is probable that a cannon, or some other piece of heavy ordinance would also have been discharged to simulate the sound of thunder along with the thunder-run, which itself would make a great deal of noise.[11]

It is, perhaps, no accident that fireworks and other pyrotechnic effects should be used to simulate lightning on the early modern stage. As we have seen, the meteorological explanation of thunder requires that a hot exhalation is trapped in the cloud. Moreover, when it escapes as lightning it is 'flying fire'.[12] The main way of creating lightning on the stage was through using what was known as, or at least subsequently came to be called, a swevel. This device is similar to a modern firework rocket, though, as John Bate describes, it also had a guiding mechanism:

> Swevels are nothing else but Rockets, having instead of a rod (to ballast them) a little cane bound fast unto them, where through the rope passeth. Note that you must be carefull to have your line strong, even & smooth, and it must be rubd over with sope that it may not burn. If you would have your Rockets to returne againe, then binde two Rockets together, with the breech of one towards the mouth of the other, and let the stouple that primeth the one, enter the breech of the other.[13]

Bate, like his fellow firework writers, markets his book for those interested in 'Triumph and Recreation'; fireworks had become a form of niche theatre in their own right.[14] Rockets, if not on cords, had been employed in civic pageants at least as far back as the 1530s,[15] but the use of swevels in the representation of storms also had a long history. Here is a description from the architect Serlio:

> You must draw a piece of wyre over the Scene, which must hang downewards, whereon you must put a squib covered over with pure gold or shining lattin which you will: and while the Bullet is rouling, you must shoote of some piece of Ordinance, and with the same giving fire to the squibs, it will worke the effect which is desired.[16]

Serlio, an Italian, died in 1554, but swevels found their way onto the English stage before his work was translated in 1611. As Philip Butterworth notes, they were evident in France, as 'during the performance of ... *Antichrist* in 1580, it is recorded that "they shall project fireworks in the air and along the cord."'[17] The royal entertainment at Elvetham in 1591 had 'many running rockets upon lines, which past between the Snail Mount and the castle in the Fort'.[18] The companies of the public playhouses in London, too, were certainly aware of the technique of swevels, and so were their audiences. In Thomas Dekker and Thomas Middleton's *The Roaring Girl* (1611), Moll refers to a 'rogue [used] like a fire-worke to run upon a line betwixt him and me'.[19] Dekker, indeed, seems to have had a fondness for the image, and used it figuratively in several plays. He also employed the technique itself: thus, in *If it Be not Good, the Devil is in it* (1612), when the stage direction calls for 'Fire-workes on Lines', swevels would have been ignited by an offstage hand.[20] When lightning was being created, the line ran from the heavens down to the stage.[21] As with several examples of theatrical pyrotechny of the period, the effect is mirrored in the language of characters: indeed in Dekker's play, the swevels are directed by a character, Ruffman, a disguised demon in the court of Naples. Ruffman dismisses the efforts of the human courtiers – 'the toyes they bragged of (Fire-works | and such light-stuffes)' – before offering his own:

> RUFFMAN   you shall see
> At opening of this hand, a thousand Balles
> Of wilde-Fire, flying round about the Aire – there.
>   *Fire-workes on Lines*
> [ALL] Rare, Rare.[22]

Whilst swevels, as this example shows, could be employed for a variety of special effects, their use in signifying lightning was well established. John Melton, in 1620, refers to Marlowe's still-popular *Doctor Faustus* in his refutation of the claims of 'astrologasters' (those who use astrology to predict the weather, amongst other things):

Another will fore-tell of Lightning and Thunder that shall happen such a day, when there are no such Inflamations seene, except men goe to the *Fortune* in *Golding-Lane*, to see the Tragedie of Doctor *Faustus*. There indeede a man may behold shagge-hayr'd Devills runne roaring over the Stages with squibs in their mouths, while Drummers make Thunder in the Tyring-house, and the twelve-penny Hirelings make artificial Lightning in their Heavens.[23]

Even as Marlowe's play approached its thirtieth birthday, the staging of it was still something to 'behold'. Melton's writing, moreover, shows how natural it was to conflate dramatic pyrotechny with genuine thunder and lightning. Whilst the effects in amphitheatres might not have been realistic, there is no confusion that in the play they represented storms.

An extensive storm, then, such as that in *Julius Caesar*, would have included quite a display of fireworks to represent lightning. Thunder, however, was heard and not seen. The chief means for producing the effect involved a heavy cannonball, and during archaeological excavations a cannonball was found at the site of the Rose playhouse.[24] At its most simplistic, the method involved rolling the ball on the floor of the heavens, to vibrate the wood and produce a thundering sound. Also available was the 'thunder run', nomenclature which postdates the drama, though early evidence for the mechanics of the 'run' is well established.[25] The device is a very simple one. A wooden trough, either on a fulcrum or sloping along the floor, contains a cannonball which, when see-sawed or released, rolls. Different levels may be built into the trough, to enable separate thunder-claps to be sounded when the ball drops down.[26] In early modern texts, the reference to use of the run is usually confined to a 'rolling bullet', as in Jonson's prologue. The effect of the run is pleasingly convincing. This realistic aspect, though, may diminish when, as suggested by Serlio, Jonson and Melton, drums contributed to the noise. All of these writers point towards the storm as a cumulative theatrical effect of fire and noise, and faithful representation of the environment is apparently less important than the production of a grand spectacle.

As I have said, *Julius Caesar* is Shakespeare's first staged storm. In the context of the theatrical competition and the financial risks of the new playhouse, the reasons for the storm's emergence at this point in the playwright's career become clearer. The fact that all the fire effects in the early modern playhouses appear to have been carried with scant regard for health and safety – as of course evidenced by the fire, ignited by the use of stage cannon, which destroyed the Globe in 1613 – indicates just how seriously the playing companies took the impact of their fire and sound. There must have been a tangible strain of fear in the audience, especially if the well-documented early modern anxiety over fire is taken into account.[27] By turns, then, electrifying and terrifying, the noise and the sight of banging and fizzing effects would have been accompanied by a strong smell of gunpowder; truly an assault on the senses. This was certainly a feat which could not be matched by the boys in St Paul's Cathedral and, very likely, was not to be found, at least on the scale of *Julius Caesar*, anywhere else in or around the City. Of the plays being staged in June 1599, most are lost, but none of those extant match Shakespeare's enthusiasm for thunder and lightning.[28] It can be concluded, then, that part of Shakespeare's purpose in writing a storm might well have been to maximise the full sensory impact of the venue and create the impression, and the hype, of the Globe as a vibrant and exciting new theatre with an effects department to outmatch its rivals.

The nearest of those rivals, and the most fierce, were the Admiral's Men at the Rose. That playhouse, as I have mentioned, was less than 50 yards from the Globe. A loud noise from one amphitheatre would have been easily audible in the other. All plays began at 2pm. It is therefore possible, or even likely, that the audience and the players at the Rose would have been disrupted and intrigued by the violent sounds coming from nearby. This point extends to audience cheering and applause: it would have been very easy for an audience member, especially one in the yard, to decide that the other playhouse sounded more entertaining and to make the short journey across the road. Of course, there is no evidence that such behaviour took place, but the sound of the Globe's cannon and rockets yards away would at least arouse the curiosity of those at the Rose. The new playhouse was still announcing its presence to the audience at its chief and nearest rival.

The storm is the most obviously spectacular element of the play's staging, but there is further evidence that Shakespeare was utilising the capability of this new theatre in his description of flourishes and alarums. The battle scenes of Act 5 of *Julius Caesar* as read in the stage directions show a sensitivity for distance which had not been evident in the playwright's earlier work, written for other playhouses. For example, in *Titus Andronicus*, a play performed at the Rose, there are eleven battle calls and flourishes, none distinguished by volume level. In *1 Henry IV*, probably first staged at the Theatre, the final act stipulates seven calls for trumpets, specified by type (e.g. 'Alarum' (5.3.0) or 'retreat' (5.4.157) but, again, not by loudness. The instruction '*Alarum afar off*' in *3 Henry VI* (5.2.77) appears in the 1623 text, but not in the 1594 text of the play. The same applies to the direction '*Drum afar off*' in *Richard III*, which is missing from the pre-1623 quartos, which nonetheless include 'The clocke striketh' in the same scene (5.3.338; 277). The early modern trumpet lacks the subtlety of the modern version, and its theatrical use was restricted to flourishes and battle calls.[29] Only in *Julius Caesar*, though, does Shakespeare begin to write directions such as 'Low alarums' (e.g. 5.5.23).

Shakespeare's interest in dictating the sound levels of the plays, then, starts to be expressed only once he has begun to write for the Globe. Whether this is coincidence, or slight evidence of some kind of backstage muting area in the playhouse, we may never tell. Certainly such distinctions in musical directions had been rare in drama before 1599. Only two similar instances are extant: in *Edward III* (1596) and Thomas Kyd's *The Spanish Tragedy* (1592). In the former, the direction for 'The battle heard afar off' (3.1.117) does not mention trumpets, and it is conceivable that the effect could be achieved with careful swordplay, especially as the 'Shot' and 'Retreat' which follow are not ascribed volume levels (122, 132). Nevertheless, it would be unwise to draw conclusions on a text which is notoriously erratic and peculiar.[30] With Kyd's play, performed at the Rose, 'a tucket afar off' (1.2.99) does refer to a trumpet. This is the sole instance in many extant Rose plays, several of which include less specific trumpet calls, as we have seen with *Titus*, and as can also be found in George Peele's *The Battle of Alcazar*, which calls for trumpets seven times. If, in the performances of Kyd's play, the trumpet was sounded 'afar', then Shakespeare's interest in the technique, like that of other playwrights, only emerged at the opening of the Globe.

Indeed, Shakespeare seems to have taken on the idea of distant battles from *Julius Caesar* onwards, soon including far off sounds in *Hamlet* and *All's Well*. In *Hamlet*, 'A march afar off' signifies the approach of Fortinbras (5.2.332); In *All's Well*, 'A march afar' accounts for the imminent arrival of 'Bertram, Parolles and the whole army' (3.5.37; 74). These uses, coming as they do, swiftly after *Julius Caesar*, lend weight to the argument that the Globe's building – or at least the fact of writing for a new playhouse – influenced Shakespeare's stage effects, and that the stage directions are not later additions.[31] Following *Julius Caesar*, other playwrights also apparently employed the effect, and it is evidenced in plays by Robert Armin, John Marston and Thomas Dekker.[32] Later in Shakespeare's Globe career, the nuance of battle sounds becomes even more developed and we find very specific sound directions, as in *Antony and Cleopatra* 'Alarum afar off, as at a sea fight' (4.12. osd). It might seem distinctly un-spectacular to us. Indeed, there is something of a contradiction in the concept of an auditory spectacle. Yet if we are to hold the oft-repeated dictum that an early modern audience went to hear a play, as we go to see a play, we must also hold that variations in sound effects, especially ones as novel as this seems to be, would have been remarkable, even spectacular. *Julius Caesar* marks a development in Shakespeare's variations of sound distance: the audience, perhaps for the first time, experienced their battles in a fully multi-dimensional soundscape.

Shakespeare's first staged storm, then, is one of a wider set of directions pointing towards an increased interest in the non-textual elements of his dramaturgy. This interest coincides with the advent of the new Globe playhouse. Either the Globe offered new capabilities for the production of special effects and sound, or Shakespeare was influenced enough by the prospect of a new theatrical space that he reconsidered his plays at a fundamental dramatic level. Whichever is the case, the Globe prompts a demonstrable shift in Shakespeare's approach to sound. The storm is one consequence of this shift and, as with the distanced sound directions, it is one that reoccurs and develops for the rest of Shakespeare's career.

If the Globe prompts a new approach to sound, then, how does this approach affect the language of the play? As we have seen, the actors in Act 1, Scene 3 would, following the stage direction for *Thunder and Lightning* enter to a cacophony of fireworks and sound effects. Given that thunder and lightning effects in early modern drama tend to occur alongside the depiction of supernatural events, whether of gods descending from the heavens or devils rising from the traps, an audience watching *Julius Caesar* might think that the characters should be worried, as Casca seems to be. But whilst he fears the 'gods [may] send destruction', no such gods appear. Rather, the stress in Casca's speech is on the novelty of this experience:

> O, Cicero,
> I have seen tempests when the scolding winds
> Have rived the knotty oaks, and I have seen
> Th'ambitious ocean swell and rage and foam
> To be exalted with the threatening clouds;
> But never till tonight, never till now,
> Did I go through a tempest dropping fire.
> Either there is civil strife in heaven,
> Or else the world, too saucy with the gods,
> Incenses them to send destruction.

> (1.3.4–14)

Instead, in relation to special effects, a striking detail emerges. The fieriness of Casca's description matches the effects of the swevels. The focus of Casca's speech – and of Cassius's when he enters – is fire, quite reasonably, as fire is indeed 'dropping' around the actors. Casca's lines do not suggest that the stage effects are a convincing simulation of a storm; instead, they revel in their unusualness: 'never till tonight, never till now | Did I go through a tempest dropping fire'. Throughout the scene, moreover, references to the pyrotechnics continue. The phrases of Cassius, for example, which depict the 'very flash of it' (52), the 'sparks' (57) and 'all these fires, all these gliding ghosts' (63) all draw attention to the stage effects. For not only is Shakespeare advertising the new playhouse as a venue for spectacular effects, he is also writing into the play images which underscore those effects. We have here, then, a stark example of environmental irony. The effects on the stage are unlike a real storm and the language of the characters celebrates their theatricality and, in the case of Casca's speech, contrasts the sights and sounds of the stage with the ostensibly real tempests 'I have seen'. This irony is surely comic. When Brutus, in the following scene, claims that 'The exhalations whizzing in the air | Give so much light that I may read by them', the irony persists, even if the rockets do not (2.1.44–5). Similarly, when the fireworks appear again, with the *thunder and lightning* of the next scene, so too does the metadramatic language, this time through the medium of Calphurnia: 'Fierce fiery warriors fight upon the clouds' (2.2.19), 'ghosts ... shriek and squeal' (19) and, evoking the sound of the drums, 'The noise of battle hurtle[s] in the air' (22).

Much has been written on the self-consciously theatrical element of the play, with a particular emphasis on Cassius's lines over Caesar's corpse: 'How many ages hence | Shall this our lofty scene be acted over | In states unborn and accents yet unknown?' (3.1.111–13). Anne Barton, for example, writes that the passage 'serves, pre-eminently, to glorify the stage'.[33] The play, as I mentioned in beginning, is invested in the interpretation and re-interpretation of spectacle, especially as a means to gaining or consolidating power and authority. In the storm, Shakespeare takes this process one level further, both in terms of the metatheatrical and the theme interpretation. The language of the play brazenly refers to the stage effects of the new playhouse. The audience is given a spectacle the like of which, the implication is, they could not have seen elsewhere: the authority of the new playhouse is foregrounded. But alongside this advertisement, the storm is taken up as something to interpret. This starts with Casca fretting about the gods, but the process is quickly co-opted by Cassius: 'No could I, Casca, name to thee a man | Most like this dreadful night | That thunders, lightens, opens graves and roars' (1.3.72–4). The second half of this chapter will concentrate on the possibilities of interpreting storms, as we see Shakespeare's play fitting into the dramatic and real environments of early modern London.

Those audience members at the opening of the Globe who were familiar with Thomas North's 1579 translation of Plutarch (there would have been several) or even the basic story of Julius Caesar (which would have been most)[34] would know that a great many unusual portents were said to have preceded the assassination. Plutarch, in North's translation, writes:

Certainly destiny may easier be foreseen than avoided, considering the strange and wonderful signs that were said to be seen before Caesar's death. For, touching the fires in the element and spirits running up and down in the night, and also the solitary birds to be seen at noondays sitting in the market-place – are not all these signs perhaps worth the noting, in such a wonderful chance as happened?[35]

'Touching the fires in the element' is as close as Plutarch, Shakespeare's principal source for the play, comes to reporting a storm.[36] Indeed, the description is as close to a theatrical storm – heavy on gunpowder and flames – as it is to an actual tempest; the playhouses might have had rockets for lightning, but relied on poetry for rain, which is notably absent in *Julius Caesar*.[37] It is from this passage that Shakespeare takes material for Casca's speech in the storm. The playwright was, in all probability, also drawing on other descriptions here. Ovid and Lucan both describe the scene, as does Virgil:

Nere flew more lightning through a welkin faire,
Nor mo portentous comets filled the aire.[38]

It is clear, then, that Shakespeare was not the first writer to make use of thunder and lightning when listing his ominous signs. Literate members of the audience would have expected storms as a result of this. It is, therefore, perhaps already unwise to assume Thomson's conclusion that an audience would expect the supernatural when hearing the sounds of thunder, when the play is an adaptation of Caesar's story. And yet there is such a theatrical legacy of the two being paired that surely for some the expectation was still there.

As we see in Casca's speech, the storm may be taken as a fearful thing, not only in itself, but in what it portends. In this regard, as I have noted, it fits in with the recurrence of the interpretation of spectacle in the play. But it is also illustrative of another wider concern of *Julius Caesar*, for this is a play which comments on the strange nature of prognostication and its obsessive desire to look forward. Brutus's soliloquy depicts not Caesar, but the Caesar that may come: 'And therefore think him as a serpent's egg | Which hatched, would as his kind grow mischievous, | And kill him in the shell'.[39] The grim accuracy of the Soothsayer's date compares starkly with the ambiguity of the storm interpretations offered by the characters who appear whilst the thunder is staged. This 'strange-disposed time' of the play extends to the crowd's response to Antony's funeral speeches, in which the resonant words suggest all of past, present and future simultaneously: 'We *will* hear the *will*'. But what of the prognostication based on the storm itself? How might a contemporary audience have reacted to a storm? How would their reaction to a staged storm be different from that to a real storm?

As has been made clear, an early modern audience who heard theatrical thunder and saw theatrical lightning would probably expect some kind of dramatic manifestation of the supernatural. Before addressing the question of this expectation, though, it is important to relate the audience's experience of the natural, especially with regards to this play. In March of 1599, whilst the Globe was being built and *Julius Caesar* was very likely being written, there was a storm in London which would find a place in the writings of several contemporary chroniclers. Robert Devereux, second Earl of Essex, was departing the city with his officers and cavalcade.[40] This was the first stage in the Earl's journey to Ireland, where he aimed to crush the rebellion of Tyrone. The fluctuating relationship between Devereux and Queen Elizabeth had resulted in the Earl's appointment to this challenging and dangerous role. There had been some delay in his departure and the rebellion was gathering strength; put bluntly, this was an eagerly anticipated moment of great significance. There would have been many who wished Devereux success, and many who hoped that his ambition, if not his life, be curtailed by the enterprise. The historian John Stow (1525–1605) provides the most complete contemporary description of the day's events:

> The 27th of March, about two of the clock in the afternoon, the right honourable Robert earl of Essex, lieutenant general, lord high marshall, etc. departed from Seething Lane, through Fenchurch Street, Grace Street, Cornhill, Cheap, etc. towards Sheldon, Highgate, and rode that night to St. Albans, towards Ireland, he had a great train of noble men, and gentlemen, on horseback before him, to accompany him on his journey, his coaches followed him. He had also (by the pleasure of God) a great shower, or twain, of rain and hail, with some claps of thunder as he rode through the city.[41]

Stow's language evokes a great spectacle. There is a certain reverence in his listing of Devereux's titles, of his companions and of the streets through which they passed. The description of the weather employs a similar syntax and thereby hints at a similar reverence. It is made explicit in the parenthetical 'by the pleasure of God'; the display is a divinely staged backdrop to the hero's departure. Note also the phrase 'He had', which, being echoed in the description of the weather from that of the company, goes further to consolidate the notion that the environment (and, therefore, God) is on the Earl's side. If there is portent to be found in this weather, it seems, Stow would have it be positive. For the sake of contextualising Stow's comments, we may contrast this description with his account of a 'tempest of wind' in November 1574:

> The eighteenth day at night, were very stormy and tempestuous winds out of the south ... These are to be received as tokens of God's wrath ready bent against the world for sin now abounding, and also of his great mercy, who doth but only show the rod wherewith we daily deserve to be beaten.[42]

Here, we may see that Stow's accounts of storms are, at least occasionally, dependent on his interpretation of God's intentions as manifest in the weather. Although both storms are unexpected, they are both harmless and Stow records no damage caused by them.[43] Nonetheless, the two storms are presented very differently. There is certainly no mention of God showing 'the rod' in the Devereux account, nor indeed, any of 'grace' in the earlier narrative. It does not seem sustainable, in light of this, that Stow wished Devereux anything bar support and admiration. It is significant that one writer should appraise two harmless storms so differently. The fickle character of weather interpretation seldom depends solely upon that weather but is bound up within broader issues: from the political to the religious, the literal climate is invariably aligned with a metaphorical climate. Stow's description of the sudden storm of Devereux's departure tells us about the weather, but his inclination to view it as bountiful tells us about his veneration of, or hope for, the Earl of Essex. Even if Stow is writing ironically, or with political reasons in mind, the point is largely similar: the description would simply be a more nuanced account of the popular apprehension of Devereux's spectacle. As Shakespeare has Cicero remark when Casca is harbouring the doom of the storm: 'men may construe things after their fashion | Clean from the purpose of the things themselves' (1.3.34–5). Cicero's comment reinforces what the Stow reports confirm: meteorology is malleable in highly idiosyncratic ways and empiricism has only a minor role to play.

Stow, with his religious language, was hardly being unusual in his descriptions. It is the significance attributed to these storms which is important. As in the play, the important thing is not only the spectacle, but also the way in which it is interpreted and symbolised as a means of consolidating and/or troubling authority. Even if there is no religious quality to the attributed significance, there is invariably still a superstitious perspective involved. An example of such superstition is provided by Leonard Digges, writing in his *Prognostication Everlasting of Right Good Effect:*

> Some write (their ground I see not) that Sunday's thunder, should
> bring the death of learned men, judges and others.
> Monday's thunder, the death of women.
> Tuesday's thunder, plenty of grain.
> Wednesday's thunder, the death of harlots, & other bloodshed.
> Thursday's thunder, plenty of sheep and corn.
> Friday's thunder, the slaughter of a great man, and other horrible murders.
> Saturday's thunder, a general pestilent plague & great death.[44]

Digges's suspicion of such beliefs ('their ground I see not') is clear, but the fact that he records them regardless is significant, and suggests that they have not vanished completely.

Another writer who notes superstitions based on thunder is Thomas Hill, whose *Contemplation of Mysteries* was published in 1574. The work is a compilation of the meteorological observations of many thinkers, edited by Hill, who notes:

> The learned *Beda* wryteth, that if thunder be first heard, comming out of the
> East quarter, the same foresheweth before the yere go about or be ended, the
> great effusion of bloud.
>   That if thunder first heard out of the West quarter, then mortalitie, and a
> grievous plague to insue.
>   That if thunder be first heard out of the South quarter, threatneth the
> death of many by shipwrack.
>   That if thunder be first heard out of the North quarter, doth then portend
> the death of wicked persons, and the overthrowe of many.[45]

Again, death is the main emphasis here; thunder portends bloodshed or disease whichever direction it comes from. Hill, in a later work on dream interpretation, writes as though to confirm the above passage: 'besides wheresoever the fyre [in the skye] shalbe or where it is carried up, as from ye North, South, West, or East, & from thense enemyes come, or els neare those regions or countryes, dearth shall be'.[46] Those who feared the omens of storms and dreams of storms cannot have been calmed by the progress of Devereux, whose crossing to Ireland was beleaguered by tempest. The superstitions outlined by Digges and Hill, and others like them, were surely held by many as parameters of the thunder that accompanied the Earl's march, whilst others would have adopted the sceptical position of Digges himself. Among the superstitious, moreover, was the possibility of taking the day's weather to be a good omen or one of evil.[47] Like all good prognostications, clarity can be safely achieved in hindsight, as with Francis Bacon who, writing many years afterwards, said that the storm 'held an ominous prodigy' and that he 'did plainly see [Essex's] overthrow chained by destiny to that journey'.[48]

The combination of strange weather and significant event ensures that both are more likely to be remembered. As Shapiro writes, the afternoon's weather:

> made so powerful an impression on the translator John Florio that, over a decade later, he included it in a dictionary as the definition of the word 'Ecnéphia': 'a kind of prodigious storm coming in summer, with furious flashings, the firmament seeming to open and burn as happened when the Earl of Essex parted from London to go for Ireland'.[49]

Nor does it appear to concern Florio that the storm by which he defines the word does not come in summer – a condition of the definition – but in March. This is testament not only to the impression that the storm made on Florio but also that which he implicitly acknowledges it has made on his reading public. It makes much more sense to use an example that is ingrained in living memory, whether or not it fits in snugly with the definition. Such is the power of remarkable weather, especially when it occurs at dramatic moments which can be easily recollected by witnesses.

Writing in his casebooks of Devereux's departure, Simon Forman gives the scene a rather different description:

> [I]t began to rain and at three 'till four there fell such a hail shower that was very great, and then it thundered withal and the wind turned to the north and after the shower was past it turned to the south-east again, and there were many mighty clouds up, but all the day before one of the clock was a very fair day and clear, and four or five days before bright and clear and very hot like summer.[50]

Here, the veneration Stow displays for Essex's progress is absent. Instead, the emphasis is on the strangeness of the weather in the episode. From the description, it seems that Forman found this particular piece of weather more remarkable than did Stow. There is no divining of meaning from the sky, merely exact description. Weather does not have to be ascribed meaning to be noteworthy, even when celebrity aristocrats are marching out to preserve the outposts of Elizabeth's empire. Unexpected weather has a hold on the human imagination and this has continued into the twenty-first century; even when the weather has little consequence beyond its surprise factor, we find front-page headlines such as 'After the Sunshine, Bolts from the Blue', reporting unexpected lightning.[51]

Regardless, then, of how it was construed by those who observed it, here was certainly a piece of weather which, by virtue of its suddenness, its scope and its timing, inhabited the imagination of Londoners and remained there for some time. In short, there could not have been a better time for Shakespeare to take theatrical thunder to hitherto unexplored realms of expression and symbolic resonance. We will likely never be certain that he saw, or did not see Devereux's cavalcade, but it is certain that many of the play-going public experienced the storm and debated its significance, and even more would have heard about it. As the storm of 27 March 1599 shows, however the weather is interpreted, and with whatever omens it is said to bring, there is likely to be disagreement. Furthermore, there is always the likelihood that the weather will be remembered long after those interpretations and omens have faded from memory. This notion has its parallel in the extended use of special effects in *Julius Caesar*, which must at least in part have been written to ensure the lasting reputation of the Globe as an exciting venue.

Early modern theatrical orthodoxy suggests that thunder and lightning provide the backdrop for heavenly or hellish creatures. In *Julius Caesar*, of course, no such creatures appear: this is a play concerned with the human interpretation of weather, just as it is concerned with the human interpretation of other properties – the will, the mantle, blood or a corpse. From the accounts of Stow, Digges, Hill, Bacon and Forman, we know that weather, especially when strange and dramatic, is held to be a significant background to important events and that interpretations of that significance can vary widely. In *Julius Caesar*, the same phenomenon is displayed. The very process of divining interpretation according to status is made explicit:

> CAESAR   Yet Caesar shall go forth, for these predictions
> Are to the world in general as to Caesar.
> CALPHURNIA When beggars die there are no comets seen;
> The heavens themselves blaze forth the death of princes.
>
> (2.2.28–31)

The storm, and indeed the numerous portents that are listed by Calphurnia are not specific enough to persuade Caesar of his fate. 'The world in general' is subject to thunder and lightning. This is why Caesar has his 'priests do present sacrifice' (2.2.5); there is purpose only in reading futures if one knows whose future is being read. Calphurnia's objection is designed both to flatter Caesar and reinforce the hierarchy inherent in such a brand of divination. Observers, likewise, feared or celebrated for Devereux: it is not surprising that there are no examples of the observers regarding that storm as significant for themselves. Just as Calphurnia elevates Caesar to be associated with the portents, so, in a different way, does Cassius:

> you shall find
> That heaven hath infused them with these spirits
> To make them instruments of fear and warning
> Unto some monstrous state.
> Now could I, Casca, name to thee a man
> Most like this dreadful night
> That thunders, lightens, opens graves, and roars.
>
> (1.3.68–74)

The play, then, utilises the practice of individual weather interpretation – the like of which we have observed in the accounts of Devereux – and the subjectivism of such interpretations is dramatically effective. Cassius's rhetoric is one aware of the metaphorical potency which the storm provides. As Calphurnia interprets the storm as foretelling Caesar's death, so Cassius views it as presaging Caesar's life; the storm is too sudden and slippery a sign to be construed evenly by each character. What is also happening here, however, is that the audience witnessing the stage effects of the storm are being reminded of the symbolic weight of expectation which those effects have been shown to carry. Cicero's remark, 'men may construe things after their fashion | Clean from the purpose of the things themselves' (1.3.34–5), may be seen to function as a caveat to the audience. Similarly the phrase of Casca's to which Cicero is replying, 'let not men say | "These are their reasons, they are natural"' (29–30) keeps alive the possibility of the supernatural, but also stages the anticipation of the supernatural which is allied to theatrical storm.

Although I do not wish to enter the debate on how *Julius Caesar* and *Henry V* may be read together, particularly with regards to Devereaux's biography, the plays share many inviting qualities. One that emerges here concerns the quality of greatness verging on tyranny, and its figurative alignment with the storm. Henry's wrath is described: 'Therefore in fierce

tempest is he coming | In thunder and in earthquake, like a Jove' (2.4.99–100).
Henry is oragious, just as Caesar is figured: 'a man | Most like this dreadful
night | That thunders, lightens ...' (1.3.71–3). Later in his career, Shakespeare
would again write from this viewpoint with Isabella in *Measure for Measure*:

> Could great men thunder
> As Jove himself does, Jove would never be quiet,
> For every pelting petty officer
> Would use his heaven for thunder, nothing but thunder.
>
> (2.2.112–15)

Isabella makes the relationship between storm, violence and power simultaneously extremely vivid and utterly vacuous. Considered alongside Henry,
the images of Angelo and Caesar are damning ones and are commentaries
on the storminess of tyranny. Again, we see the protean nature of the storm
and are reminded that the ways of thinking about Shakespeare which it
provides are never straightforward. Hence my inclination to avoid the life
of Essex in reading *Julius Caesar*, however well those examples may function with his story as context. Texts as complex as *Julius Caesar* invariably
demand that we look beyond these parallels with Elizabethan society if we
are to draw conclusions about what, and how, the plays signify. Indeed, as
Andrew Hadfield puts it, such parallels 'were routinely made in the drama
of the 1590s and would have done little on their own to distinguish the play
from numerous other works competing for the attention of the theatregoing
public'.[52] What does distinguish this play is, as we have seen, the extended
staged storm and Shakespeare's arrangement of sound.

The storm in *Julius Caesar*, then, may be read as metatheatrical, a self-
aware, self-aggrandising moment of theatre in which poetry reflects material practice. And yet there are far subtler poetic resonances in the lines.
For example, a transition takes place from supernatural judgement – that
feared by Casca – to human punishment by vigilante. Just as Cassius has
'bared [his] bosom to the thunder-stone' (1.3.49), so Brutus, attempting to
swear his constancy, says:

> When Marcus Brutus grows so covetous,
> To lock such rascal counters from his friends,
> Be ready gods with all your thunderbolts,
> Dash him to pieces!
>
> (4.3.79–82)

Brutus's lines recall the rallying cry of the vigilante Plebians who set upon
Cinna the Poet in Act 3, Scene 3. 'Tear him to pieces', says one, 'Tear him,

tear him!' another, and 'Come, brands, ho! Firebrands! To Brutus', to Cassius', burn all!' say all together (3.3.28; 35–6). Thunderbolts and fire have been physically – visually – conflated on the stage, to the extent that one may stand for the other. Thus Brutus and Cassius, in calling upon the storm to prove their justifiability, slip into a category error: the thunder they invoke is explicitly supernatural, yet there is a viscerally functional human thunder in the frenzied crowd. Casca is frightened about what the storm portends, and Cassius is empowered: each crucially misreads the environment as something other than natural. The dramatic irony noted above is therefore deeper than it first appears. In a play that is often strikingly aware of the potential of theatre, the conspirators, though explicitly aligned with the creation and the action of the drama, are represented through a naïve and basic audience response: storm equals supernatural. *Julius Caesar*, as well as delighting in, and drawing attention to, its own special effects, is a comment on this response, its crudity and its dangers, most severely in the death of Cinna. In this way, as much as in the use of spectacular effects, it establishes the basis of the rest of Shakespeare's storms.

Should an audience at the Globe have assumed the arrival of the supernatural with the sound effects of thunder, then, such assumption would have gradually eroded in the action of the play. The killing of the innocent Cinna does more than signify the extremity of mob violence: it stages the claim of the crowd to wield fire and consequently, thunder and lightning. It stages, that is, the absence of the supernatural as associated with storm. Thus the Globe's opening figures the new playhouse not only as stage for the spectacular, but also as a place in which the expected is not given. Rather than the association of storm and the supernatural, storm is explicitly linked to human violence. In this way, it takes on board the resonances of determinism that structure all of the plays of Shakespeare that are based on historical narratives.

3

Lightning

On 17 November 1606, at around ten o'clock at night, lightning struck the steeple of the church in the village of Bletchingly in Surrey. Simon Harward, a clergyman in Banstead, some nine miles away, heard rumours of the incident and was moved to visit Bletchingly, whose inhabitants had for many years shown him kindness. Harward's fears were confirmed. The spire of the church, apparently as tall again as the tower which supported it, had been consumed by fire. In the space of three hours, that fire had destroyed the steeple, and caused to 'melt to infinite fragments a goodly Ring of Bells'.[1]

Harward was obviously affected by the experience, as it moved him to write his pamphlet, *A Discourse of the Several Kinds and Causes of Lightnings*. The sympathy of the author, and his sense of wonder, is especially evident in his description of the bells which were 'before a sweet ring, and so large, that the Tenor waighed twenty hundred waight'.[2] Whilst some of the bells could perhaps be salvaged, others were 'burnt into such cinders, or intermingled with such huge heaps of cinders as it will never herafter serve to the former uses of'.[3] A clearer impression of Harwood's response, though, is gained through the time it took to produce. The preface to the text is dated 20 November, just two days after Harward could have arrived in Bletchingly. Whether motivated by genuine compassion, commercial cynicism, or the opportunity to sermonise, Harward manages in that short gestation period to produce a neat comprehensive account of ancient and contemporary lightning theory. In 1607, the pamphlet was sold at the stall of Jeffrey Chorlton, near the North door of St Paul's Cathedral. It is tempting to imagine that Chorlton's sales patter made reference to a more famous lightning strike: that which destroyed the steeple of St Paul's in 1561.

The causes of lightning are, for Harward, quite plain. Much of his pamphlet is given over to moralising through various examples of lightning strikes of the past. Hence, the 'opinions of philosophers and astronomers' on the 'naturall cause' of lightning are filtered into an appendix. More space is given to 'The causes of the greivous harmes which are often caused by lightnings' which 'are of three sorts, the first judicial, the second instructive: and the third faticidall'. When Harward does outline the natural causes of lightning, though, he is clear:

First a viscous vapour joyned with a hot exhalation is lifted up to the highest part of the middle region of aire, by virtue of the Planets: then the waterie vapour by the coldnesse both of place and of matter, is thickened into a clowd, and the exhalation (which was drawne up with it) is shut within the clowd, and driven into straights.

This hotte exhalation flying the touching of the cold clowd, doth flie into the depth of the clowd that doeth compasse it about, and courseth up and downe in the clowd seeking some passage out[.]⁴

Lightning, then, like thunder, is seen as an exhalation, or rather a vapour joined with an exhalation. At this point, it is worth remarking that Harward here is, as others before him have done, effectively describing the way in which a cloud becomes electrically charged. If this seems naïve, it should be remembered that such a process cannot accurately be described (at least without disagreement) even by today's meteorologists. Although the language of vapours and exhalations is peculiar, then, the idea that clouds are invested with a special and unusual energy before producing lightning is a curious anticipation of electricity. Moreover, the idea of the exhalation of lightning breaking through the cloud is analogous to lightning discharging its electrical energy:

[this hotte exhalation] maketh a way by force, and being kindled, by the violent motion it breaketh through the clowde. If the sides of the hollowe clowd be thicke, and the exhalation be drie and copious, then there is made both thunder and lightning: but if the clowd be thin, and the exhalation also rare and thin, then there is lightening without thunder.⁵

Harward's pamphlet, then, details with concision the established explanation of the causes of lightning. There is little disagreement between early modern writers on this basic process, and the speed with which Harward outlined it suggests that this knowledge is hardly recherché. But if the fundamental principles of lightning are straightforward, the nuances in the detail are anything but. It is a familiarity with such nuances of the early modern understanding of lightning that enriches our reading of dramatic texts. Take, for example, this passage from *Pericles*, in which Helicanus recounts the deaths of Antiochus and his daughter to Escanes:

> Even in the height and pride of all his glory,
> When he was seated in a chariot
> Of inestimable value, and his daughter with him,
> A fire from heaven came and shrivelled up
> Their bodies even to loathing for they so stunk
> That all those eyes adored them ere their fall
> Scorn now their hand should give them burial.
>
> (2.4.6–12)

Although there are many storms throughout Shakespeare's plays, and though some characters perish in shipwrecks, it is only in *Pericles* that anyone is killed by what seems to be a lightning strike. Even then, it seems unlikely that this speech is Shakespeare's, as it bears the stylistic stamps of his collaborator or co-writer George Wilkins. Still, it is necessary to consider it here not only because of its unusualness, but also because it provides a platform from which to explore the various understandings of lightning available to an audience or reader in early Jacobean London.

There is a question, though, which threatens such exploration from the start: is this 'fire from heaven' lightning? A lightning bolt is, perhaps, the likely reasoning of a modern reader, but other fires from heaven appear in early modern accounts. Hence, for example, Juliet's plea to Romeo, 'Yond light is not daylight, I know it, I. | It is some meteor that the sun exhales | To be to thee this night a torchbearer' (*R&J* 3.5.12–14). These are also the visions of Tamburlaine's image: 'So shall our swords, our lances and our shot | Fill all the aire with fiery meteors. Then when the Sky shal waxe as red as blood, It shall be said, I made it red my selfe'.[6] For all of their symbolic charge, though, and whatever form they took, such fires – the early modern term used is generally 'apparitions' – were thought of as harmless.[7] The fire that kills Antiochus and his daughter is not one of these apparitions, then, but a lightning strike.

This conclusion tallies with *The Painful Adventures of Pericles Prince of Tyre* (1608), Wilkins's prose version of the story, in which the description is less ambiguous:

> Vengeance with a deadly arrow drawne from foorth the quiver of his wrath, prepared by lightning, and shot on by thunder, hitte, and strucke dead these prowd incestuous creatures where they sate, leaving their faces blasted, and their bodies such a contemptfull object on the earth[.][8]

Wilkins here lists the several parts of a thunderbolt's action – thunder, lightning and the notion of striking – which are absent in the play's ambiguous phrasing. Similarly, in John Gower's poem, *Confessio Amantis*, the major source of the play:

> That for vengance, as god it wolde,
> Antiochus, as men mai wite,
> With thondre and lyhthnynge is forsmite;
> His doghter hath the same chaunce.[9]

Again, in Laurence Twyne's adaptation of the story, *The Pattern of Painful Adventures*, 'Antiochus and his daughter by the just judgement of God, were stroken dead with lightning from heaven'.[10]

Taking the meteorology into account, therefore, Helicanus's 'fire from heaven' seems to be a bolt of lightning. But whilst this agrees with Wilkins's prose and the poetic source material, it differs from the other main influence at work, the story of Antiochus IV Epiphanes in the Apocrypha of the Bible (hereafter Antiochus IV).[11] The Biblical connection is evidenced by both the chariot and the stink of flesh, but distinguished by the cause of death: Antiochus IV 'commanded his charet man to drive continually ... But the Lorde almightie & God of Israel smote him with an incurable and invisible plague', 'and whiles he was alive, his flesh fel of for paine and torment, and all his armie was grieved at his smell'.[12]

By opting for lightning rather than plague, Wilkins, like Gower and Twyne before him, changes the moralisation of Antiochus's death. The lightning strike – its absoluteness – ensures that Antiochus does not have the time for redemption for which Antiochus IV survives. All three writers figure the death as heavenly revenge or judgement: there is no space for Antiochus's absolution. In the play we are told of 'the most high gods not minding longer | To withhold the vengeance that they had in store' (2.4.4–5). In his *Painful Adventures*, Wilkins draws attention to what the lightning means for the victims and their fate: 'twixt his stroke and death, hee lent not so much mercy to their lives, wherein they had time to crie out; Justice, be mercifull, for we repent us'.[13]

Antiochus IV has time to become wholly contrite, but Antiochus and his daughter have no time to speak at all. Part of the appeal of the lightning strike over the Biblical disease of Antiochus IV, therefore, is the rapidity of action. So often figuratively representative of anything swift or sudden, the reality of lightning when employed for these very qualities has the urgency that only a dramatically reclaimed and reified metaphor can assume.

Until now, I have been using 'lightning' to describe the 'fire from heaven'. 'Lightning', however, is something of an umbrella term: as I have suggested, if its possible meanings are explored, then further nuances are revealed. Most of the meteorological texts classify separate kinds of lightning, but vary in their descriptions and nomenclature. The clearest available – and the text that seems to have influenced subsequent writers the most – is William Fulke's *Goodly Gallery*. Fulke distinguishes four separate types of lightning: fulgetrum, coruscation, fulgur and fulmen.[14] According to Fulke, fulgetrum, whilst 'terrible to beholde', is 'not hurtful to any thing', with the occasional exception being when 'it blasteth corne, and grasse, with other small hurt'.[15] Clearly, the fire which strikes Antiochus and his daughter is not recognisable in this description. Coruscation can also be discounted in this case, for it 'is a glistering of fyre, rather then fyre in deade, and a glymmerynge of lyghtning, rather then lightning it self'.[16] By Fulke's description, fulgur comes closer to *Pericles*'s fire from heaven, as when the thunder 'beateth against the sydes of the cloude, with the same violence, it is set on fyre, and casteth a great lyghte, whiche is séen, farre and neare'.[17] Whilst there is a certain amount of violence mentioned in the definition, however, it is, like those listed before it, 'more feareful then hurteful'.[18] This leaves fulmen, which, Fulke posits, is 'the moste dangerus, violent, & hurtfull, kinde of lightning' and which 'seldome passeth without som damage doing'.[19]

Bartholomaeus's description of fulmen, as translated by Stephen Batman in 1582, agrees with that of Fulke: 'this lyghtening smiteth, thirleth, and burneth things that it toucheth, and multiplyeth, and cleaveth and breaketh, and no bodilye thing withstandeth it'.[20] Thomas Hill, with characteristic concision, names fulmen as 'the perillousser lightning', highlighting both its danger and extremity in comparison to other forms of lightning.[21]

The danger perceived in fulmen resides chiefly in the belief that it is seen as the cause of the thunder-stone.[22] Hill describes the process:

> The fumous and somewhat black lightning, procéedeth of a verie earthly and obscure, yet a matter mightily burning, whose clowde, in that it containeth very much of the viscous moysture, is woont to fabricate or forme a black or yronnie stone, which in ye shot sent forth, burneth hastilye mightie bodyes of trées, and sundrie other most solide matters, without shewe or signe left behinde: yea, these and other matters this cleaveth, destroyeth, and utterly wasteth.[23]

The thunder-stone, then, is wholly destructive. The kind of devastation described by Hill is at stake when characters in the drama refer to this type of lightning. It is this level of danger, for example, which Cassius evokes in *Julius Caesar* as he brags, 'I have bared my bosom to the thunder-stone'

(1.3.94). This boast is contingent on the idea that the thunder-stone is the 'perillousser' sort of lightning: Cassius is speaking in extremes.

For Fulke, then, fulmen is the only type of lightning which could possibly fit Helicanus's description of the fire from heaven that kills Antiochus and his daughter. For other commentators, though, there is a further classification of lightning which is potentially deadly. Pliny termed this type clarum, which Holland translated as 'Bright and Cleare'.[24] Clarum does not appear in Fulke's list, and is not so named by many other commentators, who nonetheless describe its qualities. As Heninger notes, 'it accounted for many wonders popularly ascribed to lightning'.[25] Bartholomaeus, who does name the lightning as clarum, claims that it 'melteth golde and silver in pursses, and melteth not the pursse'.[26] Hill makes the same claim, and offers further descriptions of clarum's features, declaring that it 'burneth man inwarde, and consumeth the bodie to ashes, without harming the garments, it slayeth the yongling in the wombe, without harme to the mother ... it melteth the sworde the sheath being whole'.[27] Harward, referring to 'penetrans, a pearcing lightening', also hints at its destructive properties: 'It pearceth thorough the outward pores of the body and slayeth the vitall parts within'.[28]

Given two such deadly possibilities it would seem difficult to find a way of identifying which kind of lightning is responsible for the deaths of Antiochus and his daughter. La Primaudaye describes what happens when people are struck by lightning: 'Those who are stroken ... remain all consumed within, as if their flesh, sinews, and bones were altogether molten within their skin, it remaining sound & whole, as if they had no harme'.[29] La Primaudaye here does not name the lightning, but his details match the penetrative effects of clarum. Conversely, as we have seen in Bartholomaeus's account, 'no bodilye thing withstandeth' the power of fulmen. It may seem a minor distinction, but in Helicanus's narrative, 'A fire from heaven came and shrivelled up | Their bodies'. Here, the subtler effect of clarum is not in evidence. Moreover, the corpses in *Pericles* 'so stunk' that the citizens either refused to bury them, or bemoaned the responsibility. In Bartholomaeus's text, the author lists as a property of fulmen that 'where he burneth, he gendreth therwith full evill stench and smoak'.[30] Helicanus's fire from heaven is fulmen, or the thunder-stone.

Why does the type of lightning matter? Whilst the celerity of lightning is important in denying Antiochus time for repentance, the destructiveness is important in terms of what is left behind. Whereas a clarum strike could still be fatal, it would maintain the *appearance* of harmlessness: damaging within, but 'never toucht therewith or burnt, nor any other shewe and token ... left behind', as Pliny puts it.[31] Antiochus, a ruler who places great emphasis on appearances, is 'seated in a chariot of inestimable value' and he and his daughter are 'both apparelled all in jewels'.[32] In *Painful Adventures*, Wilkins goes further, in describing the couple as 'gazing to be gazed upon'.[33] Just as lightning leaves no time for repentance, this *type* of lightning leaves no space for these images of pompous indulgence. There is a further connection here with the Biblical account of Antiochus IV, who is castigated under similar conditions: 'Howbeit he wolde in no wise cease from his arrogancie, but swelled the more with pride'.[34] Like Antiochus and his daughter, Antiochus IV rides in his 'charet that ran swiftely'.[35] Furthermore, the moral distance between the two doomed Antiochus figures and their respective people is represented sensually: 'no man colde beare because of his stinke, him that a litle afore thoght he might reach to the starres of heaven';[36] in *Pericles*, 'so they stunk | That all those eyes adored them ere their fall | Scorn now'. And just as the striking of fulmen destroys the iconographic image of the incestuous couple of *Pericles*, so the divine plague affects the mind and belief of Antiochus IV as much as his body: 'And when he him self might not abide his owne stinke, he said these wordes, It is mete to be subject unto God, & that a man which is mortal, shulde not thinke him self equal unto God through pride'.[37] It is the capacity of fulmen to destroy Antiochus and his daughter, rendering their bodies the same state as the plague, but the symbolic resonance of lightning's swiftness confirms that there is no possibility of salvation.

The classification of lightnings in relation to dramatic texts, then, may recover poetic subtleties that the modern reader may otherwise overlook. One more example is worth looking at briefly. In *Cymbeline*, Guiderius and Aviragus lament 'Fidele', in song: 'Fear no more the lightning-flash, | Nor th'all-dreaded thunder-stone' (4.2.270–1). The thunder-stone, as we have seen, is caused by fulmen, and is justifiably 'all-dreaded'. Conversely, the lightning flash is harmless. In that it flashes, it fits most closely with coruscation, in Fulke's phrase 'a glymmerynge of lightning, rather then lightning it self', but could also be, in Fulke's words fulgetrum.[38] It is manifestly *not* fulmen, the chief characteristics of which are its downward motion and its violent force. The harmlessness is the crucial quality of the song's lightning-flash, the tendency to fear it being in its suddenness and shock value. Only with an acknowledgement of the classifications of lightning, can we appreciate that this phrase is suggestive of lightning's two extreme manifestations: a wide range of occurrences, not a single storm. Seen in this way, the phrase integrates more comfortably with the reset of the song's aesthetic, in which 'the heat o'th' sun' is juxtaposed with 'the furious winter's rages' and 'the reed is as the oak' (258–9; 267). Lightning, like the song's other examples from nature, has a range of extremes, from the frightening to the utterly destructive. Indeed, its undamaging form is recalled by Cymbeline at the play's end, as he notes that 'Posthumus anchors upon Imogen; | And she (like harmless lightning) throws her eye | On him' (5.5.394–6). This recalls the tame lightning of the lament, but also perhaps the beneficent thunderbolt thrown by the descending Jupiter in Posthumus's dream (5.4.92sd).

Elsewhere, the diction describing lightning relates much more obviously to stage effects. In addition to re-establishing the nuance of seemingly simple terms, like 'lightning', an understanding of early modern meteorology helps to clarify the language of the plays. In Julius Caesar, for example, when Brutus is brought the letter in his orchard, he claims 'The exhalations whizzing in the air | Give so much light that I may read by them' (2.1.44–5). The word 'exhalations', is often glossed as 'meteors', rather than lightning.[39] Given that 'exhalation' does, in early modern terminology, cover several types of weather, the assumption that Brutus is referring to meteors is problematic. Indeed, there is no particular cause for concluding that he is, but it is worth pointing out that in either case he is still commenting on the weather: meteors are meteorological by the same theory which holds that lightning is an exhalation. Even if we do assume that Brutus's phrase refers to meteors, there is still, in early modern thinking, a stormy element to shooting stars:

> For they say, that the starres fall out of the firmament, and that by the fall of them, both thonder and lyghtning are caused: for the lightening (say they) is nothyng els but the shyning of that starre that falleth, which falling into a watrie clowde, and being quenched in it, causeth that great thonder, even as whoat yron maketh a noyce if it be cast into colde water. But it is evident that ye starres of the firmament can not fall, for God hath set them fast for ever, he hath geven them a commaundement whiche they shal not passe.[40]

Although William Fulke is not convinced by the theory that meteors can cause thunder and lightning, his description suggests that he is at odds with the popular belief. That belief is espoused to by Pliny, who holds that storms caused by falling stars are of a special providence.[41] Despite the existence of this theory, Brutus's word, 'exhalations', much more readily refers to lightning itself – or the phenomena in the category of apparitions – than to meteors. However, the most important point is that Brutus – as with the characters of the preceding scene – is calling attention to the stage effects.

Hence 'whizzing', which is more evocative of the fireworks display of Act 1, Scene 3 than of any type of weather observed by early modern meteorologists. Of course, Brutus's line is hyperbolic or comic: whether meteor or lightning, the light is impossible to read by. Like Casca and Cassius, though, his language – and the catchall term 'exhalations' – revels in the stage effects of the Globe playhouse.

Simon Harward, William Fulke and other writers of meteorological texts understood that some clouds are invested with a particular energy which results in lightning. But whilst the understanding of lightning in early modern England was broadly agreed upon, there is a wealth of poetic resonance in the detail. Writers have long called on lightning when an image of swiftness is required, and, of course Shakespeare and his contemporaries are no different. But just as the lightning in Homer is often literal and deadly, so the manifestations of it in early modern England were terrifying, as Simon Harward found. As I have shown, lightning is much more than a representation for speed, and whether harmless or destructive, metatheatrical or metaphorical, its range of meaning provided a wide resource for writers.

4

King Lear: storm and the event

Well, well, th'event.

King Lear 1.4.344[1]

The quotation with which I begin may seem an utterly innocuous one. Spoken by the Duke of Albany at the end of a scene in which his marital relations with Goneril begin their inexorable deterioration, the words slip past almost unnoticed. They are supplementary in essence, following Albany's own formulaic rhyming couplet which has all the formal structure of a scene ending: 'How far your eyes may pierce I cannot tell; | Striving to better, oft we mar what's well' (341–2). Goneril's reply, 'Nay then', is unexpected, a seemingly artificial prolonging of a scene which has reached its natural conclusion. Albany immediately interrupts with the quotation above. I want to explore the ways in which *King Lear* is dominated by the event. The event in *Lear* is unavoidable: there is no location, there is only event. Indeed, there is just one 'event' in the play: remarkably, Albany's line is the only instance of the word. This singularity, as we shall see, is no obstacle to the strange logic of the event characterising the play.

In this chapter I will outline the ways in which *King Lear* is subtly but consistently misunderstood by the tendency to imagine the storm happening in a particular place. I propose that the storm itself is, aesthetically and structurally, what sustains the play. In the course of my argument, I will show how the storm in *King Lear* is characterised by an absence of location and the ways in which this absence is crucial to the play and its process of meaning. I will show that responses that bypass this absence of location, however briefly, necessarily fail to address the text on its own terms.

We will, moreover, see how *King Lear* continues and develops Shakespeare's characteristic approach to storm, namely the systematic troubling of the expectation of the supernatural. As this aspect of the play is explored,

I will draw on the work of critics who seek, or perhaps expect, to find the residue of supernatural cause where storm is concerned. As we have seen already, the notion that storm effects almost invariably prompted the audience to expect the supernatural is pertinent and valid with other dramatic work of the period, but is problematised by the plays of Shakespeare.[2] I will argue that whilst the audience may indeed expect the supernatural, in common with other plays I am considering, *King Lear* subverts that expectation. In this case, the subversion is carried out in particular through Lear's question 'What is the cause of thunder?' (3.4.151). The question not only introduces a sense of naturalistic meteorological inquiry, but opens the play to an investigation of the work of one of its most resonant words: 'cause'. Such investigation will form the last part of this chapter, as I explore the ways in which cause and event inform our understanding of *King Lear*.

Why the event? To begin to think about the ways *King Lear* is subject to the logic of the event, here is a definition: 'The (actual or contemplated) fact of anything happening; the occurrence of'.[3] Even in this ostensibly basic definition, the event already seems strange, occupying the real and the imaginary: the 'occurrence of' the 'contemplated' suggests that the event is a basic condition of human thought. A more obscure usage – one present in early modern English – sees event defined as 'What "becomes of" or befalls (a person or thing); fate'.[4] Thus, the event bears finality and what Jacques Derrida might term the 'to come'. Indeed, it is this quality of the event that Derrida draws upon in his own explication: 'The event must be considered in terms of the "come" ... Without this "come" there could be no experience of what is to come, of the event, of what will happen and therefore of what, since it comes from the other, lies beyond anticipation'.[5] This 'experience', I will argue, is what characterises *King Lear*. In the play, the event 'lies beyond anticipation'. Albany's phrase, with which I began, is an encapsulation of this idea: an admonition of Goneril's threat to anticipate. In several plays, Shakespeare is alive to the eccentricities of the event. Nicholas Royle has addressed uses of *event* in Shakespeare, contending that 'its appearances are consistently associated with a sense of strangeness'.[6] The three suns of *3 Henry VI* are 'but one lamp, one light, one sun. | In this the heaven figures some event' (2.1.31–2). Indeed in several of Shakespeare's plays, the event verges on the announcement of the supernatural. Hence, in *The Tempest*: 'These are not natural events: they strengthen | From strange to stranger' (5.1.228–9) and in *Macbeth*: 'dire combustion, and confus'd events, | New hatch'd to th' woeful time' (2.3.57–8).

R. A. Foakes, unlike many editors, glosses Albany's phrase – th'event –

and does so with unerring, unnerving simplicity: 'the outcome; equivalent to "we'll see"'. I want to suggest that this gloss is coloured by the logic of play – a logic which marries blindness and sight, daylight and night, 'matter and impertinency mixed', as Edgar says, 'Reason in madness' (4.1.170–1). That the event, in this idiomatic context, is revealing and structured as a promise – 'we'll see' – happily aligns it with madness, blindness and night.[7] Furthermore, there is a subtle difference between the Quarto and Folio versions of Albany's line: the former has 'the event', whilst the latter has 'the'vent'. Foakes's 'th'event' is a medium between the two. The Folio's version prompts consideration of another definition, under *event*: 'To expose to the air; hence, to cool'.[8]

For these reasons, Albany's line is the ideal starting place for a discussion of the storm in *King Lear*. To the events of blinding, maddening and darkening in the play, we may add the storm: the ironic exposure to the air of Lear's event, which does not cool, but maddens. In the case of *King Lear*, the sense of strangeness in the storm as event is brought out in its status as outcome and as occasion: it informs the meaning of the lines which run through it, sometimes seemingly in dialogue with them, yet confined to one insistent stage effect. It is, to apprehend the language of the stage direction, *still*, both in the sense of continuing and unchanging. I choose the word *event* to consider *King Lear* in general and the storm in particular to evoke the sense that 'what is happening' and 'what has happened' is prioritised in the play over issues of location. How to address the storm in *King Lear*? Only by first addressing also a tradition which depends upon the storm's marginalisation; only thereby teasing the 'we'll see' from the event. This tradition has to do with the superfluous location of the heath. The storm has often been interpreted as an external symbol of Lear's internal distress,[9] itself an indication that critics are open to readings of the play, or at least its title character, based on the event of the storm. However, rather than simply offering the storm as context, whether by aligning it with the depiction of Lear's psyche or by, for example, the gradual decline of providential pagan belief, critical responses have almost inevitably localised the storm, and hence failed to address the play on its own terms.

In using a phrase such as 'the play on its own terms', I am conscious that I leave myself open to rebuke.[10] What I hope to show, however, is that, far from attempting to reclaim a pre-critical, pre-editorial incarnation of the play, it would benefit us to recognise that criticism and editorial practices frequently represent *King Lear*, however subtly, as reliant on the poetics of location. Terence Hawkes suggests that we focus 'on the ways in which *King*

Lear is processed by a society ... rather than on any mythical "play itself"'.[11] I would submit in response that the play with which we interact, that is, the play which, as a society, we engage in processing, is one inherited from a society – the Restoration and its scenic theatre – which operated under inherently different principles and conditions than either our own or the early Jacobean theatrical culture. And whilst we cannot claim a 'real version' of the text in this way, if we are to continue to 'process' it, then we ought at least to delineate the origins of what we are processing and, as much as we are able, recognise the material conditions of its original production. The phrase 'the text itself' is meant only to indicate this indented recognition.

King Lear is, both popularly and critically, imagined as moving through madness and realisation on a heath. Articles have already been written which address the fallacy, notably by James Ogden, whose 'Lear's Blasted Heath' was first published in 1987, and by Henry S. Turner, whose '*King Lear* Without: The Heath' appeared a decade later.[12] It is a problem, however, which remains, as, even in critical discourse, when Lear is described as at a location, it is almost inevitably a heath. Or rather, *the* heath, as only the right heath will do: 'When he is on the heath, King Lear is moved to pity', writes Jonathan Dollimore, as though it were a place to visit for reawakening, a kind of spiritual retreat.[13] Hugh Grady, meanwhile, argues that 'modern subjectivity, in the guise of Cordelia, Edgar and the transformed Lear from the heath scenes on, is also the *locus* for the workings of the utopian'.[14] Again, the heath becomes complicit in the shifts in Lear's language and takes on a central role in any attempt at reconciliation at which the play, it is argued, hints. Those shifts in language are characterised chiefly by their relationship with the storm and the night, that is, by the external events, not by location. Despite this, the heath seems boundless in the argument of Arthur Kirsch, who mentions 'Gloucester's state of mind on the heath, after his blinding'.[15] The heath then, continues beyond the storm – and becomes, in Kirsch's reading, a figure for the sense of forlorn revelation which characterises the latter half of the play. For Ian W. O. House, too, the heath plays a part in characterisation, as Edgar's 'most effective disguise is to be quite openly part of the heath on which he lives'.[16] Even critics purportedly invested in analysing the play's treatment of the environment fall into the trap of the received version of the play.[17] Stephen Greenblatt offers another perspective: 'In the strange universe of *King Lear*, nothing but precipitous ruin lies on the other side of retirement, just as nothing but a bleak, featureless heath lies on the side of the castle gate'.[18] Here, the heath is more suggestive of banishment.[19] Greenblatt's conflation of location with the wider 'universe' of the play invites us to contemplate the text's characteristic absence of locality, although his employment of it as a point of comparison implies that the featurelessness of location is somehow important in the play's meaning. There is, perhaps, also an indication here that critics are, at least in their scholarly writings, beginning to move away from the fallacy: Greenblatt does not favour the heath in his more scholarly works, but seems happy to use it in popular biography, which nonetheless offers readings of the plays.[20] I would suggest that a conscious avoidance, if such is the case, of the heath in academic texts should not be coupled with a resurrection of it in popular works. Indeed, this is rather sinister, as though the heath should be a step-ladder for those unable to gain an unobstructed view of the play. A critical awareness of an imposition should, if one is to raise it, lead to a recognition of it *as* an imposition, unless we are resigned to repeating it. There is a disturbing and distorting act of displacement at work in localising meaning in *King Lear* and nowhere is this more pronounced than in the repetition of the heath. There is no location, there is only event.

There is a further danger, if we persist with the heath and its associative implications. Implicit in Turner's argument is the notion that to imagine Lear on a heath is to circumvent the very process by which the king is understood to be mad.[21] Lear's journey is one of dislocation in many senses of the word: just as his followers attempt to relocate him – either out of the storm, or, in Turner's language, to 'the world of the play' – Lear's manifest refusal to recognise the locations, or the possibility of location, serves not only to dislocate him from space but from the followers themselves.[22] Thus the notions of isolation, remoteness, or seclusion for which the heath stands are diminished as soon as the possibility of the heath – or any other location – is imagined. To locate Lear is to save him from madness. That the phrase 'Lear on the heath' has acquired the surrogate meaning of the progression of Lear's insanity is contradictory to the fact that Lear's mental state is not only catalysed by displacement but envisaged and articulated through the impossibility of re-placement. Only if Lear fails to accept his surroundings can the sense of isolation sought by the imposition of the heath be realised. Moreover, the notion that Lear is physically isolated in the storm, as only one in a wilderness can be, is manifestly false and recontextualises the scenes in an utterly unhelpful way. Lear is not alone in the storm. Indeed, Lear is never alone on the stage. This is the one title role in Shakespeare's tragedies which has no soliloquies.[23] To add to Turner's argument on the representation of madness in *King Lear*, the king's peculiar

state is that he soliloquises but his soliloquies are witnessed by others on
stage: this is dramatic madness – we might remember Ophelia and Lady
Macbeth for other examples of these witnessed soliloquies.[24] Edgar as Poor
Tom, of course, makes use of the notion, and his feigned madness would be
meaningless if he were on stage alone.[25] The phrase 'on the heath' encourages us to think of Lear as physically isolated – alone – and thereby bypasses
the dramatic context of the representation of the king's increasing insanity.

By stressing the fallacious nature of the heath, my intention is not to
nitpick, but to adhere to the demands of the text itself. Before examining
the play in closer detail, it is necessary to ask the question: is it important
to know where the action is taking place in a Shakespearean play? An illustrative comparison can be made with *Romeo and Juliet*: a reader's search for
mention of a balcony in the text will prove fruitless. It would be doctrinaire,
however, to draw conclusions from such an absence, as the demands both
of the text and its staging are that Juliet is above Romeo – 'o'er my head'
– at a 'window' (2.2.27; 1). What is traditionally referred to as the balcony
scene, then, has a perfectly appropriate, if supplementary name. The same
cannot be said of the so-called heath scenes in *King Lear*, which lack the
indications prevalent in *Romeo and Juliet*. So, how crucial is location in a
Shakespearean play? We might, in addition to the canard of *Lear*'s heath,
remember the castles of *Macbeth* and *Hamlet*; the various battlegrounds
of the histories – Shrewsbury, Harfleur, Orleans, Agincourt; *The Tempest*'s
island; forests in *As You Like It*, *A Midsummer Night's Dream* and *The Merry
Wives of Windsor*. We may recall the many ports of *Pericles* as well as Venice,
Verona, Cyprus, Bohemia, Belmont and the oddly unobtainable Milford
Haven. There are, of course, many more such instances, and alongside
them belong myriad scenes in bedrooms, courts, taverns, brothels, streets,
gardens, ships, prisons and caves. We recognise these locations, as readers
especially but as audience members also, not simply through editorial
glosses but by the same system of contextual signs that tell us that it is
'bitter cold' at the opening of *Hamlet* (1.1.6), or that 'The moon shines bright'
in the last act of *The Merchant of Venice* (5.1.1). In the storm scenes of *King
Lear*, there is a similar array of contextual signs: we are repeatedly told that
a) Lear and his followers are outside, but that shelter is not far; b) that the
weather is dreadful in every sense and c) it is night.[26] Aside from the close
proximity of the hovel, there is no contextual sign during the storm which
indicates the whereabouts of the characters. In each of the above examples
of place, the location of the characters adds nuance to their lines. In *The
Merchant of Venice*, for example, 'What news on the Rialto?' (1.3.33; 3.1.1) does

more than ally place with communication; it creates a sense of a bustling mercantile community which the play's other instances of 'the Rialto' build upon. Location informs meaning. Similarly, in *Cymbeline*, Aviragus's lines convey a strong sense of experience shaped by environment: 'how, | In this our pinching cave, shall we discourse | The freezing hours away? We have seen nothing. | We are beastly' (3.3.37–40). Without the image of the cave, restricting and cold in the double sense of pinching, Aviragus's speech loses much of its potency in conveying a life outside of civilisation. As it is, the concluding 'beastly' is reached through a construction of place which limits the speaker's humanity: the 'pinching cave' imposes a limit on 'discourse'. Belarius's response is also marked by an understanding of location's influence on the imagination: 'Did you but know the city's usuries, | And felt them knowingly' (45–6). When place is a significant factor in a character's meaning or circumstance, then, place is woven into the diction. If there is no such indication of place, it is not too much to say that the character's meaning and situation depend on other factors, whether they be another character's speech, the recognition of their own subjectivity[27] or an event not specific to location: the night, for example, or a storm. Indeed, in response to Kent's urgent question, 'Where's the King?', the Gentleman does not respond helpfully, but poetically: 'Contending with the fretful elements' (3.1.2–3).[28] This response, and the description which follows it, is made even odder when, not 50 lines later, the two characters split up to seek Lear, and odder still when Kent finds him first (49; 3.2.39). If the Gentleman knows the king's whereabouts, such a progression is ridiculous, unless the notion of a whereabouts is – as is made clear by his answer to Kent – acutely troubled. Thus, as the play moves into the third act, the importance and even validity of location continue to be undermined and destabilised. To localise Lear in the storm is to acknowledge a severe difficulty in approaching those scenes, a difficulty which can be sidestepped by forcing aesthetically apposite supplements upon them, thereby altering the meaning, and the way of meaning.

This same scene also sees the emergence of Dover, the name which echoes through the second half of the play: 'make your speed to Dover' is Kent's phrase (3.1.32). Even in the naming of the town, however, the idea of location is troubled. With the exception of the final instance – Gloucester's 'Dost thou know Dover?' (4.1.74) – every mention of Dover is prefaced, as Kent's is, either by 'to' or 'toward'.[29] Dover is a location to come, never a location which informs the play. Gloucester's phrase captures the finality of the idea inherent in reaching the location to come: 'From that place | I shall no leading need' (4.1.80–1). Following this, the name of Dover is not mentioned again: location, even in the act of naming places, remains tantalising, but intangible. Hence the *possibility* of location informs meaning, but only in the sense of a determinate negation: not, as in *The Merchant of Venice* or *Cymbeline*, defined by where the lines are spoken, but where they are not.

The paucity of place signs in the play was noted over a century ago, when A. C. Bradley wrote that in *King Lear*, 'the very vagueness in the sense of locality ... give[s] the feeling of vastness, the feeling not of a scene or particular place, but of a world; or, to speak more accurately, of a particular place which is also a world'.[30] Even as Bradley acknowledges the absence of 'particular place' in the play, then, he is moved to suggest that a 'particular place' is nonetheless conceived. Although he goes on to concede that the suggestion of vastness has 'a positive value for imagination', Bradley's overall position on *King Lear*'s characteristic 'indefiniteness' is that it is a 'defect' of the play.[31] Perhaps, then, his 'feeling' a 'particular place' is intentional, affected by the modern approach to drama which Alan Dessen has described: 'Thanks to generations of editing and typography, modern readers have ... been conditioned to expect placement of a given scene ("where" does it occur?), regardless of the fluidity or placelessness of the original context or the potential distortion in the question "where"?'[32] It is this fluidity of location which Dessen describes that characterises much of *King Lear*. And yet the various realisations and psychotic episodes which Lear goes through in Act 3 are characterised not by a fluidity of location but by a singularity of event. Whilst the 'placement of a given scene', that is, remains slippery, the event which forms the context of those scenes – the storm – is constantly reiterated. The crucial aspect is that such events may always be approached and re-imagined in the language of characters, to inform and shape their meaning. In this way, the fixedness of the storm may be seen to constitute both the expected 'placement' of a scene which Dessen describes and the definiteness which Bradley craved, in that it alters only in the language of those who apprehend it. The storm is, therefore, different from the night, as the latter is represented solely *by* the language of those who apprehend it, whereas the storm is figured as resolute by the stage machinery, and by the direction '*Storm still*' (3.1.0; 3.2.0; 3.4.3; 3.4.61; 3.4.98).

A similar clarification of the notion of 'a singularity of event' is offered when Lear awakes after the storm. Indeed, the king asks his own distorting question of where: 'Where have I been? Where am I? Fair daylight?' (4.7.52). The fair daylight, that is, introduced as the opposite to the 'tyrannous night' (3.4.147): once more, it is a language which seems to be invested in the powerlessness of location to suggest meaning. That the daylight is questionable – phrased *as* a question – that the fundamental sequence of night followed by day has become, in Lear's language, problematic, is suggestive itself of the circumstances in which the king awakes. That such singularity of event, that is, shown to be beyond the domain of the human in the storm scenes, retains the power to become slippery and doubtful in the language used to apprehend it, points indeed to the relationship of character and event in the play.

So far, I have argued that the tendency to read location into *Lear* undermines the work of the play. I have shown that location informs meaning in some plays, but *Lear* is characterised by a lack of location which is part of its disorientating aesthetic. The tradition of the heath has, in turn, its own tradition, one that credits the superfluous location to Nicholas Rowe's edition of 1709. The veracity of this conventional opinion has been questioned by Ogden, who argues, convincingly, that Rowe derived the heath from the painted scenery used in the Restoration staging of Nahum Tate's version of the play.[33] The same scenery, indeed, was used for Tate's play *The Loyal General*, and, as Ogden has shown, 'There are several similarities between [*The Loyal General*] and Tate's version of *King Lear*, which was the next play he wrote'.[34] That the idea of Lear on the heath originates in a specifically visual theatrical setting, rather than the bare stage of the Jacobean amphitheatre, should itself be a clue that when we speak of the heath, we are not addressing the Shakespearean text. Why, then, has the tradition of the heath in *King Lear* endured? Ogden's essay goes on to suggest that, in addition to originating from a visual development on the Restoration stage, the heath was perpetuated by illustration, beginning with an image in Rowe's volume.[35] This practice of illustration persists (finding its current most obvious incarnation on the cover of the 2007 Arden edition of the play, which depicts an open tract of land with a bare tree)[36] and, indeed, is furthered by cinematic versions.

But apart from this modality of the visible, there is something more alluring about the heath that has enabled it to endure. What is it about the image that appeals to our sense of understanding of the play? Can it be that, with its notions of wilderness, it carries the context of isolation in which Lear is imagined to be? The concept of wilderness itself is a pervasive one and readily fits in with the now outmoded Christian reading of the play. Christ, led by the Spirit of God, enters the wilderness and resists the temptations of the Devil.[37] Christ's wilderness fast lasts for forty days: an explicitly stormy duration, given that the rains of the Flood fall for the same length of time.[38] The heath, the wilderness, the storm and the epiphanic moment all seem happily to fit together.

There are undeniable attractions in the heath as wilderness in reading *King Lear*. In the Christian readings of the play that dominated critical approaches during much of the twentieth century, the logic of suffering and redemption finds its ideal counterpoint in 'an extensive wasteland'.[39] In the Old Testament, the heath and wilderness are conflated in a fashion particularly apposite to *King Lear*:

> Thus saith the Lord, Cursed *be* the man that trusteth in man, & maketh flesh his arme, & withdraweth his heart from the Lord. For he shalbe like the heath in the wildernes, and shal not se when *anie* good commeth, but shal inhabit the partched places in the wildernes, in a salt land, and not inhabited.[40]

It seems to me that this is the very same conflation which appeals to the implicit localising of the event which we see in the above quotations from Greenblatt, or prioritising of location in the way Grady does. As Greg Garrard has noted, wilderness is not only the location for Christ to be tempted by the Devil, but also the place of exile from Eden, and, furthermore, recognisable in early examples of monasticism as a place of retreat.[41] This is part of the symbolic heritage upon which formulations such as those of Dollimore or Kirsch draw. 'The Judaeo-Christian conception of wilderness, then', writes Garrard, 'combines connotations of trial and danger with freedom, redemption and purity, meanings that, in varying degrees, it still has'.[42] Those meanings are also to be identified in the modern employment of the heath in *Lear*. If the logic of suffering and redemption is no longer characterised as Christian allegory by critical consensus, it is nonetheless a logic which persists in some form, as Dollimore's essay goes on to show; indeed, suffering is essentialised in such interpretations as the aim of existence.[43] As such, the logic of isolation, suffering and redemption is often grounded by the force of the metaphorical inertia of the heath. The event and the wilderness constitute two distinct concepts of any putative salvation: a wilderness implies that we can seek our salvation out; an event, that it is something that happens to us.

That Lear's belated realisation of social responsibility – 'I have ta'en too little care of this' (3.4.32–3) – is imagined to take place in a wilderness allows the thought that in order for civilisation to function, we must contend with and acknowledge its limitations in the face of nature. Contained in the notion of the heath is the attractive paradox that the further Lear recedes from civilisation and companionship, the more he understands his humanity and that of others (it becomes, in this way, a parallel play to *Timon of Athens*). Wilderness is, of course, an extremely important concept for ecocriticism: it 'has an almost sacramental value: it holds out the promise of a renewed authentic relation of humanity and the earth, a post-Christian covenant, found in a space of purity, founded in an attitude of reverence and humility'.[44] In light of this level of metaphorical force, it is not difficult to see why the heath is still construed as an apposite location for the humbling of a remorseful king. The danger of a 'post-Christian covenant' attracting and endorsing further and deeper misreadings of the play based on the regurgitated fallacy of the heath should explain why a move away from considering the play in terms of location is worthwhile. Although ecocriticism may hold the concept of wilderness dear, it is a critical discourse which must increasingly represent nature as event, whether it is an event that has happened, is happening, will happen or a mixture of all three. Indeed, the qualities of nature that have been exemplified in conceptions of wilderness have themselves been problematised since the 2000s by, for example, Timothy Morton.[45] The idealised nature is, in such readings, troublesome for ecology in the same way that the heath is problematic for readings of *Lear*. In coming to terms with nature as event, we may increase our imaginative capacity to participate in climate change debates. However, we also stand to re-engage with texts which have for centuries laboured under the yoke of nature-as-location. A historically aware approach to Shakespeare is necessary for ecocriticism to learn the subtleties of Shakespeare's representations of nature, if those representations are to carry any weight in presentist discourse. I have not argued that Shakespeare represents nature as event because I feel that such a conclusion is crucial for ecocriticism, although it may well be. Rather, it is because that representation is grounded in his dramaturgy, which, in turn, is grounded in the material conditions of performance in which Shakespeare spent his daily life. *King Lear* finds Shakespeare manipulating amphitheatre drama's systems of signification, with one effect being that nature is something which happens to characters, and through that happening characters are presented as reconceiving themselves.

I have been arguing that the tradition of the heath undermines a critical approach to the play, however attractive it is with its connotations of wilderness and isolation. Instead, we should read the play and its treatment of nature in terms of event. Steve Mentz has proposed that:

Works like *King Lear* can help transform sterile dualisms and static eco-
systems into pluralized and dynamic conceptions of self and nature. Making
sense of these competing frames requires shifting from a pastoral vision,
in which nature resembles a pasture or garden, to a meteorological one, in
which nature changes constantly and challenges the body at its boundaries.[46]

The pastoral vision has its counterpart in the wilderness. Mentz's proposed
meteorological vision prioritises event. Nature 'changes constantly'; nature
happens and audiences and characters symbolise and react. If, as I propose,
it is crucial to approach *King Lear* in terms of the event, not location, then
we must begin to explore how development of Lear's character in the storm
scenes is achieved through the storm itself. Here, then, is Lear's first speech
in Act 3:

> Blow, winds and crack your cheeks! Rage, blow,
> You cataracts and hurricanes, spout
> Till you have drenched our steeples, drowned the cocks!
> You sulph'rous and thought-executing fires,
> Vaunt-couriers of oak cleaving thunderbolts,
> Singe my white head: and thou all-shaking thunder,
> Strike flat the thick rotundity o'th' world,
> Crack nature's moulds, all germens spill at once
> That makes ingrateful man.
>
> (3.2.1–9)

If I have introduced these familiar lines rather late in this chapter, it is
because they *are* familiar. By quoting them here, I hope that my argument on location and the event will allow them to be considered anew. In
the wealth of critical responses to this speech, it is rarely conceded that
Lear maintains his imaginary authority over the elements. One of the few
writers to acknowledge this is George Williams, who notes: 'These wild
lines then must be understood as direct orders to the winds, the waves,
the thunder, and the lightning. Such an interpretation accords well with
what has been seen of the character of the king'.[47] In response to Williams's
article, E. Catherine Dunn writes that this speech and the following one
'appear to be curses *upon himself*, primarily'.[48] Rather than continue such
debate, however, there is now a pattern of general agreement. Usually,
as in the case of Martin Rosenberg, there is a formulation such as 'Lear
contends against the storm, with many subtle weapons'.[49] If it is not a matter
of contending against, then it is one of defiance, or contending despite. The
Gentleman's speech from the preceding scene gives something of the same

context: as we have seen, he speaks of Lear 'Contending with the fretful element'. Indeed, it may be the case that this answer informs the reading of critics: Stephen Booth mentions that the audience have heard the description of the king contending, 'and seen him do so at the beginning of this scene'.⁵⁰ However, the Gentleman's following lines suggest a character who is actively willing the storm on: 'Bids the wind blow the earth into the sea, | Or swell the curled waters 'bove the main, | That things might change, or cease' (3.1.5–7). Soon, conversely, the speaker offers the image of a Lear who 'Strives in his little world of man to outscorn | The to-and-fro-conflicting wind and rain' (10–11),⁵¹ one that is who apparently seeks command over his own actions before those of the weather. In Lear's opening speech in the storm, there is no such antithesis. The storm here is Lear's ally; he seeks destruction and the weather is his means to it.

There is, moreover, the notable irony of Lear's language performing the storm, just as the stage effects do, so that the arrival of his realisation comes about through the missing messianic qualities of his apocalyptic tone. He comes to terms with his own powerlessness at the same time as his language creates the event. Furthermore, the speech follows on perfectly from that with which he exits Regan's house at the end of Act 2. There he promises 'such revenges' on his daughters 'That all the world shall – I will do such things – | What they are, yet I know not' (2.2.447). It is moments later that the first sound of 'storm' is directed (on this occasion, interestingly, the direction is for 'storm and tempest', 2.2.472).⁵² In the next scene, the stage machinery of the tempest fills in the gaps of Lear's aposiopetic curse: the storm constitutes, in the context of the speech of the king, the 'terrors of the earth' which he had promised. It might be remembered that in the original 'part' of Lear – the cue-script for the actor to learn – this continuity would have been readily apparent, for the gap between the curse speech and the storm speech would have been separated only by a direction to exit and enter. The passion and thoroughness implicit in the lines in the storm are indicative of the appropriateness of this completion.⁵³ It is crucial that the speech contains the first explicitly Christian imagery of the play – 'drenched our steeples' – as though Lear's 'revenges' extended into an era far beyond his own. There are other Shakespearean instances of anachronistic Christianity, but not ones that constitute curses, not to mention evoke the Biblical image of the Flood: 'What they are, yet, I know not, but they shall be the terrors of the earth'. The text, then, insists that we take the storm as complicit in Lear's meaning, whilst dismissing any impulse which would have us ask, to echo Dessen, the distorting question of *where*.

Lear's attempted command of the weather in the storm is, as we have seen, anticipated somewhat ambiguously by the Gentleman's speech to Kent. It is, however, also foreshadowed much earlier in the play, usually taking the form of a curse. 'Blasts and fogs upon thee!' (1.4.291) is one such instance, with 'blasts' open to a variety of interpretations: thunder, lightning, infection and winds, for example. Lear hints at his potential power again in rebuking Goneril: 'I do not bid the thunder-bearer shoot, | Nor tell tales of thee to high-judging Jove' (2.2.415). These curses are indicative of Lear's notion of his identity, that is, as one who can command weather – *bid*, crucially, is very different, qualitatively, from *ask*.[54] At their most developed, Lear's curses take account of contemporary meteorology as well as pagan mythology:

> You nimble lightnings, dart your blinding flames
> Into her scornful eyes! Infect her beauty,
> You fen-suck'd fogs, drawn by the powerful sun,
> To fall and blast her pride!
>
> (2.2.368)

The fogs here are vapours, raised by the sun, but the fact that they are raised from fens makes them more noxious and harmful, thus with the potential to blast (or, in the Quarto, 'blister'). The minute detail of this part of the curse surely testifies to Lear's proclaimed faith in the power of weather, whether or not it evinces his belief that he truly can summon that power. The curse is all the more effective when it is acknowledged that it is governed not by imagery, but by scientific consensus. The pagan mythology of the quotation resides in Lear's invocation of the lightnings. In pre-republic Rome, it seems kings had pretensions of god-like grandeur and perhaps thought themselves able to mimic Jupiter/Jove in creating storms, and Pliny suggests that Numa actually had such power.[55] Lear has imagined himself in this Jove-monarch mould. The image-making of the above passage should be considered in conjunction with the earlier curse:

> Hear, Nature, hear! dear goddess, hear!...
> Into her womb convey sterility.
> Dry up in her the organs of increase;
> And from her derogate body never spring
> A babe to honour her.
>
> (1.4.270)

Here invoking Nature, rather than Jove, Lear's curse is nonetheless commensurable with his later bidding of lightning. Jove's thunderbolt, those 'nimble lightnings', had the power to 'slayeth the yongling in the wombe,

without harme to the mother'.[56] Lear's curse of sterility is therefore much
the same as his later curse: the lightning of Jove would not change the outer
appearance, but would kill within. 'All the stored vengeances of heaven fall |
On her ingrateful top! Strike her young bones, | You taking airs, with lame-
ness!' (2.2.354–6) is how Lear begins his 'nimble lightnings' curse, belying
the later 'I do not bid the Thunder-bearer shoot'. The curse on fertility
reaches its zenith in the storm as Lear demands the lightning 'Strike flat the
thick rotundity o'th'world | Crack nature's moulds'. Again, the lightning, like
Jove's, is intended to 'slayeth the yongling in the wombe, without harme to
the mother': in this case rid the world of 'ingrateful man' yet leave the world
intact. The term rotundity is clearly a reference to pregnancy – the implicit
image of the ever-expecting Mother Earth. The 'terrors of the earth' then, is
finally imagined as the rendering of the earth impotent, without killing the
earth itself. As Lear commanded Nature to 'convey sterility' into Goneril,
so the curse is here extrapolated to cover the entirety of the human race,
just as the wrath following the ingratitude of his daughters is ostensibly
visited upon the whole world. The conclusion of the earlier curse is arguably still relevant here:

> If she must teem,
> Create in her a child of spleen, that it may live
> And be a thwart disnatured torment to her
>
> (1.4.273–5)

The echo of this curse is resonant in the storm. If Lear does not realise
his wish for a sterile earth, the consolation is a world of 'disnatured' and
tormenting children. The notion of nature itself producing disnature,
points to the inherent dystopian quality of the lines. If we are to extrapolate
the conclusion of the curse as Lear himself does the beginning, then, the
inference is apocalypse. Just as the storm informs meaning in the language
of curses, therefore, so it magnifies it when those curses are contextualised
by the storm as an event.

The curse on the earth has been read by Janet Adelman as the point
at which the masculine influence of the pagan aesthetic is destabilised by
female authority:

> Despite Lear's recurrent attempts to find a just thunderer in the storm, that
> is, its violence ultimately epitomizes not the just masculine authority on
> which Lear would base his own but the dark female power that everywhere
> threatens to undermine that authority. No longer under the aegis of a male
> thunderer, the very wetness of the storm threatens to undo civilization, and

manhood itself, spouting rain until it has 'drench'd the steeples, drown'd the cocks', its power an extension into the cosmos of Goneril's power to shake Lear's manhood.[57]

Adelman's reading of the storm, authorising, as it does, Goneril with the power of the weather, effectively makes the same move of pathetic fallacy as Lear himself does. As outlined by William R. Elton, it is the process of demystification of the storm which correlates to Lear's own process of forlorn realisation and acceptance.[58] In the first speech in the storm, which Adelman is citing, Lear does not concede authority over the elements to his daughters. Only as Lear declares to the storm, in his next speech, 'But yet I call you servile ministers | That will with two pernicious daughters join' (3.2.21–2), has he indeed moved from his self-conception of commander of the weather. Rather than being, as Adelman would have it, 'an extension into the cosmos of Goneril's power', however, Lear is insisting that it is an extension of his own inability to command. Adelman refuses to acknowledge that 'the very wetness of the storm' is the aspect which Lear most explicitly attempts to control: the attempt to drench the steeples and to drown the cocks is explicitly Lear's, and therefore male. The fact that the storm is not 'under the aegis of a male thunderer' is what accounts for the fact that civilisation is not undone, as Lear has threatened or sought. Furthermore, constructions of the storm as an explicitly female power have to contend with the unfortunate metaphor of spilling germens. If one truly wishes to sexualise the storm itself and not Lear's own misogyny, it becomes a kind of apocalyptic coitus interruptus with Mother Nature: 'all germens spill at once | That make ingrateful man'. Adelman's formulation of the storm as female here is preparatory work for her argument connecting it with witches.[59] However, the will to connect the event of the storm in its entirety, whether causally or metaphorically, to any character of the play, or indeed gender or god, loses sight of an important fact. It is precisely such connection which Lear repeatedly undertakes, with changing emphasis or direction, and this is how the representation of his character is developed. The storm is consistent – 'storm still' – and consistently *just a storm*: the interpretation machine which seeks its origins and meaning as a storm is the domain of the characters. If we as critics engage in the same interpretation, we inevitably alter the means by which the characters are to be imagined.

If the play's original audience expected the supernatural when the stage machinery of the storm was utilised, such expectation might have been merited given the play's source. The conflation of storm and the curse in *King Lear* owes something to one of Shakespeare's sources, the anonymous chronicle play *King Leir*, which was first published in 1605.[60] In the source play, there are flashes of lightning and rumbles of thunder, but no sustained storm. As Elton has made clear, *Leir*'s thunder is rather explicitly depicted as a divine voice:

'Thunder and lightning' create panic in the would-be murderer's intention and awaken his conscience. Noteworthy is the crucial difference between Lear's defiant challenge to the thunder, culminating in a naturalistic question regarding its origin, and the Messenger's stupefied terror: 'Oh, but my conscience for this act doth tell, | I get heavens hate, earths scorne, and paynes of hell' (ll. 1646–7). 'They bless themselves', the directions read, both assassin and victim sharing the religious mood engendered by the thunder.[61]

The storm in *Leir*, then, encourages resolution, whilst the storm in *Lear* gives succour to curses. Thus much is indisputable. Earlier in the play, Edmund plays on the naivety of Gloucester by appealing to the same correlation of storm as divine voice that occurs in *Leir*: 'I told him the revenging gods | 'Gainst parricides did all the thunder bend' (2.1.44–6). In Psalm 83, the parallel of storm and the anger of God is invoked in the same way:

As the fyer burneth the forest, and as the flame setteth the mountaines on fyre: So persecute them with thy tempest, and make them afraied with thy storme. Fil their faces with shame, that thei maie seke thy Name, ô Lord.[62]

The extraordinary marginal note which accompanies these verses in the Geneva edition is 'That is, be compelled by thy plagues to thy power'. This codicil, presumably, refers to the 'thei' who are to be the subjects of the storm, that are to be converted. There is a defiant, almost colonial ferocity to its tone; the language, that is of invasion (a term which, as I have noted, Lear uses to describe the storm).[63] Against this grain, however, the note might be read in the same imperative vein in which the rest of the extract is written. Such a reading invokes an equally ferocious, but self-fulfilling God, encouraged by his own capacities of storm to express them further. There must always be the acknowledgement that, whenever postulating the audience's expectation of the supernatural upon hearing and seeing the special effects of thunder and lightning, each storm is necessarily invested with the supernatural in that it is understood as the work – the judgement – of God. As Elton notes, 'Marlowe employs thunder as a sign of divine anger: in *Faustus* the power of generating thunder and lightning is, as in Job, a divine attribute, and Faustus's ability to "rend the clouds" and produce the effect will unseat Jove and gain him "a deity" (1.1.60–4)'.[64] Unlike Faustus, Lear's impulse is not to unseat Jove, but to invoke him, and his tempestuous instruments. Although Lear's ability to control the storm is imaginary, there is little qualitative difference in his summoning Jove and summoning the weather directly. This is the understanding with which Lear enters the storm: thunder and lightning, wind and rain, are agents of his and subject to his command, and to them he turns whenever he wishes to address the various dilemmas of his existence. His first speech in the storm is also characterised in precisely this way, but, as Elton postulates, it is a belief to which Lear cannot cling: 'By the end of Act 4 Lear's madness has run its course, as have also the tension and breakdown caused by the failure of belief on all levels; and he is ready for belief of some kind, though not, of course, for anything resembling his previous tenets'.[65] Lear's 'belief', that is, is represented in terms of his acknowledgement not only of his lack of power over the storm, but of a willingness to conceive of the notion that there may be no possibility of such a power.[66]

The 'naturalistic question' to which Elton refers occurs at 3.4.151: 'What is the cause of thunder?' It is a question which reflects on Lear's understanding of his own being, as well as that of his environment: both of which have become problematised. I will conclude this chapter by exploring this question in terms of my argument so far. Before I do, however, I will examine one of its most insistent words: *cause*.

Unlike *event*, *cause* occurs as if quite relentlessly throughout *King Lear*, and in many different ways. In Goneril's use, it is both secretive and dangerous: 'Never afflict yourself to know the cause' (1.4.238).[67] For Lear, it is bodily and emotional: 'Old fond eyes | Beweep this cause again, I'll pluck ye out' (1.4.293–4); 'No, I'll not weep. | I have full cause of weeping ...' (2.2.472–3). Elsewhere in the play, *cause* is both crime ('what was thy cause? Adultery? 4.6.109) and vindication ('your sisters | Have, as I do remember, done me wrong. You have some cause, they have not' 4.7.72–4). Perhaps ultimately, *cause* is a special kind of impossibility: 'Is there any cause in nature that make these hard hearts?' (3.6.74–5). *Cause*, like *event*, is a word invested with ambiguity by Shakespeare, throughout the plays. In *Othello*, for example, the final scene's minatory opening line operates through the word's cryptic qualities: 'It is the cause, it is the cause, my soul!' (5.2.1). In *Troilus and Cressida*, an inherent illogicality is made explicit: 'O, madness of discourse, | That cause sets up with and against itself!' (5.2.149–50). On occasion, *cause* and *event* are juxtaposed. In *King John*, this is overtly meteorological: 'No common wind, no customed event, | But they will pluck away his natural cause | And call them meteors, prodigies and signs' (3.3.155–7). In *Antony and Cleopatra* the two words are linked again:

> All strange and terrible events are welcome,
> But comforts we despise. Our size of sorrow,
> Proportioned to our cause, must be as great
> As that which makes it.
>
> (4.15.3–6)

It is this changeable quality of *cause* in Shakespeare, and its relationship to the event, which I want to focus on in Lear's question, 'What is the cause of thunder?' Several editors point out that it is a question which harks back to ancient philosophical discussions about meteorology. Wells quotes Ovid here: 'Whether Jove or else the wind in breaking clouds do thunder'.[68] There is, however, a depth to the line greater than that conventional question. 'What is the cause of thunder?' can be understood as seeking out the atmospheric conditions which produce storms, but also questioning which side is taken by thunder, which purpose thunder is advocating: it can, in short, be understood as '*whose* is the cause of thunder?' Read either way, Lear's question is indicative of the process of disillusionment that he has gone through in the storm. The more familiar reading accepts that the elements are not subject to human command and Lear seeks a reconfigured view based on that acceptance. The latter reading can be aligned with the earlier 'yet I call you servile ministers'; that is, Lear accepts that the elements are not subject to *his* command and seeks a reconsidered view based on the notion that they are subject to someone else's.

We might, also, think in terms of Aristotle's four causes, and reframe Lear's question as 'What is the *final* cause of thunder?' After all, there is an implicit teleology at work in early modern concepts of weather, and the final cause of nature is hinted at throughout the play. If we are to read *King Lear* with attention to its meteorology, then, 'What is the cause of thunder?' is one of the most pertinent and poignant lines in the play, and also part of the play's radically self-questioning identity.[69] To characterise the journey of Lear's personality in the storm as a descent into madness is, of course, to oversimplify. Rather, the structures of the king's belief are fractured. Comment has been made on how such fracturing enables Lear, apparently for the first time, to be aware of a wider societal concern which has developed under his reign: it is at this point, for example, that we may re-join Dollimore: 'When he is on the heath, King Lear is moved to pity'.[70] The meteorological aspect of Lear's demystifying inheres in a lapse from solipsism and develops into a wider understanding of the forces of nature which prompt him to pray for his lost, weather-beaten subjects. From the starting position that *he* is the cause of thunder, and that *his* is the cause of thunder, the simple stock philosophical question opens an array of implications when that premise is dismissed. In questioning the cause of thunder, Lear is humanised, paradoxically refusing to seek shelter from the storm in the very moment that he fully acknowledges his powerlessness over it.

However the double meaning of *cause* underlies a crux on which the experience of the play rests. If the audience expect the supernatural at the sound and sight of theatrical storm, then Lear's question proves a tipping point. Either this provides the naturalistic sign around which an understanding of the play can be formed with no room for the supernatural, or it provides an indication that the storm yet has the potential to take sides. Or rather, yet has the potential *to be understood* as taking sides: that is, as still with otherworldly power, with knowledge, with sway, with cause. Lear's question is left unanswered, though within ten lines the storm sounds again. 'What is the cause of thunder?' is a question which penetrates the phonic system of signification in early modern theatre. It does so, moreover, by demanding that the audience react to, understand through, the event of the storm.

5

Wind

There are some who say that wind is simply a moving current of what we call air, while cloud and water are the same air condensed; they thus assume that water and wind are of the same nature, and define wind as air in motion. And for this reason, some people, wishing to be clever, say that all the winds are one, on the ground that the air which moves is in fact one and the same whole, and only seems to differ, without differing in reality, because of the various places from which the current comes on different occasions: which is like supposing that all rivers are but one river. The unscientific views of ordinary people are preferable to scientific theories of this sort.

Aristotle[1]

Perhaps Aristotle tempted the 'ordinary people'. As this epigraph suggests, there was a good deal of disagreement over the causes of wind. Rather than provide an undisputed framework for future generations, though, Aristotle's theories remained in competition with those from other voices, who continued to propound the theories Aristotle here rebuts. Moreover, when the basic causes or nature of wind itself are contested, the finer points of understanding become an inconclusive mess. As we will see, the question of wind became a question of character. Aristotle supposed that winds were analogous to rivers in that each was a largely contained system with its own idiosyncrasies. Rather than detail exactly the way in which winds move and gain in strength, therefore, writers in early modern England followed their Classical predecessors in ascribing particular characteristics and names to each wind, often contradicting each other. The resultant confusion is made worse when, in retrospect, readers oversimplify their responses on the basis of one contested interpretation (whether 'unscientific views of ordinary people' or 'scientific theories'). I will come to such responses below, with an example from *Pericles*.[2]

Within the wider context of my study, the exploration of wind is complicated by a further peculiarity. Today, wind is seen as a constituent part of a storm. If we think of the most extreme storms of recent years, they are likely to be ones characterised by high winds – hurricanes, cyclones or gales. In the destructive face of these phenomena, lightning, if it occurs, is a lesser concern than the force of the wind; thunder even less so. Hence, the OED has wind as the defining feature of a storm: 'A violent disturbance of the atmosphere, manifested by high winds, often accompanied by heavy falls of rain, hail, or snow, by thunder and lightning, and at sea by turbulence of the waves'.[3] To measure the strength of a storm is to measure its wind speed, whether in units per hour or against a predefined scale.[4] Wind is a quantifiable phenomenon.

In early modern texts, however, the emphasis is rather different. Wind was far from being an element of the definition of storms as in today's language. Instead, 'storm' and 'tempest' are commonly employed as intensifying nouns ('a storm of thunder', for example, or 'a tempest of lightning'), especially in factual accounts. Moreover, when winds are described meteorologically, it is often the case that storm winds are not given specific attention, and there is no consensus that one wind is more associated with storms than the others. This has led to a remarkable variability in the ways in which the wind's characteristics are employed by creative writers.

Even when winds were described in meteorological terms, there was a dispute over the basic principles, as inherited from the Classical texts. As is evident in the above quotation from Aristotle, one existing theory was that wind was simply 'air in motion'. That notion, found in Hippocrates, continued to hold sway after Aristotle's contention that wind is an exhalation.[5] Aristotle's view follows from the notion that air is made up of vapour and smoke: 'being composed, as it were, of complementary factors ... because the exhalation continually increases and decreases, expands and contracts, clouds and winds are always being produced in their natural season'.[6] When Pliny the Elder came to describe wind, he added a further theory: 'So again are caverns ... from which, if you throw some light object into it, even in calm weather a gust like a whirlwind burst out'.[7] Moreover, 'windings of mountains ... and the hollow recesses of valleys ... are productive of winds'.[8]

These competing theories were resolved by William Fulke. Whilst Fulke generally accepts, and slightly embellishes inherited ideas throughout *The Goodly Gallery*, his reasoning on wind is an impressive act of imaginative diplomacy. Essentially, Fulke's solution is to allow for each theory to apply: Aristotle's in general, and the others in specific situations. Hence for Fulke, in most circumstances: 'The wynd is an *Exhalation* whote and drie, drawne up into the aire by the power of the sunne, & by reason of the wayght thereof being driven down, is laterally or sidelongs carried about the earth, & this definition is to be understanded, of general winds that blow over all the earth'.[9]

Fulke's view is that the Hippocratic wind that Aristotle complains of 'is but a soft gentile and coole moving of the ayre, and commeth from no certaine place (as the generall wind doth)'.[10] Fulke goes on to describe the pleasantness of this wind, which seems to be what we would now call a summer breeze. This phenomenon, then, is not stormy in any way; indeed, is 'properly no wind, but a moving of the ayre by some occasion'.[11] The remaining type of wind, however, is problematic. For Fulke, the Plinian cave theory is best understood as the idea that there are localised winds in certain countries, or areas: 'this aire that cannot abide to be pinned in, findeth ... as it were a mouth to breake out of, and by this meanes bloweth vehemently: yet that force & vehemency extendeth not farre'.[12] This helps explain the observation that wind in some areas 'is very violent & strong, in so much, that it overthroweth both trees and houses, yet in other countries, not very farre distant, no part of that boysterous blast is felt'.[13]

It is, therefore, difficult to conclude from Fulke's descriptions whether he believes that the high winds we now associate with storms are of the Aristotelian, exhalation group or the localised Plinian group. We might assume that Fulke would contend that storm winds might occur in any location, but this is not made explicit until much later. Only when he has fully explained thunder and lightning, does Fulke define 'Storme wynde', as 'a thycke *Exhalation* violently moved out of a cloude without inflammation or burning'.[14] The reasons for this order of the text are made clear, as Fulke likens the storm winds to lightning itself, 'all one with ye matter of lightening, that hath béen spoken of: namely it is an *Exhalation* very whot and drye, and also grosse and thycke, so that it wyll easely be set on fyre, but then it hath another name, & other effectes'.[15] This reasoning shows that it is not unlikely for storm winds and lightning (which, as we have seen, was acknowledged as producing thunder) to occur in close proximity.[16]

Fulke's approach to the causes of wind seems to have persuaded his contemporaries and followers. Perhaps this is because it allows for the combination of competing theories, or perhaps it is simply that Fulke's default position is Aristotelian. Disagreement persisted, however, in the idea of particular characters being ascribed to particular winds. From the Classical period onwards, writers have disagreed about the names and features of each wind, and even the number of winds which might, or should, be distinguished.[17] Each of the four winds of the main compass points was popularly linked to one of the four elements: south and air; east and fire; west and water; north and earth. As such, attributes of the elements – moist or dry, hot or cold – were readily matched with the wind in question. There, however, the similarities in interpretation between writers tend to become less consistent, especially with the notion that one wind in particular might result in storms. It is this notion, more than the debates on the origins of all winds, that is especially relevant in reading dramatic or poetic texts of the period (or, as Aristotle might have it, 'the unscientific views of ordinary people'). Heninger contends that 'Each wind had definite characteristics, attributes, and associations, so that an author wishing to use a wind for literary purposes necessarily took great care in choosing the proper one'.[18] However, as I will argue, the process is not so nearly refined as Heninger suggests.

To illustrate this, here is an example from *Pericles*. Unlike the almost silent daughter of Antiochus, Marina, lost daughter of Pericles, is verbose in the face of adversity. Her seemingly absent-minded conversation with Leonine draws on the story of her birth:

> MARINA   Is this wind westerly that blows?
> LEONINE   South-west.
> MARINA   When I was born the wind was in the north.
>   (4.1.49–50).

The direction of this wind and its significance has resulted in confusion amongst commentators. In an attempt to unravel the play's geography, Peter Holland, not unreasonably, writes: 'a north wind cannot blow a ship travelling from North Africa to somewhere close to Tarsus ... It is a navigational impossibility'.[19] It is, of course, no surprise to find Shakespeare careless with cartography, and within the context of the play at least, Marina is accurate: 'The grizzled north | Disgorges such a tempest forth' (3.0.47–8). Doreen DelVecchio and Antony Hammond assert that 'the south and south-west winds had negative associations for Shakespeare'.[20] This notion finds support in *2 Henry IV* ('the south | Borne with black vapour' 2.4.363–4) and *The Tempest* ('A southwest blow on ye | And blister you all o'er' 1.2.324–5) among other plays. However, if this idea is not as firmly established as DelVecchio and Hammond contend, then it is contradicted entirely in *The Winter's Tale* by Florizel's 'a prosperous south-wind friendly' (5.1.160).[21]

Roger Warren glosses Gower's note of the wind's direction as 'north wind (bringer of storms)'.[22] It is certainly true that many examples, from both poetic and factual sources, support Warren's supposition. Barnabe Barnes, in a sonnet of 1593, writes: 'The North whence stormes, with mistes and frostes proceede'.[23] In Richard Hakluyt's *Principal Navigations*, a voyage to Tripolis is described as troubled by tempest, as 'presently there arose a mighty storme, with thunder and raine, and the wind at North'.[24] Nor is the connection a novel one, for in the Biblical Apocrypha we find 'The sounde of his thonder beateth the earth: so doeth the storme of the North'.[25] However, the notion that the north wind is *the* 'bringer of storms' is undermined by at least as many incidents as support it. Taking the south wind as an example, Nicolas de Nicolay, recounting explorations of Turkey, recalls Plutarch's conviction that the desert was formed by 'sand being moved with a storme which blew out of the south'.[26] In a 1586 work of criticism, William Webbe cites Virgil: 'Looke how the tempest storme when wind out wrastling blowes at south'.[27] And the idea that the north wind is particularly tempestuous is not a Biblical one, for the south is just as dangerous: 'And the Lord shalbe seene over them, and his arrowe shal go forthe as the lightning: and the Lord God shal blowe the trumpet, and shal come forthe with the whirlewindes of the South'.[28] Clearly, then, the characterisation of winds is not as simple a process as we might casually have thought, and is further complicated by several other possibilities. The direction of the wind might, for example, be seen to have medical significance, as in this extract from Simon Harward: 'Fernelius sayth, The north wind utterly forbiddeth letting bloud, only the south wind doth best admit it in the cold time of winter'.[29] Clearly, although this quotation is from a medical text, the letting of blood in Act 4, Scene 1 has other connotations, Leonine having agreed to stab Marina.

There is a symbolic resonance to the wind in Marina's enquiry – 'is this wind westerly that blows' – owing to a tradition of the wind's agreeable, or even fertile nature. For Pliny, it is 'that spirit of generation which doth breath life into all the world'.[30] During the plagues of Egypt, the west wind is sent by God to rid Egypt of the locust (or grasshopper in the Geneva text) just as He sent them with an east wind. This was often recalled in sermons and religious tracts of the early modern period.[31] But just as with the north wind, the tradition finds itself at odds, whether in poetry or experience. In the *Odyssey*, then, 'The old Sea-tell-truth leaves the deepes, and hides | Amidst a blacke storme, when the West wind chides'.[32] In Thomas Dekker's account of the plague year of 1603, the author opines 'O world of what slight and thin stuffe is thy happinesse! Just in the midst of this jocund Hollday, a storme rises in the West'.[33] And in the Gospel of Luke, it is taken as a given that 'when ye se a cloud rise out of the West, straightaway ye say, A shower commeth: and so it is'.[34] The southwest, meanwhile, also has its threats. This applies at sea: 'the winde came Southwest, and with so great a storme, that we thought to have run upon the strand, and were forced to cut downe our maine maste'.[35] It also pertains on land: 'And when the Southwest winde doth long blow about the ende of harvest, then those persons diseased with a long sicknesse, doe shortly after die'.[36] Traditions of a wind's character, it seems, are increasingly exposed as naïve and problematic in the phenomenon of the early modern publishing industry, especially when that industry is so invested in travel narratives.

The north wind might be understood in another way, as shown by John Deacon in his 1601 work, *Dialogicall Discourses*. Deacon describes the way weather affects those suffering from melancholy madness, which 'eftsoones is encreased in the *spring*, & in *summer:* yea, & it is then the extreamest of all when the *north-winde* blowes, by reason of the *drines* thereof'.[37] It is possibly this characteristic Hamlet alludes to: 'I am but mad north-north-west. When the wind is southerly I know a hawk from a handsaw' (2.2.315–16). The dryness of the north wind is part of the association of characteristics attributed to each wind by contemporary meteorology.[38] Like its corollary element, earth, the north wind was seen to be cold and dry as it 'riseth out of watrie places, that bee froze and bounde, because they bee so farre from the circle of the Sunne'.[39] The idea of the dry north wind is expressed most clearly in the Proverb 'the Northwind driveth away raine', quoted by clergymen in sermons and repeated in ecumenical commentaries.[40] Given this, it might seem curious that a tempest should arise from a northerly wind. However, as is characteristic of early modern notions of wind, the equation is not so simple. The north wind, although dry, carries poetic associations of violence, as expressed in this sonnet of Barnabe Barnes:

> That boystrous turbulence of North winds might
> Which swels and ruffles in outragious sort:
> Those chearefull Southerne showers whose fruitefull dew
> Brings forth all sustenance for mans comfort[.][41]

Here, the rain is not oragious, but refreshing – it is the south wind's revitalising answer to the chaotic influence of the north's. The 'boystrous turbulence' of the wind in *Pericles* is clear enough: Pericles prays to the 'god of this great vast ... | ... that hast| Upon the winds command, bind them in brass' (3.1.1–3). Indeed, the violence of the wind is the reason which Pericles's crew demand that Thaisa be abandoned: 'the wind is loud and will not lie, till the ship be cleared of the dead' (3.1.48–9). The important characteristic of the north wind, then, both in the storm scene itself, and in Marina's recounting of it, is not dryness, but chaos. Just as in the Barnes poem, the quality of the north wind is understood partly through its opposite, so in *Pericles*, the text creates its own weather dynamic. Far more important than the several cultural undertones of the particular wind is the construction established in the conversation. Although the wind in the scene is 'South-west', Leonine's emphasis is on *south*, to qualify Marina's suggestion that the wind is solely from the west. Marina associates the north wind with birth, then, whilst Leonine emphasises south, thereby implicating that wind in the scene with connotations of Marina's death. In this way, opposites are used for symbolic effect: north/south, birth/death. Just as Marina connects the north wind with danger and futility ('When I was born. | Never was waves nor wind more violent' 4.1.57–8) so the other winds seem to maintain her sense of security (Lychorida seems still to live, for example, in Marina's retelling). This sense, and the narrative which results, elevates the dramatic tensions of the passage. Shakespeare eschews the learnt associations of weather and portent, just as he does the conflation of storm effects and the supernatural. As elsewhere, he is more interested in the speed and certainty with which his characters tend towards symbolising weather.[42]

6

Macbeth: supernatural storms, equivocal earthquakes

Witchcraft is in itself much more terrible in its theatrical effect than the most absurd dogmas of religion; that which is unknown, or created by supernatural intelligence, awakens fear and terror to the highest degree: in every religious system whatever, terror is carried only to a certain length, and is always at least founded upon some motive: but the chaos of magic bewilders the mind.

Anne Louise Germaine de Staël, 1800[1]

Macbeth's storms are reminiscent of storms elsewhere. In the play, we have the meaning of remarkable weather, signs and portents debated, as in *Julius Caesar*; we have magical, conjured thunder and lightning, as in *The Tempest*; we have, as in *King Lear*, the intimation of apocalypse and fatalistic doom. But this familiarity is misleading, for there is something peculiarly unsettling, subversive even, about *Macbeth*'s incidences of storm. As suggested in the epigraph above from de Staël, this unsettling quality can be traced to the play's treatment of magic. The debates of remarkable weather follow the rebellious murder, rather than forewarn it. The conjurers do not renounce their art.

The play exhibits the familiar and obvious relationship of storm and the supernatural. *Macbeth* exploits this relationship in its staging, with stage directions for *Thunder and Lightning* for each entrance of the Witches. It is also present in the play's meteorology, which suggests supernatural origins for the remarkable weather. The distinction between a natural and a supernatural storm is, I will argue, critical in a meteorological reading of *Macbeth*. And yet, in an important sense, that relationship remains secretive: at the conclusion of the play, the magic is not only un-renounced but defiant, furtive, even victorious. The incidents in *Macbeth* of weather being attributed to natural causes are invariably from characters who are not involved with the Witches. The naivety of the surviving characters on the battlefield at the end of *Macbeth* can be seen as reflected in their inability to recognise the supernatural identity of the weather. In this chapter, I will show how this conclusion is prefigured throughout the play. *Macbeth* stages storms that conform to the theatrical status quo, in that they provide a backdrop for the supernatural figures. It is then, more widely, the sense of the supernatural storm which I will examine, along with the alternative meteorologies propounded by the characters who do not meet or know of the Witches. The constant tug between these extremes is reminiscent of the play's renowned espousal of equivocation and, as my chapter title suggests, this can be viewed in relation to a particularly violent phenomenon: the earthquake. As we shall see, the early modern distinction between storm and earthquake is not a decisive one; the two phenomena are fundamentally related.

Macbeth's stormy opening is an obvious place to begin. Perhaps less obvious is the extent to which these familiar lines, along with their concurrent effects, constitute a distinctly strange instance of storm:

> *Thunder and lightning. Enter three Witches*
> 1 WITCH   When shall we three meet again?
> In thunder, lightning, or in rain?
>
> (1.1.1–2)

The use of thunder and lightning to open a play is unusual. This is Shakespeare's first such usage and *The Tempest* is the only other. Nor is there a great deal of precedent for such an opening: *Macbeth* is the earliest extant play in English to begin with the stage direction.[2] Perhaps Shakespeare, after writing *Lear*, once more recognised the dramatic potency of the stage effects and thought the idea of a loud, pyrophoric assault an excellent attention grabber. Perhaps the playwright saw the implicit connection of storm with the battleground of the following scene, as Ronald Watkins and Jeremy Lemmon have suggested:

> The noise of storm, the cries of the familiar spirits that attend upon the Witches, above all the dialogue of the Witches themselves invest the battle of the play's opening with a greater and more fateful significance than the simple issue of military victory and defeat.[3]

The relationship of storm and battle is intriguing, and may offer an insight into why Shakespeare opens with the storm. The noise of thunder and that of the battle drums must have sounded fairly similar,[4] and, as we shall see, the Captain in the second scene explicitly likens the battle to a storm. Although I will offer possible answers, the question as to why Shakespeare decides to open with storm effects is not one which we can answer with certainty.

What we can say, however, is that from this arresting opening, the storm is explicitly linked with the supernatural. In this, *Macbeth* is already qualitatively different from the other plays which we have thus far examined. It may be that the play's orthodox pairing of storm and the supernatural is the result of Thomas Middleton's revisions to the text; and the scenes with the Witches do seem to be the ones on which Middleton concentrated his efforts.[5] Even if Middleton is responsible for all of these scenes, the Witches exhibit a tendency of Shakespeare's other supernatural characters by speaking in rhyming trochaic tetrameter. The verse form is itself evocative of the workings of magic: we might remember that the same poetic structure characterises, for example, the fairies in *A Midsummer Night's Dream*: 'I do wander everywhere, | Swifter than the moon's sphere; | And I serve the Fairy Queen, | To dew her orbs upon the green' (1.2.6–9). In *The Tempest*, Prospero's epilogue takes the form, as does some of Ariel's speech and that of Juno and Ceres (4.1.44–8; 106–17).[6] To the sound of staged lightning and thunder, then, is added the sound of a verse form which is recognisably other. In beginning with a storm and with the incantatory chants of the Witches, Shakespeare (or Middleton) is drawing on a vein of reference which immediately contextualises the thunder and lightning. The weather is constructed as supernatural from the outset. That the connection of storm and the supernatural is common adds to the effect of its strangeness: the storm is thereby both usual, in that the audience recognise the context, and unusual, in that it begins the play, and in that the remarkable weather is not treated as supernatural by any of the other characters.

The use of the verse form intensifies the connection of storm and magic. As I have already noted, evil spirits and supernatural events on the Renaissance stage are frequently accompanied by thunder and lightning. I have been arguing that Shakespeare's plays do not automatically engage in the relationship of storm and the supernatural, but it must be said that *Macbeth* is not the first instance in which we find the correlation at work. Indeed, the connection is made in one of Shakespeare's earliest plays, *Henry VI, Part 2* (another play with several authorial hands). During the play, as Roger Bolinbroke summons the spirit Asnath through the witch, Margery Jordan, the spirit is accompanied by one of the earliest examples of storm in Shakespeare's work:

> The time when screech-owls cry and ban-dogs howl,
> And spirits walk, and ghosts break up their graves;
> That time best fits the work we have in hand ...

*Here do the ceremonies belonging, and make the circle; Bolingbroke or Southwell
reads, 'Conjuro te', etc. It thunders and lightens terribly, then the Spirit riseth.*

(1.4.17–21)

If this is Shakespeare's first staging of thunder and lightning, then, he immediately endows storm with a sense of the supernatural. When this sense is
problematised it is done so vigorously and for aesthetic effect. Asnath is an
explicitly evil spirit, as evidenced by his name and the 'burning lake' from
which he arises (37). The structure of the renaissance playhouse is appli-
cable here, divided as it is into three sections: the Earth of the stage between
Heaven and Hell. Evil spirits, as in these examples, nearly always rise from
below. Margery Jordan, though the text names her as a witch, invokes 'the
eternal God' to persuade Asnath to answer (24). Though a conduit for an
evil spirit, then, and thereby associated with storm, the witch is seen to
contain the evil which the presence of the spirit threatens. Asnath speaks
on her terms, and on those of God. This is manifestly different from the
Witches of *Macbeth* who are very quickly established as servants to their
spirits: 'I come, Grimalkin', 'Paddock calls' (1.1.7–8) and who certainly do *not*
appeal to God, but who do have an oragious entrance of their own.

The connection between storm and the supernatural, then, a staple
of early modern theatre, is made explicit from the beginning of *Macbeth*.
While we cannot, of course, expect characters in plays to be 'aware' of the
theatrical conditions of their representation, part of the method of *Macbeth*
is to draw attention to the different levels of meaning between characters,
and indeed, audience: again, the storm brings out dramatic irony in Shakespeare's play. It is often commented that the Witches' 'Fair is foul, and
foul is fair' (1.1.12) is echoed by Macbeth's 'So foul and fair a day I have not
seen' (1.3.36). Such an echo is indicative both of the pervasive effect of the
Witches on the climate and of the invisibility inherent in their conjuring.
Macbeth 'has not seen' such weather, but also 'has not seen' a source for
such weather. Indeed, with Banquo and, indirectly, Lady Macbeth, he is one
of the people who do see this cause. All other characters 'have not seen' and
are not capable of seeing; the supernatural identity of the catalysts of the
play's action remains invisible. This is a very precise dramatic irony given
that the connection between storm and the supernatural had been truly
visible on the stage for many years before *Macbeth*.

Of course, the alliance of supernatural and storm is not solely the preserve
of the dramatic. Indeed, it seems likely that the above stage instances were
inspired and informed by popular belief. King James, famously, was suspicious of witches (I shall explore a particular manifestation of this suspicion

later) and wrote weighty and detailed works against them. In his *Daemon-ologie* (1597), he writes 'They can rayse stormes and tempestes in the aire, either upon Sea or land, though not universally, but in such a particular place and prescribed boundes, as God will permitte them so to trouble'.[7] William Perkins (1558–1602), in drawing the difference between a 'bad witch' and 'good witch' notes that the former can 'raise tempests by sea and by land'.[8] In *A Treatise of Witchcraft* (1616), Alexander Roberts concludes: '[As f]or the Elements, it is an agreeing consent of all, that they can corrupt and infect them, procure tempests, to stirre up thunder & lightning, move violent winds, destroy the fruits of the earth'.[9] Reginald Scot, a noted sceptic, begins his *Discoverie of Witchcraft* (1584) with the subtitle *An impeachment of Witches power in meteors and elementary bodies, tending to the rebuke of such as attribute too much unto them.* Scot's lengthy work, then, is itself testament to the belief in the meteorological power of witchcraft, and he makes the point clear in his opening chapter, which is labelled 'Credulitie'. 'But let me see', writes Scot 'anie of them all rebuke and still the sea in time of tempest, as Christ did; or raise the stormie wind, as God did with his word; and I will believe in them'.[10] Such seeing – every sensationalist aspect of it – was clearly happening in the theatres of London whether Scot would have approved or not. Yet *Macbeth*'s figures are not necessarily typical stage witches. Ryan Curtis Friesen has contended that they are 'demonic and existing in ambiguous domains reachable only through acts of tyranny' and contrasted with, say, Middleton's witches who are 'a brand of entertainment industry, easy to locate and cheap to bargain with'.[11]

Given this contemporary climate, then, in the playhouses and in literature, the association of witches and storm in *Macbeth* is not surprising. Critics have long argued over what power exactly the Witches possess but they are at least constructed as being something *other* by the effects of light and sound. The fact that the Witches and thunder and lightning always appear at the same time suggests an early modern signifier – which has kept some of its identity, if not its potency – of the supernatural.[12] This, furthermore, in a play run through with storm and wind imagery.[13] If the play does not require the question to be answered of *what* the Witches are, it at least demands that we inform any reading of the play's weather with an acceptance of their role in it. In answering the questions 'what are the implications of the storm in figuring the theistic identity of the Witches?' and 'how are those implications to be read in the rest of the play?' it is crucial to bear in mind the *supernatural* force of weather which proves an immediate point of reference. Whatever power the Witches have, the extensive correlation of their appearance and the thunder and lightning identifies both them and the storm as supernatural. As we have seen, this correlation is not solely a dramatic construct. However, it is also important to remember that, for the Jacobean, weather may be thought of as being caused by either natural or supernatural causes.[14] 'Natural' causes – those attributable to 'meteors' – were deemed explainable by science or natural philosophy, which of course, witchcraft was not. Although they may have portended the same omen, storms were frequently attributed to one source or the other; the two weather systems seemed to have been imagined to work in tandem, without functioning at the same time. Hence, when King James describes the storms for which witches are responsible, he declares they are

> verie easie to be discerned from anie other naturall tempestes that are meteores, in respect of the suddaine and violent raising thereof, together with the short induring of the same. And this is likewise verie possible to their master to do, he having such affinitie with the aire as being a spirite, and having such power of the forming and mooving thereof, as ye have heard me alreadie declare.[15]

As I have noted, this distinction between a natural and a supernatural storm is important in a meteorological reading of *Macbeth*. Although James thinks it 'verie easie' to distinguish between the two, there were no clear guidelines offered by the king or his contemporaries and there are certainly accounts of storms both 'suddaine' and 'short induring' which were not deemed supernatural.[16] However, as has been made clear by many critics, the presence of witches and storms in *Macbeth* may well reflect a very particular resonance for James. In 1589 Anne of Denmark was due to sail to Scotland to marry the king. This plan had to be abandoned when a tempest struck. James, in the autumn of that year, set sail in the opposite direction to complete the marriage, and stayed at the Danish Court throughout the winter. When the newlyweds sailed for Scotland in the spring, their ships were again subject to storms – one ship was lost – and witch-hunts on both sides of the North Sea began. As Stephen Greenblatt has written, 'One of the accused, Agnes Thompson, confessed to the king and his council that on Halloween 1590 some two hundred witches had sailed to [North Berwick] in sieves'.[17] It seems likely that Shakespeare had heard of this incident, or read about it in the pamphlet *News from Scotland* (1591), for when the Witches in *Macbeth* are plotting their sea-tempest on the Tiger, one says 'in a sieve I'll thither sail' (1.3.7).[18] Numerous critics have remarked on the relationship between the king and the Witches.[19] The important point here is that storms may be understood by Jacobeans to be the result of supernatural or natural causes. The language and the actions of the Witches in *Macbeth*, dramatic and memorable as they may be, are only one side of this dichotomy. The incarnations of the Witches and their relation to the weather dominate the opening and the third scene. In the intermediate scene, however, a different stance is taken:

> As whence the sun 'gins his reflection,
> Shipwrecking storms and direful thunders strike,
> So from that spring whence comfort seemed to come,
> Discomfort swells.
>
> (1.2.25–8)[20]

The Captain here is relaying to Duncan the story of the battle. At this point in his narration, Macdonald has been slain – the 'comfort' in the simile – and the Norwegian lord is about to begin his 'fresh assault' (33). The imagery the Captain uses to introduce this assault is strictly meteorological: the storms are natural. The 'reflection' of the sun refers to its return from the zenith of the spring equinox;[21] *spring* is used here to mean both the season and *origin*. At this point in the year, it was believed that violent weather should be expected. This belief extends at least as far back as Pliny: 'Moreover also the parts of some constellations have an influence of their own – for instance at the autumnal equinox and at mid-winter, when we learn by the storms that sun is completing its orbit'.[22] Rather than the immediate pleasantness of late spring and summer, then, there is a likely period of chaos. In addition this meteorological expectation reinforcing the reading of the line, the Captain's phrasing still makes use of a kind of poetic truth. Thus, '*As* whence the sun 'gins his reflection | Shipwrecking storms and direful thunders strike' implies that this process is a given – a received truth which the audience will recognise and upon which an extended metaphor can be established.

Although the Captain is using the belief as an elaborate trope, and the elucidation of summer storms is not his aim, there is a subtle significance to his speech. Implicit in the understanding of weather systems on display here is the notion that storms and thunders are predictable. The equinox is a reliable, immovable point in the year and, therefore, so is the weather that it is thought to generate. In this way, storms become to some extent foretold, which is to say that, rather than making predictions based on the portent of thunder, thunder is already thought to have been in place. The equinox is a regular, calculable event and an equinoctial storm should therefore engender few predictions, because it would have occurred when expected. This is a far cry from the thunder and lightning of the Witches, whose weather is grounded in its sense of confusion and paradox: 'fair is foul and foul is fair'. Indeed, part of the fearfulness of the weather of the Witches is in its unpredictability and its capacity to alter the environment suddenly. Moreover, if the Captain's meteorology is descriptive and inherited, there is space in the text, surely, for a reading of the Witches' thunder and lightning as *performative* storms. 'I'll do, I'll do, and I'll do' (1.3.9). It is this performative aspect of the Witches' weather, this promise of storm, which endows their identities with further supernatural power. Although the drums, the thunder-run and the fireworks begin the Witch scenes, it is their language which continues to perform the storm, 'In thunder, lightning or in rain', 'fair is foul', 'I'll give thee a wind', 'tempest-tossed'. Their capacity to perform this storm in language sets them apart from Margery Jordan, for example, who does not maintain the oragious character of her magic in her speech. *Macbeth*'s Witches are in complete control of the weather, and this is consolidated in their use of language to perform the storm.

The difference between the Captain's storm and those of the Witches might be neatly defined in their origins, but they have the same effects. Indeed, the use of the modifiers 'direful' and 'discomfort' are indicative of the place of thunder in *Macbeth*'s aesthetic: even the most predictable storm does not lose its prophetic implications. Greenblatt has contended that, in engendering the language of *Macbeth* with storms and magic

> Shakespeare was burrowing deep into the dark fantasies that swirled about in the king's brain. It is all here: the ambiguous prophecies designed to lure men to their destruction, the 'Shipwrecking storms and direful thunders' that once threatened Anne of Denmark.[23]

As we have seen, however, the storms that Greenblatt cites here are manifestly different from those that led to James's honeymoon witch hunt. The Captain explicitly mentions a natural reason for the bad weather, however dangerous (shipwrecking) and terrible (direful) it might be. Although James's ships set sail from Denmark at around the spring equinox of 1590, the storms that sank one of them and endangered the rest were immediately attributed to witches in Denmark and soon after in Scotland. Put bluntly, the Captain's storms are natural; King James's storms are supernatural. This is not to say that Greenblatt is mistaken in his appraisal of James's 'dark fantasies': from the available evidence on James it seems likely that the king would have found *Macbeth* unsettling, and clearly leapt to conclusions about storms and witches. The dramatic irony discussed above, then, must have been especially poignant for James, for the unnatural or supernatural malicious sorcery of the Witches remains as an undercurrent to all but a few characters of the play. A reading of the Captain's imagery which, like Greenblatt's, concentrates on James's reaction, misses this irony. The Captain's understanding of storms is very different from James's, especially as these are *shipwrecking* storms. The construction of these as natural, given that James contends the opposite, creates a tension not resolved until the Witches are seen, in the following scene, plotting a shipwreck. For those characters, like the Captain who do not encounter the Witches, storms remain calculable phenomena, attributable to natural origins. This suggestion is analogous to the fact that the Witches are not even acknowledged, let alone punished in the play's conclusion: their powers and their efforts, meteorological or otherwise, are undisclosed to any character still living at the end.

The incidents in *Macbeth* of weather being attributed to natural causes come from characters who are not involved with the Witches. The Captain speaks of equinoxes resulting in storms, and yet those storms retain a certain foreboding quality. Similarly, Lennox, upon reaching Macbeth's castle after Duncan is murdered, does not leap to conclusions about the causes of the remarkable weather, yet is fearful of what it might portend:

> The night has been unruly: where we lay,
> Our chimneys were blown down, and, as they say,
> Lamentings heard i'th'air, strange screams of death
> And prophesying with accents terrible
> Of dire combustion, and confused events,
> New hatched to th'woeful time. The obscure bird
> Clamoured the livelong night. Some say, the earth
> Was feverous, and did shake.
>
> (2.3.50–7)

It is not uncommon for critics, presumably encouraged by this description, to note that there was a 'frightful hurricane of the night when Duncan was murdered'.[24] The connection between storm and omen is, of course, nothing new, as we have seen. The link is most explicitly drawn in *Julius Caesar*, in which Casca, in the midst of a storm, is troubled that 'prodigies | Do so conjointly meet' (1.3.28–9). In the same scene, Casca, like Lennox, seems to report an earthquake: 'all the sway of earth | Shakes like a thing unfirm' (3–4). Despite appearing in both plays, of all of the prodigies which Lennox lists, this last is surely the most unusual, if not the most fearful. In early modern England, an earthquake was thought to prognosticate a time of terrible upheaval. As Abraham Fleming wrote in 1580:

> But of what sorrowes to come are Earthquakes foretokens? First, to beginne, of warres, whereby it is most certaine pestilence and famine are ingendered: pestilence by the aire poisoned with the stinch of dead carcasses lieng unburied: famine by reason of husbandrie, when plough landes lie unmanured: besides other calamities full of feare, horror, and desolation.[25]

It is clear, then, that earthquakes are not to be taken lightly, whether obscure birds are clamouring or not. Although they are hardly common, it is quite possible that Shakespeare would have experienced an earthquake himself: the earthquake of 6 April 1580, which prompted Fleming and many others to write, was apparently felt throughout England.[26] Perhaps a more immediate source of reference for the significance of earthquakes, though, was the story of Jesus on the cross. If, as has been argued, Shakespeare had access to the Geneva Bible,[27] in it he would have read:

> Then Jesus cryed againe with a loude voice and yelded up the gost. And beholde, the vaile of the Temple was rent in twayne, from the top to the bottome, and the earth did quake, & the stones were cloven, and the graves did open them selves, and many bodies of the Sainctes whiche slept, arose.[28]

Fleming interprets earthquakes, not unreasonably given this context, as a sign of 'the wrath of almightie God, therewithall admonishing us to amende our evill life'. The same had been said of thunderstorms by contemporary commentators, but, as Fleming goes on to demonstrate, the Biblical allusion imbues the theory with a grim authority:

> otherwise such sorrowes are like to light upon us, as shall turne to our most miserable overthrowe and lamentable destruction: and here upon it came to passé, that when our Lord Jesus Christ was crucified, the earth quaked and trembled.[29]

Such a parallel, of course, is even more relevant when, as in 1580, the earthquake occurs in the week of Easter. Nor is Matthew's account the only Biblical reference to earthquakes; in Revelations, the apocalyptic imagery is thick with them: 'And I behelde when hee had opened the sixt seale, and loe, there was a great earthquake, and the sunne was as blacke as sackecloth of heare, & the moone was like blood'.[30] This same darkening of the sun precedes the earthquake in the Book of Joel, where we find 'the day of the Lord cometh, for it is nigh at hand: A day of darkness and of gloominess, a day of clouds and thick darkness'.[31] Indeed, this darkening of the sun will have an eerie familiarity to those who recall Ross's words in *Macbeth*:

> Thou seest the heavens, as troubled with man's act,
> Threatens his bloody stage. By th'clock 'tis day
> And yet dark night strangles the travelling lamp.
>
> (2.4.5–7)

Ross here is responding to the Old Man, who, like Lennox, is in the unfortunate position of noticing prodigious 'things strange' in hindsight rather than premonition. The sun, the travelling or *travailing* lamp,[32] is subsumed by the night, in the exact way which the Bible shows should be treated as foreboding. Drawing carefully from Raphael Holinshed's *Chronicles*, Shakespeare took as his model for Duncan's murder that which Donwald arranges of King Duff. Consequently, then, after Duff's murder, 'there appeared no sunne by day, nor moone by night ... and sometimes such outragious windes arose, with lightnings and tempests, that the people were in great fear of present destruction'.[33] Again, then, the portents appear rather too late. In *Macbeth*, the Witches seem able to foresee many things, and create storms, and so their supernatural qualities are augmented by the fact that most characters – 'natural' characters – display knowledge of meteors only in hindsight. And yet the Witches remain silent on the subject of the darkness which foretells an earthquake. Indeed, if anyone in the play shows prescience of this, it is Lady Macbeth:

> Come, thick night,
> And pall thee in the dunnest smoke of hell,
> That my keen knife see not the wound it makes,
> Nor heaven peep through the blanket of the dark,
> To cry 'Hold, hold'.
>
> (1.5.48–52)

It might be argued that Lady Macbeth here is implicitly linked with the Witches, in that she calls upon the heavens to align themselves to her own malicious purposes. This invocation of deviant darkness resonates with the supernatural and evil, especially in the light (so to speak) of its Biblical precedents. It is not too much to say that Macbeth is linguistically integrated in this effect later in the play, when he echoes the summons: 'Come, seeling night, | Scarf up the tender eye of pitiful day' (3.2.46–7). In case this ricochet of syntax is not enough, Macbeth, telepathologically perhaps, constructs the opposite of his wife's 'thick night' as a threat to their dynasty: 'Light thickens' (50).[34]

After the earthquake of 1580, the Church of England published *The Order of Prayer, and other Exercises, upon Wednesdayes and Frydayes, to Avert and Turne Gods wrath from us, Threatened by the Late Terrible Earthquake: to be used in all parish churches and housholdes throughout the realme.* This document contained the Book of Joel, in which can be found 'The earth shall tremble before him; the heavens shal shake, the sunne and the moone shalbe darke, and the stars shal withdrawe their shining'.[35] Presumably from reading Joel or from hearing these state-ordered sermons, Fleming goes on to write:

> *Before the end of the world come* (saith Christ) *iniquitie shall abound, there shalbe rumors of wars, there shalbe Earthquakes, there shalbe famine & troubles: all which if they be but the beginnings of sorrowes, alas what calamities will followe?*
> The Prophet saith that *Before the great and terrible daie of the Lord come, wonders shalbe seene in the heauens and in the earth, bloud and fire, pillers of smoke, the Sunne darkened, and the Moone turned into bloud, &c.*[36]

Fleming's work, like the Church pamphlet and several contemporary writings on the earthquake, contains a prayer specifically designed to be enunciated in times of disaster. Indeed, although Fleming's work contains passages which attempt to elucidate the *causes* of earthquakes rather than what they signify, it is clear that so-called 'naturall reasons', in the case of the quake of 1580, give way to an interpretive emphasis on the will of God. In none of the extant documents relating to the earthquake does the author contend that the disaster is down to natural causes (to the extent that the natural can be distinguished from the divine) although the majority of them list what these 'natural' causes – in the case of other earthquakes – must be. In Lennox's speech, the adjective 'feverous' is most telling: the earthquake is understood to be of natural origin. There is no element of the supernatural here, nor mention of God or the Bible, although both would offer a fearful context in which to understand the earthquake. It must also be pointed out that, for early modern thinkers, an earthquake was not due to plate tectonics. Rather, following thinkers of the Classical era, the earthquake is considered a form of storm. The general principle upon which the theory of earthquakes is based is that wind, trapped beneath the surface of the earth, rushes and swirls underground, causing the earth to shake. As Fleming writes, a natural cause of an earthquake would be 'all the winds being gotten into certeine veines, holes, and caves of the earth, and there moove by there secrete rusling'.[37] Likewise, Arthur Golding notes that

> naturally Earthquakes are sayde to be engendred by winde gotten into the bowels of the earth, or by vapors bredde and enclosed within the hollowe

caves of the earth, where, by their stryving and struggling of themselves to get oute, or being haled outwarde by the heate and operation of the Sun, they shake the earth for want of sufficient vent to issue out at.[38]

Just as the wind struggles to leave the earth, the element of fire, trapped in the watery and airy vapour of a cloud, is compelled by friction to be discharged as lightning. Pliny contends that

> Neither is this shaking in the earth any other thing, than is the thunder in the cloud: nor the gaping chinke thereof ought els, but like the clift whereout the lightening breaketh, when the spirit enclosed within, struggleth and stirreth to goe forth at libertie.[39]

For the sake of comparison, to see how closely the descriptions match, here again is Simon Harward's description of thunder and lightning:

> This hotte exhalation … courseth up and downe in the clowd, seeking some passage out, which when it cannot find, it maketh a way by force, and being kindled, by the violent motion it breaketh through the clowde.[40]

This was not simply a scientific analogy confined to the natural philosophers, but found its way into literature. In Thomas Dekker's *A Strange Horse-Race* (1613), we are told of 'thundring velocity, lightning-like violence, and earthquake'. In Edmund Spenser's *The Fairie Queen*, we find the description 'trembling with strange feare, did like an earthquake show. | As when the almightie *Jove* in wrathfull mood | … Hurles forth his thundering dart'.[41] What we have, then, is an event rich in ecclesiastical resonance and which might carry such meaning for anyone who experiences or hears of it. Rather than drawing upon this resource, however – and with the implications of the death of Christ and the apocalypse, it is a rich one – the earthquake is constructed as natural. As Harold Bloom has written: 'Macbeth rules in a cosmological emptiness where God is lost, either too far away or too far within to be summoned back'.[42] Booth notes that Macbeth, in contrast to young Siward, is denied expository rites.[43] God is almost absent from *Macbeth* or, perhaps, Macbeth eradicates belief: 'I could not say "Amen" | When they did say "God bless us"', he says of the guards he kills (2.2.31–2).[44] The impact of the earthquake cannot be free from Biblical overtones: we might call to mind one of the play's allusions: the Captain describes Macbeth and Banquo, who 'meant to bathe in reeking wounds | Or memorise another Golgotha' (1.2.39–40). Booth writes that the Golgotha image is a 'stylistic analogue to the perverse meteorological commonplace' of the Captain's equinoctial storm.[45] Of course, *meteorological* is a narrower term now – as Booth uses it – than it had been, but once included earthquakes. Golgotha, the site of Christ's crucifixion, which is to say, an earthquake's epicentre, is indelibly linked with violence and with death but also the heroism of victorious leaders. Despite occurrences such as this, however, there is something quite systematic about the absence of faith in the text. Indeed the lack of any mention of God in relation to the storms and the earthquake, if anything, augments the supernatural power of the Witches to command the elements and to see the future.

The idea that earthquakes were the result of the trapping of winds was evidently a theory to which Shakespeare gave credence. In *Venus and Adonis*, lines describing the goddess's feelings on seeing the injured youth display both the early seismology and the emotions which earthquakes engender in the victims. Venus

> quakes;
> As when the wind, imprisoned in the ground,
> Struggling for passage, earth's foundation shakes,
> Which with cold terror doth men's minds confound.
>
> (1045–8)

Lennox's 'feverous' is indicative that he is subscribing to the scientific explanation of the earthquake, rather than attributing it to supernatural causes. The personification of the Earth was a common notion, with its fever's symptoms being the trapped wind and the shaking. We find the same personification, and fever, articulated in *1 Henry IV*:

> GLENDOWER I say the earth did shake when I was born.
> HOTSPUR And I say the earth was not of my mind,
>   If you suppose as fearing you it shook.
> GLENDOWER The heavens were all on fire, the earth did tremble –
> HOTSPUR O, then the earth shook to see the heavens on fire,
>   And not in fear of your nativity.
>   Diseased nature oftentimes breaks forth
>   In strange eruptions, oft the teeming earth
>   Is with a kind of colic pinch'd and vex'd
>   By the imprisoning of unruly wind
>   Within her womb, which for enlargement striving
>   Shakes the old bedlam earth, and topples down
>   Steeples and moss-grown towers.
>
> (3.1.18–30)

Although Glendower's aggrandising of the portentousness of this earthquake is met with mockery by Hotspur, the latter's comments still betray something of the fear of the earthquake phenomenon. The 'colic' and 'unruly wind', as well as aligning Hotspur's speech with Lennox's 'feverous', point towards a fear arising from the meteorology of earthquakes. As S. K. Heninger puts it, 'not the least terror invoked by earthquakes was the possibility that stagnant infectious airs ... might be released by this rending of the earth's surface'.[46] This calls to mind that phrase of Fleming's, 'most certaine pestilence ... is ingendered'.[47]

However, if we are to take the influence of contemporary meteorology into account, we must also point out that there is still something rather unusual about Lennox's description. To illustrate this, here are some quotations concerning the weather conditions which were thought to accompany a feverous earth:

> Againe, wheras in Earthquakes that procéede of naturall causes, certaine signes and tokens are reported to go before them, as, a tempestuous working and raging of the sea, the wether being fair, temperate, and unwindie, calmenesse of the aire matched with great colde: dimnesse of the Sunne for certaine dayes.[48]

> [T]he earth is never wont to quake, but when the sea is so calme, and the aire so still, that nether ships can saile, nor birdes flie[.][49]

> If any earthquake bee at hand, the Sea will give manifest tokens thereof unto the skilfull Marriner, for though no wind be stirring, the sea will swell and mount with billowes and great waves as in a Tempest and storme[.][50]

These writers are, again, extending a tradition dating back to Aristotle, who contends that 'the majority of earthquakes and the greatest occur in calm weather. For the exhalation being continuous in general follows its initial impulse and tends either to flow inwards at once or all outwards'.[51]

It is clear that for these thinkers the air must be still for the earth to quake, whilst the sea either rages in the still air or remains still itself. Nowhere in contemporary theories of earthquakes is there any parallel to Lennox's opening gambit: 'The night has been unruly' or 'chimneys were blown down' and certainly not anything approaching the 'hurricane' of Bradley. Indeed, the very opposite is almost always the case. Motionlessness, silence, immobility. Lennox's earthquake, then, is a kind of hyperstorm. That which afflicts the earth and makes it feverous has also afflicted the air. Neither element is safe. The chimneys that were blown down, the 'Lamentings heard i'th air; strange screams of death', the 'accents terrible | Of dire combustion and confus'd events', this is not the calm of which the natural philosophers write. The images are vivid enough for a modern audience to appreciate, but for a Renaissance audience, who believed their wind to be moving through one realm at a time, the impact of the final omen of the earthquake must have been truly apocalyptic. Casca, in *Julius Caesar*, had the words to express this impact: 'Let not men say | "These are their reasons", "they are natural"' (1.3.29–30). This is not expressed as succinctly in *Macbeth*, but is shown through the overwhelming horror of Lennox's description. Lennox's 'natural reasons', though he strives to maintain them, are undone by the completeness of the disasters he describes. The dramatic irony of the Witches' complicity in the weather – the fact that there are two meteorological levels of meaning in the text – allows, or even persuades the audience to dismiss Lennox's naivety: these storms, like the events they relate to, are strictly supernatural in their origin. Whilst in *Julius Caesar*, the possibly supernatural storm is eventually understood not to be betokening a spirit, devil, a god or God, in *Macbeth* the opposite is the case: the ostensibly natural storms in descriptions are troubled by the supernatural storms on stage.

In Lennox's speech, this strange sense of augury after the fact is deeply ironic. For him, 'th' woeful time' is indeed one of violence and rebellion, but Macbeth, through his violent prowess, is the curtailer of rebellion, not its instigator.[52] In the face of all of the portents he lists, then, Lennox must feel secure to reach the castle of the king's most celebrated defender. This irony, obvious though it is, is nonetheless underlined by Macbeth's lines as he leaves the stage to kill Duncan:

> Now o'er the one half-world
> Nature seems dead[...]
> Thou sure and firm-set earth,
> Hear not my steps, which way they walk, for fear
> The very stones prate of my whereabout,
> And take the present horror from the time,
> Which now suits with it.

> (2.1.49–50; 56–60)

These lines offer a complete contradiction to Lennox's. Nature seems dead: the silence that is described here is, as we have seen, that very state which is opposed in Lennox's description. Furthermore, the speech has several more quiet qualifiers: 'stealthy', 'Moves like a ghost', 'Hear not' and 'Hear it not' are all within the space of ten lines (54–63). Moreover, 'present horror' is generally taken to be indicative of 'terrible stillness':[53] Braunmuller glosses the phrase as 'the silence that would be broken by speaking stones'.[54] The sounds that Macbeth mentions – the wolf and the bell – both act as 'alarum' calls (53, 62) for him to act. There is nothing, to use Lennox's vocabulary, strange or clamouring about these noises. Rather, they have a direct and specific purpose. Even more brazen than these oppositions, however, is the image of the 'firm-set earth'. In the history of *Macbeth* criticism, a well-worn theme is that of equivocation.[55] The equivocality of the earthquake is explicit in the examples of the speeches of Macbeth and Lennox: the earth described as firm-set and simultaneously as shaking. Equivocation, like the earthquake, can be construed as a catalyst of terror. The infamy of the gunpowder plotters and their equivocal defence is generally taken to be the foremost reason behind the play's concern with the equivocal.[56] If we take the earthquake lines to be indicative of Lennox's fear of the 'woeful time', then it is clear that Macbeth is speaking out of 'fear' of the very portent of which Lennox has heard. That Macbeth should mention the earth in his expression of this fear is distinctly unusual, as earthquakes and speaking stones are particularly rare.[57] When Macbeth delivers his lines, if dwelled upon, they seem strange and curious. Prating stones? Macbeth's plea for silence rests on ordinary things: an earth which doesn't move, a night which is quiet, stones which don't gossip easily. Lennox's speech is characterised by the unusual, particularly the noisy unusual. His description seems to will the very silence which Macbeth is invoking. Yet for all of Macbeth's fear, even the exact opposite of the climate he wished for has betrayed neither his intentions nor his actions. The earth has shaken and he is undiscovered. Curiously, this might call to mind another Biblical verse: 'There shal come as an earthquake, but the place where thou standest, shall not be moved'.[58] Macbeth, with his supernatural seismograph alert, has enough foresight to fear the prognosticatory potential of the earthquake but does not feel its effect, either literally or metaphorically. The action which the audience understands to cause the earthquake requires a firm-set earth.

The contrast with Lennox's speech is profound and yet, the effect of that contrast rests on the order of the statements: had Lennox's lines been placed before Macbeth's, the result would be noticeably different. The firm-set earth is innocuous, it is lodged at the end of a highly decorative speech, a part of Macbeth's self-propagandising invective, and the audience may be forgiven for still musing on the phantom dagger. This would not be the case if Lennox had already mentioned the earthquake. Context and linearity here are crucial. And yet Macbeth's 'firm-set earth' does provide a context in which to hear of Lennox's portents. Aside from the contradiction of the description of the earth itself, Lennox's words are haunted by

Macbeth's. The virtue of the steadiness of the thane's lines, their calm decisiveness, their unshakeability. Macbeth's phrase has the effect of a ghostly presence, haunting the invocation of the earthquake. Macbeth himself opens the possibility of the firm-set earth being disrupted, being shaken, being heard again in a new context. Macbeth is portrayed as requiring an inhabiting of the equivocal in order to bring himself to regicide: 'The eye wink at the hand. Yet let that be | Which the eye fears when it is done to see' (1.4.52–3). The full impact of the earthquake, then, might be felt in the extent to which Macbeth succumbs to meteorological equivocation, seeming to will the earth to be still as it is later said to be shaking. The thrill of this particular case is that we are carried along on Macbeth's firm-set earth, only afterwards to be exposed to the fissures and faultiness of his tumultuous quake.

Lest this is thought slender textual evidence or merely a solitary chance reference, we see that later in the play, when Macbeth himself is shaking, he once more invokes the surety of the earth: 'Then comes my fit again: I had else been perfect; | Whole as the marble, founded as the rock' (3.4.20–1). Yet the ambiguity is also apparent later in the same scene: 'Stones have been known to move, and trees to speak' (122). The distinction between the shaking earth and the founded is one of the many things over which Macbeth loses control.

When the Witches vanish before Banquo and Macbeth, the former's thought is a line which is eerily informed by the science of the earthquake: 'The earth hath bubbles, as the water has, | And these are of them' (1.3.77–8). Science in *Macbeth* is established in opposition to the supernatural, or indeed God. The pull of equivocation permeates the language of the play in this opposition as well as the other, more notable equivocal instances. Here, however, the scientific cause is given a supernatural flavour – not one of wrath or benevolence, but one of knowing, of disappearance, of something to come: the storm of the Witches in the air, but then the sea and then the ground. They continue to perform their storm, even in the language of characters who do not know of their existence. An iterable storm. A storm to transcend elements. This troubling, unsettling quality of the storm in *Macbeth* is, indeed akin to the quality of equivocation which has been shown to characterise the play. Banquo's shift from a witness of the Witches to a victim of their supernatural directive is, appropriately enough, finalised in a weather-based phrase: 'It will be rain tonight' (3.3.16). The reply he receives from his unseen audience, the murderers, is one which furthers, or re-iterates, the malevolence of *Macbeth*'s storm, one which fulfils Banquo's part in the Witches' prophecy, one which modifies Banquo's naturalistic meaning and draws blood: 'Let it come down'. Weather dominates *Macbeth*; and its origins, its effects and its meaning are always subject to the equivocal play of terror.

7

Rain

The quality of mercy is not strain'd,
It droppeth as the gentle rain from heaven
Upon the place beneath

The Merchant of Venice 4.1.182–3

The meteorological phenomena that I have examined so far – thunder, lightning and wind – are all the result, in Aristotelian terms, of exhalations. Of the various elements which we now consider to make up storms then, only rain and the related hail or snow, are categorised as vapours. Perhaps it is this irregular status that ensures that rain alone never stands for a storm in Shakespeare's work. Another element is required to form a compound image of a storm, as in, for example, 'the to and fro conflicting wind and rain' of *King Lear* (3.1.11). For this reason, I will not dwell on it for as long as I have the other parts of a storm. It is, however, still worth looking at briefly.[1]

If rain is invoked alone, then it is usually moderate or, as in Portia's speech above, an image of gentleness. Most often of all, rain is part of the poetic commonplace of tears as rainy or tempestuous (as in *King Lear*'s 'he holp the heavens to rain' or *3 Henry VI*'s 'And when the rage allays, the rain begins | These tears are my sweet Rutland's obsequies' (3.7.61; 1.4.146–7). Rain, therefore finds itself part of a remarkable range of figures, from the deeply embedded pathetic fallacy, through nourishment and replenishing, to wild storms. This quality, I will argue, is attributable not only to the variety of rains to which England was – and is – exposed, but also to the way in which rain itself is understood.

As with thunder and lightning, rain was known to result from clouds:

After the generation of cloudes is wel knowen, it shall not be hard to learn, from whence the rayne commeth. For after the matter of the cloud being drawn up, and by cold made thick (as is sayde before) heate followynge, which is moste commenlye of the Southerne wynde, or any other wynde of hotte temper, doth resolve it againe into water, so it falleth in droppes.[2]

Some heat, then, normally from wind, is needed to produce rain, as it melts the cloud. Fulke's model of the weather explains neatly why storms should include rain. He views storm winds as 'very whote and drye', and so it is no surprise that rain should accompany them if rain is 'resolved ... again into water' by warm air. The same process outlined here accounts for hail, snow and dew, depending, as each does, on the temperature of the region of air. As Fulke continues, the simplicity of the meteorology of rain is evident:

> There bee small showers, of small, drops, & there be great stormes, of great drops. The showers with small drops, proceede eyther of the small heate that resolveth the clouds, or else of ye great distance of the clouds from the earth. The streames with great drops, contrariwise doe come of great heate, resolving or melting the cloud, or else of small distance from the earth.[3]

There is no inherent complexity in rain, nor is there any ferocity. The other stormy elements are forceful and violent: we have seen thunder rattling and breaking, lightning piercing and striking, wind disgorging. Rain simply *resolves* itself. Alone, then, it is beneficial and only when joined with other weather phenomena is to be feared:

> Also a cloud is profitable to the earth, when he is resolves and fallen into raine. But hée is full gréevous and noisfull when he tourneth into winde: for then he gendereth groan tempest both in sea and in lande.[4]

The idea of a rain being a 'resolution' of itself fits in with the overarching theory of Aristotle. In describing the 'cycle of changes' that accounts for the air's moisture he gives this image:

> One should think of it as a river with a circular course, which rises and falls and is composed of a mixture of water and air. For when the sun is near the stream of vapour rises, when it recedes it falls again. And in this order the cycle continues indefinitely. And if there is any hidden meaning in the 'river of Ocean' of the ancients, they may well have meant this river which flows in a circle round the earth.[5]

Rain is a crucial element of the replenishing sequence of order which characterises Aristotle's system of understanding.

The language used to describe rain is more well-known outside of its meteorological context, though, as it forms a familiar editorial crux. In the 1604 Quarto of *Hamlet*, we find 'O that this too too sallied flesh would melt, | Thaw and resolve it self into a dewe'.[6] When using the Quarto as a base text, editors frequently change *sallied* to *sullied* (*Hamlet*, 1.2.129). As such, Hamlet's flesh is contaminated, and the possibility of resolving to dew figures both cleansing and annihilation into the metaphor. In the Folio text, however, *sallied* is replaced with *solid*: vapour, that is, that has formed together into something tangible. In this case, Hamlet's wish is to 'return' to water (rather than 'become' it), which makes the image slightly more in tune with meteorological language. Moreover, his flesh in this description is, by implication, figuratively a cloud. Such an image resonates with the Claudius's parting statement:

> in grace whereof
> No jocund health that Denmark drinks today
> But the great cannon to the clouds shall tell,
> And the King's rouse the heaven shall bruit again,
> Re-speaking earthly thunder.

(1.2.123–8)

The fantasy of becoming dew is simultaneously the wish to not become implicit in Claudius's threatened thunder. Either rendering of the text gives a self-sustaining image, then, but the Folio version offers a meteorologically sound counterpart to Claudius's bombast. Such is the equalising nature of rain in early modern imagery.

8

Pericles: storm and scripture

Enter Pericles *on shipboard*
The god of this great vast, rebuke these surges
Which wash both heaven and hell, and thou that hast
Upon the winds command, bind them in brass,
Having called them from the deep.

Pericles 3.1.1–4

These lines mark a turning point. This much is noted by almost all recent commentators who linger on *Pericles* for long enough. These critics, bound up by the fine textual questions which concern the play's dual authorship, broadly agree that the play is Shakespeare's from Act 3 onwards, with the first two acts belonging to George Wilkins.[1] Hence, when Pericles appears in this sea-storm, raging at the elements from the deck of his ship, the play suddenly feels very different. We are reading, or hearing, for the first time in the story the poetry of the writer who overshadows our language like no other. Here is the touchstone of literary and dramatic merit at work, we are told. Consequently, perhaps, in this storm we feel in safe hands.

But there is something of greater importance here. Shakespeare had collaborated before, and there are similar, debatable moments of his 'entry' in other plays. In this, his first scene in *Pericles*, he tries something new. He has written sea-storms before, but they have been narrated, as in *Comedy of Errors*, illustrated through exposition, as (we assume) in *Twelfth Night*, or given a simultaneous commentary, as in *Othello*. Here, Shakespeare takes a further step and brings the ship itself into the theatre ('*Enter* Pericles *on shipboard*'). Lost in the search for Shakespearean indicators and similar Shakespearean scenes, then – lost, indeed, in the attempt to isolate the singular stamp of Shakespeare – is the important realisation that the storm of *Pericles* is inherently different, dramatically, from anything which the playwright has thus far attempted.

The immediacy and the intimacy of Shakespeare's scene are, I will argue, indicative of fundamental differences in the approach of the two playwrights. For the play contains another shipwreck, the storm in Act 2, Scene 1 written by Wilkins. This gives us the opportunity to compare the storm of Shakespeare with that of a contemporary writing the same play. In exploring the different ways in which the two playwrights develop storms in the play, we can move beyond studies of attribution, and the details of each writer's staging and phraseology. The storms, I will show, enclose both ideological and aesthetic stances. Wilkins takes an approach which allies the storm to heavenly judgement. I have already examined the 'fire from heaven' which kills Antiochus and his daughter, from a meteorological perspective.[2] In this chapter, I want to draw it into a wider discussion of the storm's signification in the play. I will examine the ways in which Shakespeare's storm is weighted towards human experience rather than heavenly judgement. The fact that Shakespeare stages the sea-storm as it happens suggests that this focus on the lived experience of the storm is an important concern, emphasised in several ways. In Shakespeare's storm there is no interventionist god; the prince, the seamen and the audience experience the storm together.

G. Wilson Knight maintained that 'To analyse the tempests in *Pericles* would be to analyse the whole play'.[3] More recently, the sea has been described as 'the play's second protagonist, facilitator of and actor in Pericles's imperial story'.[4] Each of these remarks points to a continuity in the play which may otherwise be thought lacking: in diction, aesthetic and a retrospectively judged quality, it is obviously in two sections, that of George Wilkins preceding that of Shakespeare. In tempest and sea, however, the play has its constants and both writers employ them discretely and distinctively. To the constants of sea and storm, I will introduce another, the Bible. This is for three basic reasons. Firstly, scripture informs and colours more in the play than has previously been addressed in the necessary detail. Secondly, John Gower's *Confessio Amantis* notwithstanding, the Bible is one text which can be said with a relative degree of certainty to have been encountered by both playwrights.[5] Thirdly, as I will argue, by reading the storms of each writer in the context of their Biblical allusions we can more precisely discern each writer's approach. Although the relevant sections share a great deal in terms of trope and allusion, the way in which the two playwrights develop them is distinctive. The continual use of the storm enables *Pericles* to represent these shifting perspectives at once delicately and forcefully.

That vengeance should be associated with storm, thunder and lightning is a characteristically Old Testament notion. Most obviously, it is
formulated in Exodus, as hail is the seventh of the ten plagues of Egypt:
'for upon all the men, and the beastes, which are founde in the field, and
not brought home, the haile shal fall upon them, and they shall dye ... Then
Moses stretched out his rod toward heaven, and the Lord sent thundre and
haile, and lightening upon the grounde: and the Lorde caused haile to raine
upon the land of Egypt'.[6] However, the further one explores the similarities
between the heavenly retribution of the Biblical God and that of *Pericles*
and, especially, Wilkins's prose version of the story, *Painful Adventures*, the
more it is apparent that the examples of Wilkins are extreme. In Exodus, the
ten sequential plagues provide a platform for God to deliver his message
– 'that thou maiest know that there is none like me in all the earth' – the
successful transmission of which, is, after all, one of the overarching themes
of the entire Old Testament.[7] In Wilkins's examples, there is no room for
that message to be apprehended by the recipient, and this is made explicit,
especially in comparison to John Gower, who relates the death of Antiochus 'as men mai wite' and little more.[8] Wilkins's description of Antiochus's
demise builds a narrative tension so that, rather than being offered forgive-
ness, he is struck 'in the height and pride of all his glory' (2.4.6). Perhaps this
is a feature of the author's representation of a pagan world, one, that is, that
operates under the principle that pre-Christians need not be offered Christian redemption. Perhaps, for dramatic effect, Wilkins merely augmented
the episode taken from his source.

Whatever the author's reason, it is worth pointing out that lightning
is rarely fatal in the Bible. Naseeb Shaheen lists several different Biblical
formulations of 'fire from heaven', of varying interest in relation to *Pericles*.[9] The most detailed account of a fatal lightning strike in the Bible
is in II Kings, as the prophet Elijah turns away the followers of the king
of Samaria.[10] If any Biblical instance of lightning had an influence on the
diction of Helicanus in *Pericles*, it is this one: 'If that I be a man of God, let
fyre come downe from the heaven, and devoure thee and thy fyftie. So fyre
came downe from the heaven and devoured him and his fiftie.'[11] The phrase
'fyre came downe from the heaven' and its variations are repeated several
times during the first chapter of II Kings, its victims described, according to
various early modern translations, as devoured, 'consumed' or 'burnt up'.[12]
Given that the Biblical phrase is so close to *Pericles*'s 'A fire from heaven
came' and that each describes deadly lightning strikes, it is curious that the
play's commentators have not examined this episode, as they have that of II

Maccabees. Both Wilkins and II Kings present the very kind of unequivocal relationship of lightning to judgement, wrath or indeed heavenly powers that we consistently find Shakespeare endeavouring to keep ambiguous. It would be churlish and simplistic to argue that all storm in the Bible is a result of God's anger or demonstration of his power (especially, as we shall see, given the case of Jonah). But in II Kings, the case is very much of a defined line of good and evil, or at least, the Hebrew God and 'Baal-zebub the God of Ekron'.[13] In the story, it is the belief in Baal-zebub that acts to legitimise the deaths by lightning of the one hundred and two people so killed. Each death serves rapidly to convert the captain of the final fifty:

> And the thirde captaine over fifty went up, and came, and fel on his knees before Elijah, and besoght him, and said unto him, O man of God, I pray thee, let my life and the life of these thy fifty servantes be precious in thy sight. Beholde, there came fyre downe from the heaven and devoured the two former captaines over fifty with their fifties: therefore let my life now be precious in thy sight.[14]

The power of God's weather teaches various kinds of lessons through the Bible, this example being, perhaps, the most extreme after the Flood of Genesis. Only those who are willing to accede to the power of the God of Israel are judged in II Kings to be safe from a lightning strike. This severe line is paralleled by Wilkins: lightning and judgement correlate directly. Shakespeare, as we will see, avoids anything so certain.

As if to reinforce the link between storm and judgement, Helicanus follows his report of the lightning with a conclusive, unapologetic statement:

> yet but justice; for,
> Though this king were great, his greatness was no guard
> To bar heaven's shaft, but sin had his reward.
>
> (2.4.13–15)

Helicanus's final word on the matter, as well as remembering the fatal lightning, is a continuation of the play's tendency to marginalise the daughter of Antiochus. Whenever mentioned, this character is constructed as an object. The very fact that she remains nameless is indicative of this, but she is also figured as a sexual prize by Gower from the outset: 'many princes thither frame | To seek her as a bedfellow' (1.0.32–3). As a prize, she is ideal for the romantic hero Pericles's risky adventure: he 'Think[s] death no hazard in this enterprise' and warnings of the 'danger of the task' only serve to 'embolden' him (1.1.2–5). Very quickly then, and before the daughter has entered, a vivid association between danger and sexual objectivity is clearly established.

Of course, the danger in the scene is not restricted to Pericles; the Princess of Antioch has been subject to the proclivity of her father – the 'evil should be done by none', as Gower puts it (1.0.28) – and is condemned to the relationship. Sexual violation is, like the storm, a theme recurrent throughout Shakespeare's romances: *Cymbeline* has Iachimo's illicit undressing of Imogen, and Cloten's attempted rape of the same (2.3.37–8; 3.5.138–9); the plot of *The Winter's Tale* depends on imagined adultery; in *The Tempest*, Caliban is imprisoned for his attempted rape of Miranda (1.2.348–52). It is in *Pericles*, however, that the idea of violation is most resonant and, indeed, most thoroughly connected with the violence of the storm. As his daughter enters, Antiochus describes her as 'clothed like a bride | For the embracements even of Jove himself' (1.1.8). Many commentators, remembering Jove's affairs, have found distinct sexual overtones in Antiochus's description of his daughter.[15] Jove is, in addition to being associated with sexual domination, also a father figure in Roman mythology. As Gossett notes, 'It is characteristic of Antiochus's self-assurance that he compares himself to the king of gods'.[16] Antiochus's image is thereby loaded with various threats. But Jove is not only a father god and a sexual predator; he is also the god of lightning. The minatory sexual identity of Antiochus is therefore conflated with lightning here. As I have shown, the 'fire from heaven' that kills Antiochus is best understood as *fulmen*.[17] Richard Huloet, in his Latin dictionary of 1572, offers a translation of 'Lightning' as both 'Fulmen' and 'Fulgur', going on to note that '*Also* Fulmen *is ascribed to* Jupiter'.[18] Storm is a crucial danger in the play, and results in many deaths, and is inextricably linked to desire from the start. Here, the danger of Jove provides a wonderfully concise image with many resonances: in addition to the patriarchal character of the king of gods chiming with that of Antiochus, and each figure an intimidating lustful threat, the metaphor also presages the daughter's ultimate death by thunderbolt.

The connection between desire, danger and the weather is expounded as Pericles declines to answer the riddle but persists with the connection between Antiochus and Jove:

> For vice repeated is like the wandering wind.
> Blows dust in others' eyes, to spread itself;
> And yet the end of all is bought thus dear:
> The breath is gone, and the sore eyes see clear:
> To stop the air would hurt them …

Kings are earth's gods; in vice their law's their will;
And, if Jove stray, who dares say Jove doth ill?

(97–105)[19]

Here, we can find senses of storm, king and Jove in the response to the realisation of the violation that has taken place. The image of the wandering wind is resonant with the play's themes of travel and Fortune as well as its weather patterns; the notion that it is commensurate with vice lends a meteorological aspect to the sexual violence.

Many critical responses to the play focus on its geography and its aesthetic reliance upon borders.[20] Here, it is vice itself, personified as Jove, which transgresses those borders, and it is subject to, or *imagined through* the very force which physically separates and divides the characters. The codes of societal and sexual conduct are thereby represented as liminal, just as the port towns in which the play is set. Only once such a conjunction is established, does Pericles mention the true 'wind' of vice – breath. The shifting between the societal, the meteorological and the bodily ends in the image of the eyes seeing clear 'to stop the air would hurt them'. Once more, the tone is meteorological – as in King Lear's curse 'Strike her young bones, | You taking airs, with lameness!' (2.2.354–6) – the air itself as well as the repetition of vice is harmful. As societal, meteorological and bodily are conflated, so, again, are Antiochus and Jove in the final couplet of the speech. Following the elaborate metaphors outlined above, the phrase 'in vice their law's their will' endows the king with a godlike power – in the reverberation of vice/storm – to match his authority. This is made concrete in the return to the specific god who embodies both storm and sexual transgression: 'if Jove stray, who dares say Jove doth ill?' In refusing to name Antiochus's act of incest, then, Pericles's speech figures him as an irreverent thunderer who operates on a level closed to questioning.[21] The transparent riddle in this way may be seen as a godlike declaration of invulnerability, one that reverberates in the demise of Antiochus and his daughter quoted above. It is remarkable that, in the parts of the play which are ascribed to him, Shakespeare makes no mention of Jove. This may be coincidental, but it is surely undeniable that the force and insistence with which Wilkins uses the name, and the effectiveness with which Antiochus is finished, do complete a powerful image which concludes the beginning of the play.

I have been arguing that Wilkins's approach to the storm is one invested in metaphor, as well as heavenly judgement. The figure of Jove ties together themes of the first two acts, and Wilkins's aesthetic inheres in the allusion and suggestiveness of his images. This same aesthetic is also to be found in the play's first storm proper, at the start of Act 2. The scene is often compared unfavourably to that at the beginning of Act 3 as a means of highlighting the collaborative process. Roger Warren describes Wilkins's storm speech as 'functional enough, as long as there is nothing better to compare it with'.[22] But comparisons appear hard to resist. Gossett notes 'the indubitably greater power of the [later] speech', whilst Raphael Lyne claims that the 'language [of the first storm] is sterile in comparison with the relentless fertility of the other'.[23] Because commentators and editors regard the collaborative aspects of the play as one of its most intriguing features, though, analysis of how this speech fits in to the work of the storm in the play is lacking. Here is the speech in full:

> Yet cease your ire, you angry stars of heaven!
> Wind, rain and thunder, remember earthly man
> Is but a substance that must yield to you,
> And I, as fits my nature, do obey you.
> Alas, the seas hath cast me on the rocks,
> Washed me from shore to shore, and left me breath
> Nothing to think on but ensuing death.
> Let it suffice the greatness of your powers
> To have bereft a prince of all his fortunes,
> And, having thrown him from your watery grave,
> Here to have death in peace is all he'll crave.
>
> (2.1.1–11)

Pericles's speech is clearly occupied by thoughts of his own demise: 'must yield' and 'ensuing death' being indications that 'to have death in peace is all he'll crave'. A death, that is, unlike that of his compatriots who have perished at sea.[24] Ruth Nevo regards this as 'a total submission, a capitulation' and points out the lack of 'any reference to the trauma of the wreck itself'.[25] One answer to this is that the lack of reference to the wreck is an acknowledgement of its traumatic nature. In any case, Pericles's language is that of the sole survivor, whether he mentions the crew or not. As I will show in the final chapter, this generic language is played upon in *The Tempest*. But in terms of the meteorology of the play, and of locating Wilkins's approach, the crucial portion of the speech is the rhyming couplet in the centre, not the end. We have already seen examples of *breath* constructed as *wind* and as *vice*; we might begin now to appreciate the way in which the word echoes across the first two acts, the section of the play belonging to Wilkins. Here *breath* is apparently synonymous with *life*: Pericles ruminates on the irony that he is only alive enough to contemplate death.[26] The breath, which had been dangerous in its propensity to spread vice, is now ostensibly at the limits of speech. Including the two examples noted, there are seven incidents of *breath* in the play, and it is always pertinent to the surrounding sense. Indeed, its signification has a story arc all of its own:

> For death remembered should be like a mirror,
> Who tells us life's but breath, to trust it error. (1.1.46–7)

> The breath is gone, and the sore eyes see clear (1.1.100)

> Let your breath cool yourself, telling your haste. (1.1.160)

> Our woes into the air; our eyes do weep,
> Till tongues fetch breath that may proclaim them louder (1.4.14–15)

> I'll then discourse our woes, felt several years,
> And wanting breath to speak help me with tears. (1.4.18–9)

>   left me breath
> Nothing to think on but ensuing death. (2.1.6–7)

> But if the prince do live, let us salute him,
> Or know what ground's made happy by his breath. (2.4.27–8)

To begin with, then, breath is, proverbially, life.[27] The indistinctness of the metaphor, however, complicates the proverb somewhat. Simultaneously, 'death remembered' is a prompt to consider one's mortality; is obscuring, like breath on a mirror; and is itself a validation of life, again like breath on a mirror.[28] Breath is the basis of this dispersion of meaning. Next, we have the construction of breath/wind/spreader of vice as discussed above. The following instance – 'Let your breath cool yourself' – is an example of that construction made literal, as Antiochus implores the Messenger both to be refreshed by his own conversation and to ensure that Antiochus 'sees clear'. The subsequent two examples, with Cleon lamenting the demise of Tarsus, figure breath as failing – a necessary, but absent means to communicate 'woes'. Thus breath does not spread vice or danger, as before, but is tantalisingly absent at the time of need to signal emergency. By the time we reach the example in the storm, the word has assumed a panoply of meanings and associations. The final instance, spoken about Pericles, envisions breath as indicative of a semi-materialistic afterlife, as though the wandering wind which had carried the prince could be buried with him.

The commonplace of tears as rainy/tempestuous here finds its counterpart in the breath as wind.[29] It is much more common to find such a correlation with sighing as in *Coriolanus*: 'I have been blown out of your gates with sighs' (5.2.73–4) or *Titus*: 'Then must my sea be moved with her sighs'

(3.1.228) or *Antony and Cleopatra*: 'we cannot call her winds and waters sighs and tears; they are greater storms and tempests than almanacs can report' (1.2.152–4). Wilkins's section of *Pericles*, however, is less precise in preferring *breath*, and consequently constructs a lasting parallel which finds the wind more closely connected to bodily existence – the very substantive elements of life, rather than emotional expression. When Pericles employs the word in the storm, he is entangling himself in a nuanced system of signifiers which implicates him in the cause as well as the effect of the shipwreck: his is the life of which he speaks and the wind which blows it. The editorial emendation, 'left *me* breath' – as opposed to 'left *my* breath' – has the attractive quality of briefly rendering Pericles as breath and nothing more. The Quarto phrase imagines a breath which can think – hence the emendation – and this, given the range of meanings to which the word is put, is perhaps not out of the question: either way, the point remains the same, with Pericles as breath. As Gossett notes, *breath* is not used beyond the second act and is therefore only in the section of the play ascribed to George Wilkins.[30] Curiously, Wilkins only uses *breath* once in *Painful Adventures*. Another play of Wilkins's, though, *The Miseries of Inforst Mariage* (1607) contains a phrase which would not be out of place in *Pericles*: 'As neere to misery had bin our breath, | As where the thundring pellet strikes is death'.[31] For Wilkins, it seems, the cause and effect of breath is never too far from meteorological consequence. Indeed, it might be said that the self-imposed silence which Pericles enters in the second half of the play is a direct response to each kind of breath which had hitherto been imagined: he avoids speech and is wholly committed to 'the wandering wind'. I shall return to this idea, and its resonance in the Shakespearean section of the play, below.

So far, I have shown that in Wilkins's section of the play we find a network of allusions centred on the storm. Jove acts as a figure for illicit sexual activity as well as lightning. Lightning, moreover, purges that sexual activity. Similarly, the image of breath for Wilkins is replete with associations: it is life, wind, vice and death at various points. Wilkins's employment of the storm inheres in these complex protean metaphors. Through them, a punitive, moralising aesthetic emerges.

As I have noted, the point at which Shakespeare is now usually conceded to assume the major creative role in the play is the storm of Act 3, Scene 1. Here, editors find 'Shakespearean indicators' in the opening speech, and comment on the complexity of the verse.[32] Gossett recalls the opening of *King Lear*'s Act 3, Scene 2, drawing attention to similarities and differences. Occasionally, the storm of 3.1 is taken as some sort of manifestation of authorial advent, as by Raphael Lyne:

> [T]here may be a special moment of traumatic arrival in *Pericles* as Shake-speare takes over the play, using an excessively pivotal speech as a coded way of announcing his presence; so at least it may seem to readers and audiences of romances who know that storms come at critical junctures, as in *The Tempest* and *The Winter's Tale*.[33]

The readers and audiences to whom Lyne is referring are necessarily thinking retrospectively, at least with regard to the plays he mentions, which postdate *Pericles*. Such readers would also need conveniently to forget the earlier storm in the play. If there is a 'traumatic arrival' here, it is surely the result of the immediacy of the storm. The Senecan technique of relating various violent situations and atrocities rather than acting them is abandoned, again drawing comparisons with *King Lear*, which brings such actions on to the stage (not only in the storm scenes, of course, but in the loss of Gloucester's eyes). The audience have already seen the surviving Pericles ashore and wishing for death. Here, they join him in the storm, desperate for life – his own, Thaisa's and the unborn Marina:

> The god of this great vast, rebuke these surges
> Which wash both heaven and hell, and thou that hast
> Upon the winds command, bind them in brass,
> Having called them from the deep. O, still
> Thy deafening dreadful thunders; gently quench
> Thy nimble sulphurous flashes! O, how, Lychorida!
> How does my queen? – Thou stormest venomously;
> Wilt thou spit all thyself? The seaman's whistle
> Is as a whisper in the ears of death,
> Unheard. Lychorida! – Lucina, O,
> Divinest patroness and midwife gentle
> To those that cry by night, convey thy deity
> Aboard our dancing boat; make swift the pangs
> Of my queen's travails!
>
> (3.1.1–14)

The tenor of Pericles's speech depends on the fact that, unlike those characters in, say, *King Lear* and *Julius Caesar* who exhibit fear and defiance, he is in considerable danger of death. Of course, the death that looms largest is not his own, but Thaisa's, and the subtleties of Pericles's soliloquy make use of the juxtaposed dangers of tempest and childbirth. As we have seen, Wilkins managed to conflate the sexual identity of Antiochus's daughter with ideas of the threat of Jove in terms of rape and, ultimately, storm. Here,

Shakespeare introduces the notion that the dangers of storm and labour are metaphorically resonant. It is this very juxtaposition which adds to the complexity of the verse, a characteristic which is important in the critical case for Shakespeare's composing hand.[34] 'How does my queen? – Thou stormest venomously' is a clear example of how the competing forces of Pericles's fears jostle for space in the formulaic boundaries of iambic pentameter. Neither concern can develop fully because of the urgency of the other. Clearer still is the implicit connection drawn between storm and childbirth by the invocation of a deity for each. Thus 'god of this great vast' and 'thou that hast | Upon the winds command' are called upon, referring, presumably, to Aeolus, Neptune or Tempestates, just as Lucina, goddess of childbirth is summoned. As Wilkins called on Jove to conflate storm and sexual violence, then, so Shakespeare alludes to pagan gods of sea, storm and childbirth. But for all the reference to gods, each writer prioritises the human experience of the storm. Antiochus is struck with Jove's lightning bolt, and Pericles's cries are representations of his inability to take control. For it is no accident here that Pericles's invocations are rendered as impotent through diction such as 'deafening' and 'whisper ... | Unheard'. Nor is it coincidental that the 'nimble sulphurous flashes' of lightning compare unfavourably to Thaisa's 'pangs' which Pericles wishes Lucina could 'make swift'. Each god in Pericles's speech is wished as 'gentle' or 'gently'. The wish seems forlorn as the initial long assonant sounds of 'vast', 'hast' and 'brass' give way to the guttural insistence of the three desperate 'O's. Meanwhile, the relentless alliteration ('god/great', 'heaven/hell/hast', 'deafening/dreadful', 'whistle/whisper', 'Lychorida/Lucina', 'cry convey') seems to punctuate – or puncture – those cries. If breath for Wilkins is an idea replete with metaphorical possibilities, then for Shakespeare here it is the actor's voice, subject to, and interrupted by, the movement of the storm just as his words create it.

Pericles himself is subjected to the elements more than most Shakespearean characters. Wilkins's storms compare to those of II Maccabees and II Kings, and we can continue such comparison with Shakespeare's scenes. As others have pointed out, the storm at the beginning of Act 3 recalls the account, in the book of Luke, of Jesus calming the sea at Galilee: 'And he arose, and rebuked the winde, and the waves of water: and they ceased, and it was calme'.[35] The crucial component of those New Testament verses in relation to *Pericles* is the use of the word 'rebuked', which is apparently echoed by Pericles: 'The god of this great vast, rebuke these surges' (3.1.1). Given that Jesus calms the seas and Pericles merely yells at them, such linguistic parallels are important if we are to maintain the significance of the allusion. 'Rebuke', however, is elsewhere used in the Bible in relation to controlling the elements, as Malone pointed out glossing the same line, quoting from Psalms: 'the waters wolde stand above the mountaines. But at thy rebuke they flee: at the voice of thy thunder thei haste away'.[36] The marginal note of the Geneva Bible offers the interpretation 'If by thy power thou didest not bridle the rage of the waters, it were not possible, but the whole worlde shulde be destroied'. Rebuke, then, is readily understood in elemental terms. Even though the Psalm describes the Creation, not a storm, it does not follow that Luke's instance of rebuke used in the storm should be acknowledged as an influence on Pericles. For, as we have seen with Wilkins's storms, the Biblical reference is not so direct and simple. Pericles's Act 3, Scene 1, in addition to, perhaps more than the passage from Luke, bears a similarity to the book of Jonah.[37] This similarity is found not simply in terms of its narrative – the storm is constructed as dependent upon a passenger of a ship – but also in the way that the weather is imagined. Rather than figuring the storm as a manifestation of God's anger or vengefulness, the passage allows for greater complexity:

> Then said thei unto him, What shal we do unto thee, that the sea maie be calme unto us? (for the sea wrought and was troublous) And he said unto them, Take me, and cast me into the sea: so shal the sea be calme unto you: for I knowe that for my sake this great tempest is upon you.[38]

Pericles's main parallel with the story of Jonah is clear enough: a passenger is thrown into the sea in order to calm it. In the play, of course, it is Thaisa, whether presumed or actually dead, who is cast into the water: 'Sir, your queen must overboard. The sea works high, the wind is loud and will not lie till the ship be cleared of the dead' (47–9). An important difference between the two texts is that the sailors of Pericles are determined to carry out the action, certain that they are correct in determining the cause of the storm, whereas in Jonah, the crew draw lots to establish why the tempest has arisen. Once Jonah has drawn the lot, the sailors are still unwilling to carry out his prophetic advice, but attempt to approach the shore: 'Nevertheles, the men rowed to bring it to the land, but thei colde not: for the sea wrought, and was troublous against them'.[39] This is in contrast with Pericles's meek response to the Master's demand: 'That's your superstition' (50). Despite these differences, the threat to the ship in Jonah is great, just as in Pericles, and in each case the storm is attributed to supernatural causes, and subdued by the casting of a passenger overboard.

Pericles in each half of the play rails at the elements, and the stars or gods responsible for them. For Wilkins, those elements are decisive. We see Pericles after the shipwreck; we learn of the swift death of Antiochus and his daughter. For Shakespeare, the storm is not as certain. We witness the lived experience of Pericles on the ship, and the gods to whom he alludes do not manifest themselves. Rather, Shakespeare's emphasis is on the narrative of human agency within the storm. There is a parallel distinction in the Bible verses. Whereas in II Kings and Exodus the action and diction of the storms tend to emphasise God's message and power, and in Luke, Jesus's ability to calm the elements, the depiction of the sea-storm in Jonah is weighted towards the human experience. Although the tempest is decidedly the work of God,[40] the bulk of the chapter deals with the coping strategies of the crew and Jonah. The fear of the sailors is emphasised repeatedly: 'the mariners were afraied, and cryed everie man unto his god', 'Then were the men exceedingly afraid', 'Then the men feared the Lord exceedingly'.[41] Similarly, the calm resolution of Jonah is shown to contrast with that fear.[42] Gone is the narrator of II Kings and Exodus who depicted the voice and motives of God alongside the storm; instead that voice and those motives are expounded by the figures in the storm, who are necessarily emotional. Just as the strong judgemental tones of Gower and Helicanus seem to echo the Biblical accounts given, so the Shakespearean section of the text resonates with the methodology of Jonah. Shakespeare here, characteristically, is reluctant to direct blame or offer judgement and instead portrays a scene which owes its nuance to the experiential dialogue of its many characters. This is evident, for example, in the language of the mariners:

> MASTER Slack the bowlines there! – Thou wilt not, wilt thou?
> Blow and split thyself.
> SAILOR But sea-room, an the brine and cloudy billow kiss the
> moon, I care not.
>
> (43–6)

The immediacy of such lines is not apparent in the play's first sea-storm; although Wilkins has Pericles entering 'wet', the many voices of Shakespeare's storm are reduced to that of Pericles and the spectating fishermen. Furthermore the imperative and present tenses of Shakespeare's lines are not to be found in those of Wilkins, removing the audience from the propinquity of the storm. The frenetic activity of mariners in Act 3, Scene 1 is also found in Jonah: they 'cast the wares that were in the ship, into the sea to lighten it of them'.[43] As in the play, the emotions of the sailors in the biblical text are depicted through the structure of their speech, for example in the frustrated guise of the rhetorical question: 'Then were the men exceedingly afrayde, and said unto him, Why hast thou done this?'[44] Both Wilkins's and Shakespeare's approaches to the storm operate on a metaphorical level, then, but Shakespeare's is also characterised by its practicality, both in the fact that it is played out on stage and in the language of the characters who do so.

There are phrases in both Shakespeare's section of the play and that of Wilkins which allude more explicitly to the Book of Jonah. In Act 3, Scene 1, addressing the body of Thaisa, Pericles laments: 'the belching whale | And humming water must o'erwhelm thy corpse' (3.1.62–3). As Gossett has pointed out, the fact that Jonah is described as though dead strengthens the connection between the two texts: 'Being now swallowed up of death … he was in the fishes belly as in a grave or place of darkness'.[45] The Biblical story had also been touched upon after the play's first shipwreck:

> I can compare our rich misers to nothing so fitly as to a whale: 'a plays and tumbles, driving the poor fry before him, and at last devours them all at a mouthful … he should have swallowed me too, and when I had been in his belly I would have kept such a jangling of the bells that he should never have left till he cast bells, steeple, church and parish up again. (2.1.29–42)

The story of Jonah here is explicit enough, although the Geneva Bible mentions the creature as a fish, not a whale. What makes this passage more noteworthy is not only that it anticipates the reappearance of themes from the Book of Jonah later on, but also that it follows the Fisherman's allusion to the porpoise as a predictor of storms. The sight of dolphins or porpoises playing near land is mentioned as a precursor of tempests in several ancient meteorological texts and the phenomenon had found its way into proverbial English.[46] The significant point here is that this discussion leads into a scenario in which the world is under threat from the whale (here, simply the biggest fish) and that a Deluge-like scenario is played out in metaphor. The storm precedes the fish just as the fish foretell the storm. This, of course, is very much the case for Jonah, whose complex irony inheres in his situation of finding safety from the tempest inside the creature whose appearance would predict the tempest, as much as it inheres in finding a dry room in the sea. The storm precedes the fish. That the Fishermen's discussion overlays the simple structures of the Deluge and the story of Jonah with an intricate argument on the greed of humankind is illustrative of the play's insistence on appropriating Biblical text. This being Wilkins's work, it should not be surprising, even in this moment of light relief, to find a binary ethic with simplistic answers: ring the religious bell to curtail – even reverse – the greedy destruction. As Richard Halpern writes, Wilkins here 'seems to invoke this typological framework in the fishermen's image of salvation through the ringing of the church bells and through the fishermen themselves, from whose profession Jesus recruited his disciples'.[47] What Halpern does not take into account is that, in contrast, when Shakespeare uses the story, it is to contextualise the death of the innocent Thaisa. The requisition of the strands of the Jonah story for starkly differing ends is a neat illustration of the approach of the two playwrights. Just as in Jonah, Shakespeare emphasises the human experience of storm, the strategies of bargaining and the development of fear, acceptance and resolution, rather than the indelicate message from the heavens found elsewhere in the Bible, and elsewhere in *Pericles*.

As with Wilkins, Shakespeare's storm is not confined to a single scene in the play. I have already looked in detail at the brief conversation between Marina and Leonine and the ways in which a self-sustaining understanding of the wind is formed.[48] This scene (4.1) also reflects the same approach to the storm I have been proposing. Marina's evoking of the direction of the wind at the time of her birth accords with the shift of tense as she moves from soliloquy to conversation and into narration. 'When I was born the wind was in the north', establishes a sense of impossible recollection and a testament to the power of the story: the curious minutiae of the scene bear the characteristic of received understanding, as there is no possibility of Marina remembering the night, let alone the detail. As the supplier of this knowledge, Marina's nurse Lychorida, is invoked, the tense alters: 'My father, as nurse says, did never fear' (51). Again, this bears the touch both of the impossible and its relation to storytelling – Lychorida is recently deceased, but her story is still current, still voiced. Indeed, it is a story Marina immediately begins to retell, or more accurately, since it is still *being* told, to maintain. The events are told in the past tense and this is continued for several lines, until Marina moves from conversation into fully developed narration. 'When I was born. | Never was waves nor wind more violent' (57–8) is her response to Leonine's question, but as her story becomes more detailed, she returns to the present tense:

> And from the ladder tackle washes off
> A canvas climber. 'Ha' says one, 'wolt out?'
> And with a dropping industry they skip
> From stem to stern. The boatswain whistles, and
> The master calls and trebles their confusion.
>
> (60–3)

The shift into the present tense again ensures that minute details of the scene are again made vivid, again experienced. The reported dialogue of the seamen, their frantic activity and the disorder of the storm are all conveyed. Furthermore, Marina has knowledge of mariners' terms and nautical collo-quialisms. Partly, this may be attributed to the feeling, formulated by many, that *Pericles* is 'a play controlled by the sustained awareness of the sea', or that the sea 'has the part of a principal character'.[49] The proximity of the scene to the sea is also relevant, and is emphasised by Dionyza (25). More significant than these factors, however, is the way in which Marina seems to inhabit her story: it is clear from a comparison of this speech and the scene it recollects that Marina's details have not appeared on stage earlier.[50] Appar-ently having learned the story from Lychorida, Marina is supplementing the staged version of the storm as though it were *still* onstage. The tense and the detail are both complicit in reifying Marina's earlier pronouncement, 'This world to me is as a lasting storm' (18). If the sea is a principal character of the play, the storm is that character's personality: just as the characters continue to use the diction of the sea, so they consistently identify with its oragious character and ensure that the waves are never still. Wilkins symbolises; Shakespeare dramatises the human capacity to symbolise.

In *Pericles*, therefore, we may see Shakespeare's storms in a direct comparison with those of his collaborator. We have seen the ways in which the same source is used differently by each writer, with regard to the Bible. Bardolatry and canonicism may prescribe to the modern reader the idea of which of the play's sections is more valuable, but in *Pericles*'s storms the separate approaches allow each example to function differently without becoming repetitive. For just as it is no coincidence that we find two distinct voices in the play, it is no surprise that they seem to evince two discrete world views: the judgemental diction and absolutes of Gower, Helicanus and the Pericles of the first two acts are juxtaposed with the moral exonera-tion of Lysimachus and Bolt; Wilkins's providential lightning is replaced by the ethical intricacy of Shakespeare's storm; the omniscient narration of Gower and Helicanus gives way to a generically sustained narrative ignorance and silence. Rather than form a hierarchy with regard to the two sections of the play, we might, more helpfully, conclude that the continual use of the storm enables *Pericles* to represent these shifting perspectives at once delicately and forcefully.

Whilst it is a fragmented play in many respects, the treatment of storm imparts a certain continuity. The audience are introduced to the storm *ex post facto*: it has delivered Pericles to Pentapolis; it has killed Antiochus and his daughter. In the first acts of the play, the storm is compartmentalised and ripe for unopposed moralisation. From the third act on, however, the audience encounter the storm *in medias res* and are necessarily implicated. We apprehend, but also imagine it; witness it but also create it (as implored to by Gower). *Pericles* stages the received sea-storms of *Comedy of Errors*, *Twelfth Night* and *Othello* and then progresses beyond them. Marina's image of the world as a 'lasting storm' is more than a metaphor: it is the play's performance aesthetic.

9

The Tempest and theatrical reality

In the first few pages of this book, I recalled the story of my fellow audience member, confused by the rain in a performance of *King Lear*. Her question, 'how are they doing this' pertains as much to *The Tempest* as to *Lear*. For as the Boatswain in the opening of *The Tempest* argues with the courtiers, who are 'louder than the weather', his exasperation is articulated in the phrase 'if you can command these elements'.[1] An innocuous expression, perhaps, lost as it may be in the tumult and commotion of the scene, and yet, on reflection, it is a line which echoes throughout the play. As the meticulous presentation of the storm gives way to more and more obvious magic, the Boatswain's phrase, the desperate futility of the desire to control the weather, becomes less and less unreasonable. In this chapter, I will explore the ways in which the play's opening storm allows for a reading of the rest of the weather in the text. I will give particular attention in the first part of my argument to the staging of the storm, in an effort to expose the implications of its realism. It is my contention, furthermore, that the first scene of *The Tempest* must be read in conjunction with Shakespeare's previous directions for *thunder and lightning*, if we are to attempt to come to terms with the process of meaning in which the storm is engaged.

In *Back To Nature* (2006), Robert N. Watson, exploring *As You Like It*, 'interprets the longing for reunion with the world of nature as a sentimental manifestation of a philosophical problem: the suspicion that our cognitive mechanisms allow us to know things only as we liken them'.[2] Watson finds in the imagery of the play 'the impulse of the human family to impose its familiarities'.[3] Because Watson's study is broadly concerned with the pastoral, it does not examine *The Tempest* in depth. However, an approach comparable to that which Watson takes with *As You Like It* is rewarding in reading *The Tempest*. *As You Like It* is involved in, and examines, pastoral fantasy and the human will both to succumb to nature and to re-appropriate it through language. Similarly, *The Tempest* is concerned with, and implicated in, strategies of representation of the natural world and the human will to power over it. In the second half of this chapter, I will argue that the possibilities and the connotations of the theatrical storm are repeatedly investigated during the play and that this process is part of *The Tempest*'s wider concern with the dramatic representation of nature. Although the ecocritical will become more explicit in the latter part of this chapter, however, it is always at stake in this reading, not least in the following paragraphs, which examine the play's first scene.

> *A tempestuous noise of thunder and lightning heard;*
>   *enter a Shipmaster and a Boatswain.*
> MASTER Boatswain!
> BOATSWAIN Here master. What cheer?
> MASTER Good, speak to th' mariners. Fall to it yarely or we run
> ourselves aground.
>   *Exit.*
> BOATSWAIN Heigh, my hearts; cheerly, cheerly, my hearts! Yare!
> Yare! Take in the topsail. Tend to the master's whistle! Blow till
> thou burst thy wind, if room enough.
>   (1.1.0–8)

The opening storm of *The Tempest* can be read as an example of what Timothy Morton has termed 'rendering'.[4] For Morton, rendering is a 'main element', and indeed a 'result' of 'ambient poetics' or 'ecomimesis', that is, the critical language developed in *Ecology Without Nature* that deals with the environmental form of art.[5] This vocabulary of ambient poetics, Morton contends, is necessary if we are to discuss the environmental form of literature without falling prey to its ostensible ecological content. Hence rendering, along with other elements of ecomimesis, is one way of critically evaluating works of art from an ecocritical direction, and this will become clearer below. Morton's source for the concept of rendering is cinematic theory and it is clarified by Michel Chion.[6] Chion stresses the need to 'distinguish between the notions of *rendering* and *reproduction*', arguing that for cinematic 'sounds to be truthful, effective and fitting', film should less 'reproduce what would be heard in the same situation in reality' and more 'render (convey, express) the feelings associated with the situation'.[7] Whereas Chion's definition of rendering is restricted to 'use of sounds', Morton's use of the term is extrapolated to all texts and media.[8] Morton, then, asserts that rendering 'attempts to simulate reality itself: to tear to pieces the aesthetic screen that separates the perceiving subject from the object'.[9] Morton concentrates mainly on Romantic poetry for his literary examples, but this concept of rendering may apply to any medium and, as Morton elaborates on the idea, its pertinence to theatre becomes clearer:

> When ecomimesis renders an environment, it is implicitly saying: 'This environment is real; do not think that there is an aesthetic framework here'. All signals that we are in a constructed realm have been minimized. Alternatively, even when the perceiver proceeds by 'cynical reason', we know very well that we are being deceived, but our disbelief is willingly suspended. Or we choose to enjoy the rendering as if it were not artificial. Rendering encourages us to switch off our aesthetic vigilance. But even if we know very well that it is a special effect, we enjoy the deception.[10]

This is how I wish to use the term *rendering* in my argument, that is, as a name for the process by which a text presents itself as reality and encourages the reader or audience to accept it as such. This is a helpful way to think about *The Tempest*'s first scene for two main reasons, each of which is important in an ecocritical approach to the play. The first reason is that however the King's Men staged the storm, everything in the text points towards an attempt to present a theatrical tempest which is as close to a real one as possible. In so doing, the scene works to diminish the obviousness of its own 'aesthetic framework'; that is the mechanics of representation which draw attention to the drama's artificiality. The second reason that rendering is a helpful concept in reading the play is that the 'aesthetic vigilance' which Morton describes is distracted – or 'switched off' as Morton puts it – not only by the scene itself, but by the history of Shakespeare's storms and their relationship with the supernatural. Thus, it is more likely that an audience will accept the scene as a 'natural' and therefore non-theatrical, perfectly rendered storm, if they are familiar with Shakespeare's tendency to stage storms without theophanies or devils. Doubtless this may appear to be too sophisticated an audience for some. In response, I suggest that the regular Jacobean theatregoer, having seen popular plays such as *Julius Caesar* and *Pericles*, and possibly *King Lear*, may justifiably accept *The Tempest*'s storm as 'natural' thanks to the 'natural' storms which recur in the earlier work of the playwright.[11] These reasons outline the ways in which Act 1, Scene 1 of *The Tempest* can be seen as inviting a reading informed by Morton's concept of rendering. In order to develop such a reading, I will deal with each of these points in detail.

In his essay '*The Tempest*'s Tempest at Blackfriars' (1989), Andrew Gurr discusses the various possibilities for staging the play's first scene.[12] Although, as with any attempted explication of early modern staging,

Gurr is necessarily speculative, his closing remarks are persuasive: 'If *The Tempest* truly was the first play Shakespeare planned for the Blackfriars, his opening scene was a model of how to *épater les gallants* [startle the fashionable gentlemen]. The shock of the opening's realism is transformed into magic the moment Miranda enters'.[13] As with *Julius Caesar* and the Globe, the notion that the storm could define the character of the playhouse is an attractive one. Gurr's approach may appear to reflect this notion, but a crucial difference is that the indoor theatre already had an established mode of practice when Shakespeare's play was staged there. The Children of the Queen's Revels played there from 1600 to 1608. As Sarah Dustagheer has shown, 'the Children of the Queen's Revels' repertory at the Blackfriars did *not* contain extensive and integral use of sound effects. The plays written for the indoor theatre between 1600 and 1608 are remarkably quiet in comparison to the Globe repertory'.[14] Hence, the impact of the storm in Shakespeare's play is as much to do with surprise as with impressive spectacle. It is less a matter of the play determining an aesthetic for a *new* playhouse (as was the case in *Julius Caesar*); more a matter of subverting the expectations of any audience member familiar with the pre-existing character of Blackfriars performances.

The stage direction '*tempestuous noise of thunder and lightning heard*' was probably written by the scrivener Ralph Crane, who seems to have prepared the script of *The Tempest* for publication.[15] If we are to take it literally, as 'the earliest evidence we have of how the play was staged by the King's Company', then it is unusual in specifying lightning as an *auditory* effect.[16] John Jowett has proposed that 'this is a possible indication of an original direction having been reworded' and implies that a visual lightning effect was likely.[17] However, as Gurr notes, 'Fireworks [were] unpopular at the halls because of the stink', and so the offstage noise of the stage direction was unlikely to include pyrotechnics.[18] Given that lightning is a visual effect (i.e. not '*heard*') elsewhere in contemporary drama, it is more likely that Crane used 'thunder and lightning' as a phrase to casually depict the noise of a storm. The formulation was a commonplace occurrence in early modern English: a pamphlet of 'strange newes' roughly contemporaneous with *The Tempest*, for example, describes 'a horrible noyse of both of thunder and lightning'; John Foxe writes of a 'warre ... presignified by terrible thundering and lightning heard all England over' and Leo Africanus describes a mountain that 'is called ... lyon in regard of the dreadfull thunders and lightnings which are continually heard from the top thereof'.[19] 'Thunder' and 'lightning' are different theatrical effects, but 'thunder and lightning' is a compound phrase synonymous with 'storm'.[20] There is, therefore, no decisive contradiction in the stage direction for '*thunder and lightning heard*'. In light of this, and the unpopularity of indoor fireworks, the '*tempestuous noise*' is likely to have been *only* a noise. This might, in the context of the spectacular pyrotechnics of the open-air playhouses, seem disappointing. However, it is important that whilst lightning effects are a visual extravagance, the noise of a rolling cannonball to represent thunder is convincing and accurate. This fact, and the notion that the cannonball was the only noise effect in the opening scene, supports my reading of the scene as invested in rendering the storm. As I will argue, this realistic quality of the noise is necessary for the aesthetic of the play; if the play's language, as well as the stage effects, is considered, it becomes clear that accuracy of representation is a priority of the play's opening.

Once again, Shakespeare is careful to complement the staging of the storm effects with the dramatic language of his characters. Although the storm is an illusion, the actions and diction of the crew are firmly grounded in Jacobean reality. Shakespeare paid great attention to the accurate portrayal of contemporary nautical procedures in his writing of the scene. The Boatswain's instructions to the crew reveal a determination on the part of the playwright to be as precise as possible: 'Take in the topsail', 'Down with the topmast', 'Bring her to try with the main course' and 'Set her two courses off to sea again! Lay her off!' are all valid instructions (1.1.6, 33, 34, 48). In fact, the extent to which Shakespeare deals in nautical technicalities is remarkable, as A. F. Falconer, in *Shakespeare and the Sea* has explained. In response to the commands of the Boatswain, Falconer writes:

> The ship is sound, the seamen are disciplined, the right orders are given. Some of the newer manoeuvres of the day, even one that was debateable, have been tried, but all without success ... Shakespeare could not have written a scene of this kind without taking great pains to grasp completely how a ship beset with these difficulties would have to be handled.[21]

This detail of the scene is indicative of the authenticity at which Shakespeare is apparently aiming. Why the playwright would adhere to such specifications is puzzling: it is certainly highly unusual in Jacobean drama.[22] Perhaps there is a concern that mariners in the audience would need to be as convinced by the scene as the rest of the crowd. Perhaps the possibility that there would be, amongst the audience, theatregoing gentlemen who had been to sea and absorbed some knowledge of shipping, was of greater bearing. Whatever the reason, it is apparent that the scene draws attention away from its aesthetic framework by including valid nautical commands in a correct and justifiable order. We might fruitfully contrast this with Shakespeare's anatopisms elsewhere, not least his notorious propensity to insert coastlines and seaports on to landlocked countries and inland towns.[23] Whilst Shakespeare is so often casual with the factual accuracy of his details, *The Tempest*'s opening scene presents a precision perhaps unmatched in the rest of his work. In this precision lies the singular aesthetic of the play: the minutely detailed storm that is unravelled in subsequent scenes.

The consideration with which the ship in the storm is rendered is made even clearer as Falconer goes on:

> [Shakespeare] has not only worked out a series of manoeuvres, but has made exact use of the professional language of seamanship, knowing that if this were not strictly used aboard ship, the seamen would not know what they were required to do; and that, without it, the scene would not be realistic and lifelike. He could not have come by this knowledge from books, for there were no works on seamanship in his day, nor were there any nautical word lists.[24]

The scene, then, represents a ship in a storm by going through the motions of nautical manoeuvres, but does not draw those manoeuvres from stage practice, nor even from public literature. Falconer makes clear that these particular manoeuvres are only described in print in nautical texts that postdate the play.[25] The first of such texts, Henry Mainwairing's *Seaman's Dictionary*, published in 1623, when Shakespeare had been dead for seven years, advertises its novelty even at that late date:

> To understand the art of navigation is far easier learned than to know the practice and mechanical working of ships, with the proper terms belonging to them, in respect that there are helps for the first by many books ... but for the other, till this, there was not so much as a means thought of, to inform any one in it.[26]

So Shakespeare was employing language that was not found in other plays or printed texts. The framework of the scene is therefore hidden by the fact that it is not a recognisable, book-based framework. By employing language not associated with theatre or with the written word, Shakespeare here relies on the fact that associations with artistic forms and with factual literature are concealed. Whether the manoeuvres were learned from a private manuscript, or Shakespeare gained his knowledge from conversation, the point is the same: the scene effectively broadcasts 'this is not taken from drama, this is not taken from books; this scene is not the descendant of any kind of artificial world: what you are watching is real'. To recall Morton's definition of rendering, 'All signals that we are in a constructed realm have been minimized'.[27] Whether or not this rendering is recognised by the audience, this is the way in which the scene operates. The success of rendering depends not on the exactitude of the illusion but on the ease, facilitated by *The Tempest*'s use of stage effects, with which the audience is enabled to accept it as reality: the convincing noises are heard, but, as I have suggested, the extravagant – unrealistic – fireworks are absent.

The scene minimises 'signals that we are in a constructed realm', then, through its use of stage effects and its unprecedented nautical precision. Moreover, this rendering is not simply found in the accuracy of the Boatswain's commands, but extends to the way in which they are expressed. Figurative language barely makes an appearance for the majority of the Boatswain's speech, and the imagery he uses when speaking to the nobles, or to the Mariners when his orders have failed, is pointedly contrasting: 'What cares these roarers for the name of king?' and 'What, must our mouths be cold?' (16–17, 51). When the Boatswain does use figurative language, that is, he puts it in the form of a rhetorical question; the nautical imperatives have no answer but action, the imagery no answer at all. In the Boatswain's speech, the survival of those on board is dependent on the absence of metaphor: the language of his commands is therefore direct and unambiguous. Figurative language, then, is portrayed in the scene as an extravagance. This has the result of making the storm as convincing as possible: by prioritising the technical terms and by isolating the imagery, the Boatswain's language conceals the aesthetic framework of the drama as a whole, and its special effects.

In order to illustrate this further, it is helpful to compare the scene with its counterpart in John Fletcher's *The Sea Voyage* (1622). Although Fletcher's work alludes repeatedly to *The Tempest*, the difference in terms of the figurative language of the two plays is clear in the first speech. As in Shakespeare's play, there are stage directions for a storm and the Master speaks first:

> *A Tempest, Thunder and Lightning.*
> *Enter Master and two Saylors.*
> MASTER Lay her aloofe, the Sea grows dangerous,
> How it spits against the clouds, how it capers,
> And how the fiery Element frights it back!
> There be devils dancing in the aire, I think
> I saw a Dolphin hang ith'hornes of the moone

Shot from a wave: hey day, hey day,
How she kicks and yerks?
Down with'e main Mast, lay her at hull,
Farle up all her Linnens, and let her ride it out.[28]

Despite the concern that 'Fletcher's scene is designed to be an immediately recognisable echo and development of Shakespeare's and therefore cannot be compared too closely with it', this speech in fact embellishes the language of its predecessor.[29] As in *The Tempest*, the nautical commands are evident, but here they merely bookend the speech rather than dominate it. For the majority of the speech, the imagery of the sea, the clouds, the dolphin and the fiery element give the lines an entirely alternative focus. *The Sea-Voyage* uses elaborate conceits to portray the storm whilst *The Tempest*, as Christopher Cobb has remarked, 'withholds poetic descriptions of both the storm and the suffering of those caught in it'.[30] This is not to dismiss Fletcher's scene, merely to point out that it is inherently different from the scene on which it is based. *The Tempest*'s opening keeps the extravagant stage effects to a minimum, and this is reflected in its unadorned, practical language. The stylised language of Fletcher's Master is precisely the sort avoided by Shakespeare's Boatswain.

Implicit in all of the above arguments is the recognition that the aesthetic of the opening of *The Tempest* is dependent upon the language of the scene more than upon the stage effects of thunder and lightning. With any of Shakespeare's storms the stage effects – however realistic drums, cannonballs and fireworks are – have a necessarily limited contribution to the overall effect of the scene. The reason for this is that Shakespeare's storms are never simply storms. The representation of the weather is never the only priority of the storm scenes; rather, as I have argued throughout, the scenes are always concerned with human perception. Naturally, the title of the play is of key importance here also. Given that the first scene represents – and relies upon – a convincing presentation of a storm (even though afterwards the fiction will reveal the storm to have been derived from magic), *The Tempest*'s title is designed to misdirect the audience before the play begins: the tempest is not a 'real' one, *except* in the title and the opening scene. The audience are presented with the human apprehension of a storm; only later will they learn the extra-human force behind it.

Having explored the ways in which the scene in question relies on a faithful depiction of nautical procedures, I will now turn to the importance of Shakespeare's earlier storms for the reading of this one. I have already noted that the sea-storms in Shakespeare's plays, when considered in chronological order, become increasingly involved in spectatorship.[31] It is also apparent that, when the storms that occur on stage are considered, the simplistic conclusion that thunder and lightning indicates supernatural activity is troubled. I propose that *The Tempest*'s engagement with storm relies on a career of complex approaches to that theatrical commonplace. Moreover, the ways in which the opening scene of the play builds on earlier storms once more point to what, following Morton, I want to call rendering. In order to show this, it is necessary to recall briefly each occurrence of thunder and lightning in Shakespeare's plays and how each one engages with the supernatural.

In the *Henry VI* plays, staged thunder and lightning is dealt with in two different ways. In *Henry VI Part 2*, the effects straightforwardly accompany the rise of Asnath, and therefore follow the formula proposed by Leslie Thomson.[32] In *Part 1*, however, the effects follow Talbot's oaths and, whilst the possibility of divine intervention is thereby alluded to, it is not realised on stage until Joan Puzel summons the fiends (1.4.97; 5.3). From the very start of his playwriting career, then, Shakespeare destabilises the expected association of storm and the supernatural.

In *Julius Caesar*, the next play in which directions for thunder and lightning are found, no supernatural element is forthcoming (at least until the ghost of Caesar appears, long after the storm). Whilst the possibility of portent and 'unnatural ... things' is raised during the storm, such lines are balanced within the characters' dialogue, with Casca credulous and Cicero sceptical. The storm in *Julius Caesar* shows an awareness of its theatrical context in its allusion to the supernatural, but is at odds with that context in that it does not stage a supernatural figure.

If the sound of thunder was a part of the original performance of *Othello*, then subsequent editors, from the First Quarto of 1622 onwards, have not recognised it in stage directions. However, the beginning of Act 2, Scene 1 takes place during a storm, and the characters in it comment on the weather: 'Methinks the wind hath spoke about at land. | A fuller blast ne'er shook our battlements' (2.1.5–6). Perhaps because there are no storm effects, or perhaps in spite of them, there is scarcely any allusion to the work of the supernatural during the tempest. Cassio's hopeful lines come closest: 'Great Jove, Othello guard, | And swell his sail with thine own powerful breath' (78–9). Once again then, if the audience have expectations of the meaning of a storm on stage, Shakespeare has refused to meet them.

The same applies to the next staged storm in Shakespeare's plays, that in *King Lear*. At no point is there a supernatural figure or apparition on stage during the storm, but, as in *Julius Caesar*, the scenes nonetheless can be helpfully read as alluding to a wider supernatural theatrical context. In *Macbeth*, of course, the effects of thunder and lightning are unambiguously charged with the supernatural, occurring as they do at each appearance of the Witches. Rather than consolidate the idea that an audience witnessing a staged storm would expect a supernatural element, however, the storms in *Macbeth* illustrate the extent to which Shakespeare is able to manipulate and utilise expectations. This is especially obvious in the light of the play's composition and first performance being so close to those of *Lear*. For the original Shakespearean audiences, that is, the playwright's storms had meaning specific to each play. In the wider context of other plays, this meaning was inevitably complicated and not readily transferable.

With Shakespeare's romances, the relationship of storm and the supernatural is perhaps even more complex than in the tragedies. As with *Othello*, the storms of *The Winter's Tale* and *Pericles* are not introduced with stage directions for thunder and lightning in their respective editions. However, there is a persuasive case for concluding that those effects would have been used, particularly in the case of *Pericles*, the text of which ultimately derives only from a problematic Quarto edition and which, in Act 3, Scene 1, stages a shipboard scene which seems to cry out for storm effects. In terms of the present question viz. the supernatural, Pericles is persuaded to throw the body of Thaisa overboard in order to calm the elements, but there is no apparition of the supernatural in the scene. In the following scene, however, Thaisa is revived by Cerimon, who claims knowledge of 'an Egyptian | That had nine hours lien dead, | Who was by good appliance recovered' (3.2.86–7). Storm and magic are thus delineated in the two scenes. Only when the noise of thunder and lightning has faded does the work of the supernatural commence. *Cymbeline*, however, sees the familiar descent of the heavenly figure: '*Jupiter descends in thunder and lightning, sitting upon an eagle. He throws a thunderbolt*' (5.4.93). Although, as we have seen, directions such as these are not unusual in early modern theatre, this is the first time in Shakespeare's works in which thunder and lightning accompanies a descent.[33] Storm and the supernatural, then, are once more conflated and simultaneous. As ever, this is not a position on which Shakespeare rests, for in *The Winter's Tale*'s storm is as earthly as *Cymbeline*'s is heavenly. Moreover, this is a play in which the withholding of 'magic' is essential for the dénouement: the reappearance of Hermione. As in *Pericles*, the storm and the supernatural are delineated, but here several scenes separate them. The immediate appearance of the supernatural following the storm in *Pericles* is an explicit separation: each is informed by the absence of the other, and the harm done during the storm is rectified by the magic which follows it. In *The Winter's Tale*, the effect is completely different. The deaths caused by the storm are not revisited, and the intimations of the supernatural are not related to the shipwreck. Any expectations of a theophany during the storm would introduce the idea of a *deus ex machina* too early for the play's finale to be dramatically effective.

It is possible of course that the chronology of Shakespeare's plays differs slightly from the order above. Perhaps *The Tempest* was written before, for example, *The Winter's Tale*, or both of those plays appeared before *Cymbeline*. I have listed the various approaches of the plays, however, in order to make apparent the extent to which any implicit notion of the supernatural in staged storms is destabilised by Shakespeare. This is an important realisation in reading the storm *qua* supernatural in *The Tempest*; and, whether the play was Shakespeare's last of sole authorship or whether others appeared afterwards, the playwright's earlier storms have already established the pattern.

With this in mind, I want to examine the part of Leslie Thomson's essay which deals with *The Tempest*. Until her reading of *The Tempest*, Thomson's argument has been fairly unequivocal, asserting that, '[in] the case of *thunder and lightning*, the audience was almost invariably prompted to expect the supernatural – and got what it expected'.[34] When approaching *The Tempest*, however, it becomes clear that the play already presents for Thomson a departure from the established theatrical practice which is the subject of her essay:

> until Miranda begins the second scene by saying to Prospero, 'If by your art, my dearest father, you have | Put the wild waters in this roar, allay them', it is likely that the audience would not have questioned the tragic event, given the effects they heard and saw while listening to the desperate sailors.[35]

This statement points to a complexity of audience response which is not in keeping with the 'invariable prompting' of the former assertion. Effectively, Thomson concludes that with an appropriate degree of realism in effects, dialogue and acting, the '*tempestuous noise of thunder and lightning heard*' need not suggest the supernatural. Moreover that same realism is enough to convince the audience that the storm is a portrayal of a natural phenomenon. It is my contention that an audience familiar with Shakespeare's plays would be prepared for a storm which withholds its character according to a binary supernatural/natural categorisation. Again, this is not simply a case of how effectively the storm effects are staged, but relies on a career's worth of the meaning of *thunder and lightning* being destabilised. Whilst Thomson's point about the supernatural quality of the storm being realised only through the speech of Miranda is true, then, it complicates her earlier claims over what an audience would expect as the special effects begin the play. The storm is more readily rendered because Shakespeare has, in earlier plays, already troubled the aesthetic framework which rendering seeks to conceal.

So far, I have attempted to show how the opening scene of *The Tempest* is replete with strategies of rendering, and how these strategies work in the scene itself and in relation to earlier plays of Shakespeare's. I will now examine the effect the rendering of the storm in Act 1, Scene 1 has on the rest of the play. In Act 1, Scene 2, Miranda's lines, which open the scene, immediately raise the possibility that the storm itself was, anyway, an illusion. It is seldom acknowledged, however, that the lines simultaneously suggest that the storm is still taking place:

> If by your art, my dearest father, you have
> Put the wild waters in this roar, allay them.
> The sky, it seems, would pour down stinking pitch
> But that the sea, mounting to th' welkin's cheek,
> Dashes the fire out.
>
> (1.2.1–6)

The second line of the speech, with its deictic 'this roar' and its imperative 'allay them' gives the impression, maintained throughout the passage, that the storm has not finished. This is the moment at which the provenance of the storm is revealed, but this revelation is not in retrospect: Miranda's lines allow the audience to experience the storm in the context of the supernatural, then, rather prompting the audience to reimagine it retrospectively. The scene is the point in the play at which the aesthetic framework, hitherto concealed, starts to become acknowledged – a process that continues through to the metadrama of the masque in Act 4, Scene 1. There are no directions for stage effects in Act 1, Scene 2: the shift from the presentation of the storm as natural to magical is apparently dependent on the qualities of Miranda's language. The audience can experience the storm both as natural and supernatural whilst it is occurring. Importantly, the present tense and extended imagery of the passage relates its content to accounts of storms from other plays. In this regard, the description is consciously theatrical in the very way that, I have argued, the opening scene is not. Thus Miranda's speech is related to the Mariner's in *The Winter's Tale*, 'The heavens that we have in hand are angry, | And frown upon's' (3.3.5–6) and Pericles's in *Pericles*, 'O, still | Thy deaf'ning, dreadful thunders; gently quench | Thy nimble sulphurous flashes! [...] the seaman's whistle | is a whisper in the ears of death | Unheard' (3.1.4–10).[36] The extensive imagery of Miranda's speech locates it in this stylistic tradition of characters narrating storms as they occur, a tradition which is resisted in the opening scene of *The Tempest*. One particular image will have been especially familiar to a contemporary audience: the literary conceit of the sea touching the sky. A similar idea is used by William Strachey, whose *True Repertory* is a probable source for *The Tempest*: 'the Sea swelled above the Clouds, and gave battell unto Heaven. It could not be said to raine, the waters like whole Rivers did flood in the ayre'.[37] The image, however, is widespread; taking translations of Ovid as an example, we may see some variations on the theme in the following extracts:

> The surges mounting up aloft did seeme too mate the skye,
> And with theyr sprinckling for too wet the clowdes that hang on hye.[38]

> What boysterous billowes now (O wretch) amids the waves we spye,
> As I forthwith should have bene hev'de to touch the Azure skye.[39]

> Joves indignation and his wrath began to grow so hot.
> That for to quench the rage thereof, his Heaven suffisde not.
> His brother Neptune with his waves was faine to doe him ease.[40]

In including imagery in this vein, then, Miranda's speech is identifiably engaging in a literary tradition. This is exactly the type of allusion that the first scene of the play sought to avoid. The structure of Miranda's speech – the iambic pentameter, the florid description and the familiar, allusive metaphor – signals to the audience that they are watching an aesthetic construction. Just as Miranda intimates, then, that the storm is 'art', so art becomes acknowledged through its formal qualities. The opening scene withholds the poetic; the second scene revels in it.

After the detailed and careful rendering of the storm in the play's opening, then, why have a speech which, in its diction, imagery and allusiveness, undoes the entire process? Surely, the fact that Miranda's lines intimate that the storm is not real, whilst simultaneously employing language suggestive of a *theatrical* storm, is not a coincidence. In the speech, form is reflective of content, and vice versa. Miranda's lines belong to the aesthetic framework which the first scene has been shown to hide.

If Miranda's speech highlights the aesthetic framework fleetingly, then Ariel's description of the storm consolidates the shift in emphasis:

> I boarded the King's ship: now on the beak,
> Now in the waist, the deck, in every cabin
> I flamed amazement. Sometime I'd divide,
> And burn in many places – on the topmast,
> The yards, and bowsprit would I flame distinctly,
> Then meet and join. Jove's lightning, the precursors
> O'th' dreadful thunderclaps, more momentary
> And sight-outrunning were not; the fire and cracks
> Of sulphurous roaring, the most mighty Neptune
> Seem to besiege and make his bold waves tremble,
> Yea, his dread trident shake.
>
> (1.2.196–206)

As in Act 1, Scene 1, there is a certain amount of nautical knowledge on display here, which, though less obscure than that in the first scene, is nonetheless exact. Falconer comments that Ariel 'makes his report, naming the different parts of a tall ship correctly' and, moreover, 'in order' and, as with the manoeuvres in the storm, this is apparently a knowledge gained through experience or conversation rather than books.[41] This, however, is where the similarity with the earlier scene ends, for Ariel's speech, like Miranda's, is thick with figurative language and allusion. Gabriel Egan has pointed out the similarities between these lines and Lear's in the storm:

> The compound adjectives 'thought-executing' and 'sight-outrunning' are not just grammatically alike ... but also convey in different ways the sense of a human faculty (thinking, seeing) surpassed by the instantaneous brightness of lightning flashes that are advance warnings ('vaunt-couriers', 'precursors') of the boom of thunder that will follow.[42]

Again, then, the second scene of *The Tempest* is allusive in ways which the first scene circumvents. One word in particular which Egan notes is shared by Lear and Ariel is 'sulphurous'. In fact, it is a relatively frequent word used by Shakespeare in describing storms, and in particular, in evoking Jove. As well as Pericles's 'nimble sulphurous flashes' (3.1.6), we have Isabella's comparison of Angelo and Jove: 'Thou rather with thy sharp and sulphurous bolt | Splits the unwedgeable and gnarled oak' (*Measure* 2.2.116–17). In *Cymbeline*, Jupiter 'came in thunder; his celestial breath | Was sulphurous to smell' (5.4.114–15). In choosing this word, however, Shakespeare is not simply imbuing Ariel's lines with a favourite description, but referring to the practical elements of staging lightning. Gurr contends that 'Fireworks or rosin for lightning flashes were available at the amphitheatres but unpopular at the halls because of the stink'.[43] That stink was, very often at least, attributable to the ingredients of the fireworks being based around sulphur, which is able to burn independently and is also a constituent of gunpowder.[44] Ariel's lines, then, can be read as referring to an effect absent in the first scene. If, as I have argued, the storm was staged through noise effects alone, then 'sulphurous' functions as a reminder of the inadequacy of such effects in rendering the visual phenomenon of lightning. If my conjecture is false, and fireworks were used, then Ariel's 'sulphurous' is a reminder of their smell, which has probably only recently faded when Ariel is speaking. In this way, it points towards the artificiality of the lightning which the fireworks would have been intended to mimic. In either case, the word may be understood as being informed by the practicalities of staging, and thus, in Ariel's speech, is engaged in the process of highlighting the storm's theatricality. The same can be said for the examples from *Pericles* and *Cymbeline*, of course, but in *The Tempest*, the word amounts to a further suggestion that the second scene underscores what the first scene secretes.

Whatever the various permutations of 'sulphurous' in the speech may be, it seems extremely unlikely that the staging of the storm extended to the spectacular displays of flame which Ariel describes.[45] Unlikely, that is, partly because an effect as distinctive as this would surely be mentioned in a detailed stage direction and partly because no flames are mentioned in the first scene. Perhaps the most pertinent point here, however, relates to the rendering of Act 1, Scene 1 being achieved, as we have seen, with carefully practical language. Ariel's speech is not simply figurative for the sake of fulfilling an opportunity for heightened language, but in order to contrast with the earlier storm. In this way, in its hyperbolic style, it points to a system of theatrical representation which is spectacular, that is, one which draws attention to itself and to its aesthetic form. By reshaping the content of the storm, the form of the storm is brought to light: 'As if we would stage something like that', the speech seems to say, 'when the whole point was to make you think the storm was real'. This reaches a climax in Ariel's next speech, in which, in addition to even more elaborate effects, there is reported speech which is not in the first scene:

> All but mariners
> Plunged into the foaming brine and quit the vessel;
> Then all afire with me, the King's son Ferdinand,
> [...]

Was the first man that leapt, cried 'Hell is empty,
And all the devils are here'.

(210–15)

Ariel's speeches here, moreover, are significant for another, rather different reason. Having been engaged in tempestuous imagery and staging throughout his writing, Shakespeare here indulges in the ultimate pathetic fallacy by giving the storm a voice. Ariel's speech is a detailed, first person narration, that approaches the representation of weather by focussing on, as it were, the I of the storm. The closest I have found to an appraisal of this is concerned with the masque and not the storm, in an essay by Robert Egan: 'the goddesses are being played by spirits who are, in fact, elemental creatures of nature – the real nature surrounding Prospero – and are compelled, possibly against their wills, to enact a natural order which is not their own, but Prospero's "pathetic fallacy"'.[46] Egan's remark indicates the ways in which notions of pathetic fallacy are helpful in explicating the play's approach to the representation of nature, and this applies equally to Ariel as to the spirits of the masque. I will return to this in the final section of the chapter, as it has important connotations for an ecocritical appraisal of the play and is, as I will show, best examined in that light.

The Tempest's staging of thunder and lightning is not restricted to the opening scene, however. There are two more scenes with storm effects in the play and in each of them the illusion of the first scene affects the way the audience is encouraged to respond. Because of the introductory storm, and its subsequent re-imagining by Miranda and Ariel, the sound of thunder in the play is questionable: its origin and hence its qualities, supernatural or other, are unclear.[47] Having witnessed a natural storm, which immediately becomes a supernatural storm, the audience is not in a position decisively to judge the next incidence of thunder:

> *Enter Caliban, with a burden of wood;*
> *a noise of thunder heard.*
> All the infections that the sun sucks up
> From bogs, fens, flats, on Prosper fall, and make him
> By inchmeal a disease! His spirits hear me,
> And yet I needs must curse.

(2.2.1–4)

Having established the possibility that thunder has a supernatural origin, the play consolidates the idea by directing the sound effects to be produced again. Thus the tension between natural and supernatural is created, and a hierarchical relationship between the two is brought about: the 'natural' in the play is subsumed by, and subject to the work of, the supernatural. Commenting on these lines, Gabriel Egan writes: 'Caliban has developed the recognisable symptom of the mentally traumatised ... This is why he responds to perfectly ordinary thunder as though it were the reaction of Prospero's agents to his cursing'.[48] As in Thomson's argument above, Egan's notion of 'perfectly ordinary thunder' is undermined by his earlier assumptions of the simplistic relationship of storm and the supernatural. Moreover, the impetus of Caliban's lines relies on the fact that neither the natural nor supernatural assignment of the sound of thunder here is possible. However, Caliban's curses, like Lear's before him, are formed from 'his' – or, rather, Shakespeare's – understanding of early modern meteorology.[49] According to this set of theories, as we have seen, the sun caused 'vapours' to rise towards it, much as we now understand moisture to be formed into clouds.[50] If those vapours were from a noxious source, like a bog, then when they fell to earth as rain, they would spread their disease. This curse of Caliban's, then, requires a slight acquaintance with the Jacobean understanding of the weather.[51]

The significance of the meteorological source of the later curse is that Caliban speaks following the sound of thunder. The weather in the play has been exposed as magically derived rather than natural. Caliban's curses rely on authentic natural processes: the sun drawing up vapours which eventually fall, a notion to which the Jacobean audience subscribed. Seen in this way, the curses evoke the futility of Caliban's position regarding authority: they are optimistic fantasies that require a weather system outside the control of Prospero, but such a weather system is precisely what is being exposed as unavailable. Caliban acknowledges the 'spirits' making the thunder yet hopelessly invokes a natural weather event. Nature is represented by the play not only as subject to human control but also as generating the reference points for the language through which its enslavement is expressed. Even though they may still make sense without the concept of supernatural thunder, Caliban's curses would thereby lose a wide nexus of allusive connotations. As with the opening scene, the use of sound effects provides a backdrop for the representation of the perception of a storm. The difference is that the audience now understands the play's weather as supernatural and Caliban's curse is all the more futile for it.

Continuing his argument on Caliban's traumatic state, Gabriel Egan makes the following proposition:

It is in this light that we should consider the transformatory power of Prospero's terrifying theatrical illusions. The first illusion is the tempest itself that made the 'bold waves tremble' ... and was intended to 'infect [the] reason' to cause 'a fever of the mad' in Prospero's enemies [who] thereafter take the natural for the supernatural.[52]

If we follow the hypothesis that the thunder in Act 2, Scene 2 is 'natural', then this is persuasive, although we might wonder what other 'natural' incidences Egan is referring to here. However, as I have shown, there is something more fundamental happening here in the play's representation of representation. The opening scene's determined rendering has given way to a clearly acknowledged aesthetic framework, one which makes it impossible to categorise the thunder in this scene as an 'illusion of an illusion' or as an 'illusion of the real'. The way in which Caliban's speech approaches the sound of thunder is indicative of the two separate strands of understanding. He recognises the possibility that the thunder is an indication that Prospero's spirits are listening, but meets that supernatural apprehension of the storm with diction grounded in a natural understanding of the weather. In this way, the sound of thunder questions the representation of the natural in a dramatic context: it is not simply Caliban's curses which are impotent, but the possibility of rendering a natural environment in the supernatural aesthetic which the play has established. This is, moreover, once again, a metadramatic quality: that supernatural aesthetic is the framework within which the play operates, and by highlighting it, the text necessarily foregrounds its theatricality. Much has already been written on the metadramatic in *The Tempest*, but in this way, as we shall see, such self-reflexivity has implications for an ecocritical reading of the play.

There is one more scene in *The Tempest* in which thunder is staged, and, unlike the first two scenes, there are two stage directions for it:

> *Thunder and lightning. Enter Ariel, like a harpy, claps his wings upon the table, and with a quaint device the banquet vanishes.* (3.3.52)

> *He vanishes in thunder. Then, to soft music, enter the shapes again and dance with mocks and mows, and carry out the table.* (3.3.82)

Ariel's appearance and disappearance are part of a series of theatrical miniatures which convince both the onstage and offstage audience that the scene is, as Sebastian puts it, 'a living drollery' (21). It is clear enough from these directions and from the above discussion that, in the course of the play, the sound of thunder has shifted in meaning from one extreme to another: in the first scene it signified a meticulously rendered natural storm, but here it represents a commonplace theophany which revels in its theatrical tricks. Even with the basic effects of a noise of thunder, Shakespeare can achieve a bewildering array of variations in what it signifies. But if we are to take the stage directions of the play literally, then the pyrotechnics absent in the first scene and in Act 2, Scene 2, here accompany Ariel's entrance. It is surely no coincidence that such an act of theatricalising nature is simultaneous with the play's own zenith of display: the 'quaint device' with which 'the banquet vanishes'. The shifting signification of storm effects is in balance with the representation of magic. In the opening scene, the magic is kept hidden, as the representation of nature takes the stage. As Ariel descends, nature is marginalised as magic is not only foregrounded but, with a quaint device, performed. The storm in the play, therefore, signifies both nature and supernature; both realism and magic.

Addressing the staged thunder in *The Tempest*, Leslie Thomson writes that following the first scene, 'occurrences of the effects in the play, although in the context of Prospero's white magic, are nonetheless potent reminders of its darker uses, which would probably have helped to convey – more clearly to the original playgoers than to us – that Prospero is on the edge between one force and another'.[53] 'On the edge', however, is the way in which *The Tempest* represents nature throughout. At its core, the play may be understood as an investigation of the drive to dominate nature, and the fantasies in which that desire is expressed. In order to see this quality more clearly, it should be read alongside more conservative readings of the play. As with all of Shakespeare's storms, those in *The Tempest* are reliant upon – and probing of – the processes of theatrical meaning. They can thereby be read as metatheatrical. We have seen this in varying ways throughout the other plays I have explored. In *The Tempest*, however, we find a play with a critical legacy of metatheatrical readings. How should my reading of the play's storms be handled in relationship with this tradition? Approaches to *The Tempest*'s concern with metatheatre have tended to concentrate on Prospero's character as a dramatist, and in particular on the masque of Act 4, Scene 1. Kiernan Ryan, for example, contends that '[t]he play's ideals are expansively celebrated in the masque' by representing empathy and concession.[54] As Stephen Orgel points out, the masque 'is re-enacting central concerns of the play as a whole'.[55] With these qualities in mind, the appropriateness of the masque for the focus of metatheatrical readings is evident, although the approaches are still open to various conclusions.[56] However, if the metadramatic is to be properly addressed, then we must take account not only of the masque, but of the storm of the opening scene.

Like the masque, the storm of the first scene can be thought of as reflecting *The Tempest*'s concerns. As well as identifying immediately with the title of the play, the storm portrays social upheaval and confusion. As a work of magic, it establishes the idea – which the masque, of course, makes explicit – of Prospero as dramatist, simultaneously controlling the events of the play and commenting on their illusory nature.[57] Although it is arguable that the storm in the first scene makes the metadramatic at once explicit and unstable from the start, such an argument would not fully take account of the detail with which that scene is rendered. It is possible for the scene to operate on both levels of meaning, that is, concerned both with naturalistic theatre and with metatheatre. Whilst the opening storm is retrospectively metatheatrical, we must also acknowledge that – at least in the initial reading or viewing – the concealment of the storm as a work of illusion serves to camouflage the metadramatic aspects. The rendering of storm, then, involves a representation of nature as wild and free, only subsequently to be claimed as under the domain of a supernaturally endowed human, or indeed under the domain of theatre. Part of the play's concern with its own process of producing meaning inheres in its concealing that process for the time it takes for viable alternative processes to be consolidated. By rendering the storm as thoroughly as possible, the foundations are in place for the play to carry out a formal investigation of the meaning of thunder and lightning on the Jacobean stage. This investigation can only take place if the opening storm insists on its non-theatricality. In this way, the implications of the storm – both in terms of what it means and how it means – can be extended, as we have seen, through the speech of Miranda, and culminate in the language of Ariel.

As I have already suggested, the fact that the play gives a voice for the storm is of great significance to an ecocritical approach to the text. But it is crucial that it is Ariel who speaks with this voice, for the ecocritical approach is invested with similar interests as those that ground postcolonial readings. In the readings of the play which formed the bulk of late twentieth-century responses, postcolonial studies tended to focus on Caliban, as a native of the island ruled by the invading Prospero.[58] The postcolonial and the ecocritical have already been shown to share concerns by Gabriel Egan. Egan's chapter on *The Tempest* in *Green Shakespeare* explores Prospero's apparent deforestation of the island, carried out through the enslaved Caliban who is constantly made to deliver wood, and relates this environmental question to the similar policies of Jacobean English forces in Ireland.[59] Although Egan's argument is persuasive (and can also be applied to Ferdinand – an imperial, rather than a native, challenge to Prospero's domination in a postcolonial reading), its scope is limited by the focus on Caliban. Clearly an ecocritical approach finds more of interest in Ariel, a recognisable non-human, who is nonetheless enslaved and made super-naturally to carry out, indeed to supplant, the work of nature.

Ariel's domination by Prospero is encapsulated both before and after his descriptions of the storm. His first lines display a willing subservience: 'All hail, great master; grave sir, hail! I come | To answer thy best pleasure' (1.2.189–90). The simplicity of this is troubled by the later exchange with Prospero, whose question 'What is't thou canst demand?' is met with a forthright 'My liberty' (1.2.245). The extent to which Prospero has control over Ariel is evident in the language of intimidation. The threat with which he forces the slave to work is based on Ariel's once being trapped in a pine tree by Sycorax: 'If thou more murmer'st, I will rend an oak | And peg thee in his knotty entrails' (1.2.294–5). The punishment which Prospero threatens is couched in both natural and mythological terms, the oak tree being sugges-tive both of the strength of nature and its associations with Jove.[60] Ariel's involvement in the natural world is simultaneously one of control and subservience. Moreover, the strength of Ariel's lightning is apparently not the most powerful on the island, if Prospero's later claims are to be taken at face value.[61]

As with the threat of the oak, Prospero's encouragement to Ariel is figured in terms of the natural: 'Thou shalt be as free | As mountain winds' (1.2.499–500). Indeed, the same can be seen in much of the language used to describe Ariel and his actions. Prospero also speaks of the tasks 'to tread the ooze | Of the salt deep, | To run upon the sharp wind of the north, | To do me business in the veins o'th' earth | When it is baked with frost' (1.2.252–6). Significantly, after Ariel's speech in which he claims to have 'flamed amazement', Prospero here associates the spirit with the three remaining elements – the water of the sea, the air of the wind and the earth of the ground – in quick succession. Ariel thereby stands for a codified version of nature in its discrete parts. If we isolate one of Prospero's phrases – 'To do me business in the veins o'th' earth' – we can see several potential inter-pretations. For example, if the veins of the earth refer to metallic ore, as is clearly one possible meaning, then the phrase figures capitalism as ravaging nature – 'To do me *business* in the veins o'th' earth'. Simultaneously, though, *veins* is a word which figures the earth as mammalian, even human – there is a symbolic bridge between the earth and the human here: making the ravaging of nature more explicit, more cruel. Prospero's lines are surely related to Ariel's first phrases: 'I come| to answer thy best pleasure, be't to fly, | To swim, to dive into the fire, | To ride | On the curled clouds' (1.2.189–92). Indeed, as Prospero defines Ariel, so Ariel often speaks of himself in imagery drawn from the natural world: 'Where the bee sucks, there suck I | In a cowslip's bell I lie; | There I couch when owls do cry. | On the bat's back I do fly' (5.1.88–91). The imprisoning methods of Sycorax ensured that Ariel's 'groans | Did make wolves howl and penetrate the breasts of ever angry bears' (1.2.287–9).[62] Ariel's entry in thunder is not simply the zenith of the play's gradual conflation of storm and the supernatural, then, but also of Ariel's identification with natural forces which become subject to the supernatural in theatrical representation.

In depicting Ariel both as a slave and as a personification of weather, *The Tempest* demands to be read in ecocritical terms: the fantasy of new-world domination is necessarily also a fantasy of domination over nature. Moreover, the way in which the ostensibly 'real' storm is thoroughly shown to be an illusion within the world of the play as well as within the world of the theatre, provokes the thought that all theatrical representations of nature share this same fantasy. In his chapter on *As You Like It*, Robert N. Watson remarks that the 'difficulty of knowing nature objectively becomes part of the entire subject-object problem, as well as the problem of other minds'.[63] Watson argues that *As You Like It* addresses such problems through a strategy of relentless simile, which foreground, rather than conceal, the difficulty:

> The irreducible distances between likeness and identity, and between the human and the natural, are (though the term has become anathema to Shakespeare scholars) themes of the play, recurring – often in parallel – with a remarkable frequency and intricacy quite apart from any necessities of plot or realistic characterisation.[64]

If we are to accept Watson's argument as far as *As You Like It* is concerned, then we might be intrigued by the ways in which it may be applied to *The Tempest*. *As You Like It* supports such a reading largely because of its form: the 'difficulty of knowing nature' is a condition of the early modern human experience, and is a challenge which is, according to Watson, ironically reducible to a pastoral fantasy of a prelapsarian existence. In *The Tempest*, however, nature is not represented in the same nostalgic way: the environment is presented either as destructive or as supernatural. It is furthermore, as we have seen, figured as theatrical, neatly encapsulated in Prospero's question to Ariel: 'Hast thou, spirit, | Performed to point the tempest that I bade thee?' (1.2.193–4). Whereas *As You Like It* draws attention to the difference between the human and the natural through its imagery, then, *The Tempest* does so through its metatheatricality. The only form of nature which *The Tempest* is capable of representing is that which is controlled by the human. Paradoxically, it is the first scene – the most carefully 'natural' nature –which is the most rigorously exposed as an illusion: humankind can only represent nature *as* theatre, for to represent it *through* theatre is to mistakenly conclude that it is possible to know nature objectively. According to Watson, then, in *As You Like It*, 'Shakespeare begins to explore some modern anxieties about our ability to know the world itself, to move beyond comparison into truth, to see the absolute face to face, as we feel we should and once did'.[65] In *The Tempest*, however, such an approach is problematic not because language is a barrier, but because the play is ultimately concerned with approaching theatrical representation and not nature. Rather than 'see the absolute' of nature 'face to face', *The Tempest* seeks to expose the structures of illusion on which theatre depends as the only absolute available to us. For Watson, poetic representation functions as a screen between human experience and 'real' nature: nature is presented as knowable in *As You Like It* via the medium of figurative language. The artificiality of this language conceals the fantasy of knowing nature on its own terms. Similarly, *The Tempest* presents nature as subject to human control through the medium of theatricality.

For this reason, the personification of the storm as Ariel is the summit of the play's approach to the problem of representing nature on the stage. In the speeches in which Ariel describes the storm, nature has a voice, a language, a narrative, the very qualities through which anthropocentric thought is expressed, and therefore through which the irreducible barrier between nature and the human is maintained. The fantasy of the supernatural agent, then, is one in which a dialogue with nature is possible. Crucially, such a dialogue is presented as hierarchical: the voice of nature in Ariel is subject to the voice of the human in Prospero. This hierarchy is maintained throughout the play after the first scene. Indeed, it may even be argued that the ferocity of the storm in the first scene is a way of retrospectively establishing the notion that even at its most extreme, *The Tempest*'s weather is the subject of human control. It is in the conversation between Ariel and Prospero that the relationship of human and nature is most explicitly played out, but there are incidents elsewhere which support the points I have made. The notable irony, for example, of Prospero's characterisation of Antonio as 'unnatural' rests on Prospero's entire character being founded on the subjugation of nature, or indeed the 'unnaturalisation' of nature (5.1.79).[66] Watson's account of the Renaissance maintains that 'the elite intellectual culture appeared obsessed with getting back to nature, hoping there and thereby to regain unmediated contact with simple reality – which that culture could no longer comfortably identify'.[67] In *The Tempest*, however, the obsession is not with getting back to nature, but with controlling it.[68] Moreover, the notion of a 'simple reality' with which culture might gain 'unmediated contact' is made to seem ridiculous: in its place is a complex theatricality, which addresses the attempts to identify with anything simpler – more 'natural' – as futile. This complexity inheres in the drama's capacity to recognise its own dramatic qualities after, of course, it has hidden them during the storm.

The last speech of the play has been read as superfluous. The recent Arden editors assert that the 'Epilogue is not required for a coherent reading or production because the play's action is complete. Shakespeare may have added it for special performances, perhaps at court'.[69] By way of coming to a conclusion, I would like to turn to the Epilogue with these remarks in mind, and to argue that the speech is indeed vital for a coherent reading of the play and can be shown as completing the action rather than commenting upon it.

> Now my charms are all o'erthrown,
> And what strength I have's mine own,
> Which is most faint. Now, 'tis true
> I must be here confined by you,
> Or sent to Naples. Let me not,
> Since I have my dukedom got
> And pardoned the deceiver, dwell
> In this bare island by your spell;
> But release me from my bands
> With the help of your good hands.
> Gentle breath of yours my sails
> Must fill, or else my project fails,
> Which was to please. Now I want
> Spirits to enforce, art to enchant;
> And my ending is despair,
> Unless I be relieved by prayer,
> Which pierces so that it assaults
> Mercy itself, and frees all faults.
> As you from crimes would pardoned be,
> Let your indulgence set me free.

Despite the content of the speech, its form betrays magic overtones: rhyming couplets in trochaic tetrameter is, as we have seen, the structure used for *Macbeth*'s Witches and *A Midsummer Night's Dream*'s fairies.[70] As an epilogue, Puck's is similarly arranged and is, like Prospero's, concerned with the liminal boundary of theatre and audience imagination. *The Tempest*'s Epilogue, however, is unusual for maintaining the character of Prospero: as Stephen Orgel remarks, it 'is unique in the Shakespeare canon in that its speaker declares himself not an actor in a play but a character in a fiction'.[71] How does this idiosyncrasy reflect on the play as a whole? I have argued that the storm in the first scene is deliberately written to draw attention away from the aesthetic framework of the play. Surely, something similar is happening in the Epilogue if Prospero remains in character? Remarking on this quality, Robert Egan asserts that 'The Epilogue of *The Tempest* ... specifically does away with this perspective, purposefully eliminating any barrier between the play-world and the real'.[72] The 'charms' and the 'strength' in the speech ostensibly refer to the supernatural powers which Prospero has surrendered, and yet are also evidently applicable to the power of the theatre and the play. By remaining in character, this anthropomorphic Epilogue readdresses the play's concern that our contact with reality cannot be unmediated. This is made clearer as the speech continues, as further aspects of the play I have highlighted re-emerge. In the phrase 'I must be here confined by you', for example, the language of slavery is revisited. Orgel notes that here: 'Prospero puts himself in the position of Ariel, Caliban, Ferdinand and the other shipwreck victims throughout the play, threatened with confinement, pleading for release from bondage'.[73] This much is clear. However, in addition to imagining Prospero as slave, what this phrase also does is figure the audience as enslaver. Audience become both master and dramatist: they are implicated in the same strategies of control which Prospero has espoused throughout the play.[74] Moreover, this is not simply an identification of the audience that applies only in the Epilogue. Rather, the implication is of a hierarchy which has persisted for the length of the drama. In the final speech, then, the fantasy of theatrical control over nature is made explicit again, and the audience's part in it is formalised: 'Gentle breath of yours my sails | Must fill' follows the importuning of 'the help of your good hands'. The extent to which these phrases figure the audience not simply as controlling of nature but as complicit in the play's magic – and therefore in the storm – is made clearer when they are compared to Prospero's last lines before the Epilogue:

> I'll deliver all,
> And promise you calm seas, auspicious gales
> And sail so expeditious that shall catch
> Your royal fleet far off. My Ariel, chick,
> That is thy charge. Then to the elements
> Be free, and fare thou well!
>
>   (5.1.314–19)

What the Epilogue offers, then, is a formal alignment of the audience's magical powers with those of Ariel: just as Ariel is charged with creating the 'auspicious gales', so the audience 'must fill' the sails with their 'Gentle breath' and applause. Just as Ariel is to return 'to the elements', so the audience is ultimately responsible for the means through which he is imprisoned: 'this bare island by *your* spell', a phrase which neatly implicates the audience as well as drawing attention to the bareness of the stage itself. I have argued that the play presents nature as only accessible through a distorted theatrical lens, one which reflects both subject and object through its self-awareness. The final component of that fantastical representation is the acknowledgement that any such lens necessarily requires the audience's guilty subjugation of the elements, its wilful abandonment of the natural. If the longing to get 'back to nature' is fuelled by the characterisation of nature as 'real', *The Tempest* subverts the desire by highlighting the dramatic quality of its presentation of nature. In order to achieve this, the storm in the first scene must be as 'real' as possible, for only then is the theatricality of the human apprehension of nature exposed.

Conclusion

It is not an exaggeration to say that storms have influenced the course of history, both in the period in which Shakespeare lived and today, in the ongoing storms associated with climate change. Without one notable thunderstorm in 1505, for example, it is conceivable that the entire modern era of the West would have been radically different. It was in the summer of that year that a young Martin Luther was caught in a violent storm and, fearing for his life, exclaimed the oath, 'Help me, Saint Anna, and I shall become a monk'.[1] A fortnight later, Luther entered the Augustinian monastery at Erfurt, thus beginning in earnest the theological life which would shape so much of the Reformation. If it is too much to say that the storm engendered religious upheaval, it must surely be acknowledged as a catalyst.

Unsurprisingly, just as the characters in Shakespeare's plays offer different accounts of storms, descriptions of Luther's experience vary. In 1581, the English theologian Robert Parsons wrote that 'MARTIN LUTHER walking in his youth in a certain medowe, was stroken with a thunder boolt, & therupon sodaynlie for verie feare made hym selfe an Austen fryer'.[2] The notion that Luther was actually struck by lightning lends an element of hyperbolic dynamism to a story hardly deficient in symbol. Thunder and lightning, figured since antiquity as the instruments of divinity, are constructed in Parsons's description as capable of conferring divinity on their target. The speed, both literal and figurative, of lightning lends itself neatly to the apparent rapidity of Luther's epiphany.

The storm of 1505 was not the only important storm of Luther's life. It seems that he had a susceptibility to the weather and that it substantially affected his temperament. Whilst still a novice, in the chapel at Erfurt, during a service and whilst a storm raged outside, Luther fell to the floor in a fit, shouting 'It is not I' or, according to Parsons, 'I am not, I am not dume, I wil speake yet unto the world'.[3] The episode marked the end of Luther's novitiate, and, at the invitation of Erfurt's seniors, the beginning of his career in the priesthood. As the first storm had ushered his career towards religion, so the second refined that career and imbued it, crucially, with a public voice. As Nathaniel Pallone and James Hennessy remark, explanations of Luther's experience vary according to 'the theological vs. the psychopathological'.[4] Pallone and Hennessy add to such variations with 'neurochemical interpretation': 'Severe thunderstorms release vast quantities of nitrogen … among susceptible persons, such rapid infusion may trigger episodes of "nitrogen narcosis," a short-lived condition resembling acute alcoholic intoxication'.[5]

The events of Luther's life are a helpful way to think about what this book has shown. If one were imagining lost elements of Shakespeare's life in order to read his works, then it would be tempting to speculate that he had experience, either direct or anecdotal, of some episode of nitrogen narcosis whilst working on *King Lear*. In reading the plays, however, such a conjecture would be less apposite for its explanation of Lear's raging and hallucinations than for its implicit acknowledgement of the relationship between environment and identity. It is this relationship that Shakespeare's storms highlight and elucidate.

Shakespeare probes the minutiae of the relationship between theatrical and meteorological understanding: the capacity for a character, or an audience member, simultaneously to represent or experience storms on several levels is part of the detailed complexity of Shakespeare's dramatic meteorology. Whether in the extreme manifestations of weather in *Lear* which are matched with extremes of expression by the king, or whether, as in *The Tempest*, thunder and lightning act as a looking glass through which representations of the weather are examined, Shakespeare remains alive to the environmental conditions of human experience.

Crucially, as with Luther and nitrogen narcosis, those conditions accrue layers of interpretation. As Cicero remarks in *Julius Caesar*, in what amounts to a précis of much of Shakespeare's storm dialogue, 'men may construe things after their fashion | Clean from the purpose of the things themselves' (1.3.34–5). During the early modern period, Luther was described approvingly as 'that sonne of thunder', and condemned as one who 'hath stered a mighty storme and tempest in the chirche'.[6] As we have seen, Shakespeare's attention to the contradictions and mutability of weather interpretation is evident in all of his storm plays, and particularly in *Julius Caesar*. The relationship between human and environment, then, is understood not only as integral to expression, as in *Lear*, but subject to manipulation through that expression. Thus, the storm is a conduit for symbol, as when, for Cassius, Caesar is figured as 'a man | Most like this dreadful night | That thunders, lightens, opens graves, and roars' (1.3.72–4) or for *Pericles*'s Marina, 'born in a tempest' and for whom 'This world ... is as a lasting storm' (4.1.18–19). It is the very protean nature of the Shakespearean storm that eludes critics who seek to integrate it into a comprehensive equation or code.[7]

Storms are an important metaphorical figure throughout Shakespeare's plays, and especially for those characters who, like Cassius and Marina, are subjected to them. However, the poetic implications of storms are not the only reason for their recurrence. Shakespeare seriously considered the impact of the special effects of thunder and lightning when writing staged storms, whether creating the sense of the new Globe or using the Blackfriars' to gull the audience.

Ultimately, Shakespeare is invested in the theatricality of the human apprehension of nature. Whilst theatre as a form is developing rapidly, he is aware of the codes of practice being established, and able to use them aesthetically and ironically. The recognition of audience expectation in Elizabethan and Jacobean theatre is, I believe, an area which merits a great deal of further work, and it is in such cases that Shakespeare's storms are at their most intriguing. It is through the manipulation of the expected that Shakespeare achieves the unexpected. In the storms, we have inevitably found separation, violence, beauty and loss. What this book has demonstrated, however, is that the storms also show Shakespeare testing the limits of theatre and audience before those limits are established.

Notes

Introduction

1 Although the chronology of the plays is a contentious topic, the plays in question are relatively widely spaced. The only sticking point is in the order of *The Winter's Tale* and *The Tempest*. I have opted for a more conservative arrangement, in which *The Tempest* is later, in agreement with Oxford and Arden editors.

2 A similar effect is achieved in *Twelfth Night*: 'Sebastian, are you? ... How hast thou made division of yourself?' (5.1.217–19).

3 Perhaps there is even a little signal of mortality in Shakespeare's diction. The playwright uses 'bodkin' only three times including here. Each time there is a certain conflation of danger and death involved: ('DUMAINE: The head of a bodkin. BEROWNE: A death's face in a ring'; 'he himself might his quietus make | With a bare bodkin'. *Love's Labour's Lost* 5.2.607–8, *Hamlet* 3.1.75–6).

4 See, for example, H. H. Huxley, 'Storm and Shipwreck in Roman Literature', *Greece and Rome* 21:63 (Oct. 1952), 117–24.

5 Lucretius, *On the Nature of the Universe*, trans. R. E. Latham (London: Penguin, 1951), p. 60.

6 Miguel de Montaigne, *Essays done into English, according to the last French edition, by John Florio* (London: Melch. Bradwood for Edward Blount and William Baret, 1631), p. 443.

7 Ibid., p. 443.

8 Hans Blumenberg, *Shipwreck With Spectator*, trans. Steven Rendall (Cambridge, MA: MIT Press, 1997), p. 26.

9 Ibid., p. 64.

10 Though I am using examples from the third Globe to illustrate this principle, it applies of course to any open-air performance.

11 In the performance I saw (18 July 2012), this too was greeted with laughter and applause, and I'm confident that it got the same response in each of its early performances. The weather – which finally (though briefly) became warmer on 21 July – had been something of a national joke for several months. Clearly, this encouraged the response.

12 Leslie Thomson, 'The Meaning of *Thunder and Lightning*: Stage Directions and Audience Expectations', *Early Theatre* 2 (1999), 11–24 (11).

13 Ibid.

14 Ibid.

15 Not least in the work of James VI and I. See below, p. 90.

16 See Philip Butterworth, *Theatre of Fire: Special Effects in Early English and Scottish Theatre* (London: Society for Theatre Research, 1998), pp. 41–53.

17 Barnabe Barnes, *The Divils Charter a Tragedie* (London: G. E. for John Wright, 1607), sig. A2v

18 Ibid., sig. A2v (my emphases).

19 Ibid., sig. A2v.

20 Ibid., sigs. G1v–G2r; M2v.

21 Ibid., sig. B1v.

22 Ibid., sig. D3v.

23 Ibid., sig. D3v.

24 In David Bevington et al. (eds), *English Renaissance Drama: A Norton Anthology* (New York: Norton, 2002), pp. 134–83.

25 *Robert Greene, Friar Bacon* 11.76.

26 Ibid., 9.83.

27 The authorship of the play has been the subject of much debate – it was, for example, first published as 'written by W. S.' and included in an impression of the third Folio edition of Shakespeare's works – but has most recently been included as one of Thomas Middleton's works. See Gary Taylor et al. (eds), *Thomas Middleton: The Collected Works* (Oxford: Oxford University Press, 2007), pp. 509–43.

28 W. S., *The Puritaine* (London by G. ELD., 1607), sig. G2v.

29 Thomson, 'The Meaning of *Thunder and Lightning*', p. 18.

30 R[obert] A[rmin], *The Valiant Welshman, or, The True Chronicle History of the Life and Valiant Deeds of Caradoc the Great, King of Cambria* (London: George Furslowe for *Robert Lownes*, 1615), sig. A4r.

31 Ibid.

32 Ibid., sig. F1r.

33 Ibid.

34 See Ibid., sigs. F1v and G1r.

35 Thomas Dekker, *If it Be not Good, the Devil is in it*, 4.2.33.

36 John Fletcher, *The Mad Lover*, in Francis Beaumont and John Fletcher, *Comedies and Tragedies* (London, 1647), fols. 1–23 (fol. 19).

37 Ibid., fol. 19.

38 Only *The Iron Age Part II* lacks the stage direction.

39 Thomas Heywood, *The Golden Age. Or The Lives of Jupiter and Saturne, with the Defining of the Heathen Gods* (London: William Barrenger, 1611), sig. K2v.

40 Ibid., sig. K2v.

41 Thomas Heywood, *The Silver Age* (London: Nicholas Okes, 1613), sig. C3r.

42 Thomas Heywood, *The Brazen Age* (London: Nicholas Okes, 1613), sig. L3r.

43 Thomas Heywood, *The Iron Age* (London: Nicholas Okes, 1632), sig. H4r. This text contains both parts of the play.

44 Heywood, *The Iron Age*, sig. H4r.

45 Thomson claims that 'only once is the effect [*thunder*] for weather only: "It snows, and rains, thunders"'. See Thomas Drout, *The Life of the Dutches of Suffolke* (London: A. M[atthews] for Jasper Emery, 1631), sig. F2v; Alan C. Dessen and Leslie Thomson, *A Dictionary of Stage Directions in English Drama 1580–1642* (Cambridge: Cambridge University Press, 1999), p. 230. In attributing the quotation to Thomson, I am following the note in her essay, 22n2.

46 Heywood, *The Iron Age*, sig. H4v.

47 Edward Burns (ed.), *Henry VI, Part 1* (London: Thomson Learning, 2001), 1.4.97sdn.

48 See ibid., pp. 33–7.

49 Ibid., p. 33.

50 The mention of the Ghosts is a reminder that the scene is already suffused with supernatural context, the spirits having entered to 'Solemn music' (30), which, as in the above examples, may function in a similar way to the storm effects.

51 Thomson relies partly on a perceived difference between the direction for *storm* and that for *thunder and lightning*. Storm, Thomson argues, 'however accidentally' illustrates that the effect called for is one of bad weather, rather than one to be associated with supernatural activity. In the case of *Lear*, then, 'the use of "*storm*" in the stage direction implicitly confirms that Lear is wrong to assume supernatural intervention; it *is* only a storm – even if thunder and lightning are among the special effects at this point in the play' (p. 16, Thomson's emphasis).

52 Sharon O'Dair, 'Is it Shakespearean Ecocriticism if it isn't Presentist?', in Lynne Bruckner and Dan Brayton (eds), *Ecocritical Shakespeare* (Farnham: Ashgate, 2011), pp. 71–85 (71).

53 Ibid., p. 75.

54 The 2007–09 RSC production, dir. Trevor Nunn, for example, had both stage rain and thunder.

55 Timothy Morton, *The Ecological Thought* (Cambridge, MA: Harvard University Press, 2010), p. 17.

56 Simon C. Estok, *Ecocriticism and Shakespeare: Reading Ecophobia* (New York: Palgrave Macmillan, 2011), p. 1.

57 Simon C. Estok, 'Afterword: Ecocriticism on the Lip of a Lion', in Bruckner and Brayton (eds), *Ecocritical Shakespeare*, pp. 239–46 (240).

58 See Morton, *The Ecological Thought*.

59 Ibid., p. 17.

60 Robert N. Watson, *Back to Nature: The Green and the Real in the Late Renaissance* (Philadelphia: University of Pennsylvania Press, 2006).

61 Ibid., p. 5.

62 Ibid., p. 6.

63 Timothy Morton, *Ecology Without Nature: Rethinking Environmental Aesthetics* (Cambridge, MA: Harvard University Press, 2007), p. 204.

64 Gabriel Egan, *Green Shakespeare: From Ecopolitics to Ecocriticism* (Abingdon: Routledge, 2006), p. 139.

1 Thunder

1 OED fig. *calm before the storm* (also *tempest*). The instance given is from Sutton's *Disce Vivere*, 1602.

2 See R. W. Dent, *Shakespeare's Proverbial Language: An Index* (Berkeley, CA: University of California Press, 1981), C24; S908. According to Dent, 'After a storm comes a calm' is proverbial from 1538 onwards, whilst 'After a calm comes a storm' started to appear in 1572.

3 In sixteenth-century continental Europe, there were various moves to elaborate upon or counter Aristotelian meteorological theories with alchemical and other practices: a true challenge to Aristotle's work. Writers of meteorological texts in England, however, continued to conceive of weather within the confines of an Aristotelian framework, and that is the framework subscribed to by England's creative writers in the period. For a detailed account of the development of continental meteorology and its relationship with natural philosophy, see Craig Martin, *Renaissance Meteorology: Pomponazzi to Descartes* (Baltimore: Johns Hopkins University Press, 2011).

4 Aristotle, *Meteorologica*, trans. H. D. P. Lee (Portsmouth, NH: Heinemann, 1952). For the initial outlining of the arguments on exhalations and vapours, see 340b. The terminology used by Aristotle varies, and at various points the terms 'vapour' and 'exhalation' can be misleading. For my purposes, the distinction as I outline it is sufficient. For a more detailed discussion, see Martin, *Renaissance Meteorology*, pp. 6–8.

5 See Aristotle, *Meteorologica*, 371b.

6 S. K. Heninger, *A Handbook of Renaissance Meteorology, with Particular Reference to Elizabethan and Jacobean Literature* (New York: Greenwood Press, 1968), p. 12.

7 Ibid., p. 72.

8 William Fulke, *A Goodly Gallery with a most Pleasant Prospect* (London: William Griffith, 1563), fol. 101.

9 Pliny, the Elder, *Natural History*, trans. H. Rackham (Bury St Edmunds: Loeb, 1997), 2:43; Aristotle, *Meteorologica*, 346b–347a.

10 Pliny, *Natural History*, 2:21.

11 Aristotle, *Meteorologica*, 340a.

12 Fulke, *A Goodly Gallery*, fol. 50.

13 Aristotle, *Meteorologica*, 369a–b.

14 See, for example, Pliny, *Natural History*, 2:43. Pliny differentiates storms caused by falling stars from those which result from exhalations trapped in clouds: the latter 'are accidental – they cause mere senseless and ineffectual thunder-claps, as their coming obeys no principle of nature – they merely cleave mountains and seas, and all their other blows are ineffectual; but the former are prophetical and sent from on high, they come by fixed causes and from their own stars.' See below, p. 57.

15 Fulke, *A Goodly Gallery*, fol. 8r.

16 See below, pp. 52, 87ff.

17 The Hebrew word קוֹל (*qol*, or *kole*) can be used to mean *voice* and *sound*, but also *thunder*.

2 Storm and the spectacular: *Julius Caesar*

1 Though debates on the plays' chronology have raged for many years and will rage for many more, this viewpoint should find few opponents. David Daniell terms it 'Shakespeare's first extended thunder' (*Julius Caesar*, Arden 3rd Series (London: Thomson Learning, 2005)), p. 3. All quotations are taken from Daniell's text, unless otherwise indicated. I have also made use of A. Humphreys (ed.), *Julius Caesar* (Oxford: Oxford University Press, 1984) and Martin Spevack's New Cambridge edition (Cambridge: Cambridge University Press, 2003). I have departed from Daniell in preferring the spelling of 'Casca' over 'Caska', for no other reason than I find the latter jarring. Daniell is of course correct that 'Caska' is the version in the 1623 Folio, but I'm comfortable extending the modernisation of the Folio's spelling to include names. One further caveat: my argument in this chapter concerns stage directions and possible theatrical practices of the Elizabethan playing companies and there will be a necessary amount of speculation. I assume, for example, that the stage directions in *Julius Caesar* are at least descriptive of the 1599 production of the play, rather than being additions made for the text's only publication in the Folio. I contend that the Globe playhouse allowed for certain possibilities in terms of theatrical effect which were not available in earlier auditoria, and that the stage directions of *Julius Caesar* show these possibilities being realised in a play written for a particular place. Although my speculations will be fairly self-evident, I will highlight them as they become important, and I will explain my reasons for supposing them to be true.

2 See, for example, Richard Wilson, '"Is this a Holiday?" Shakespeare's Roman Carnival', *English Literary History* 54 (1987), 31–44.

3 See, for example, Steve Sohmer, *Shakespeare's Mystery Play: The Opening of the Globe Theatre 1599* (Manchester: Manchester University Press, 1999), *passim*. Sohmer's compelling argument concludes that the most likely date of the theatre's opening is 12 June 1599 (Julian) and explores the many fragments of evidence suggesting the play was *Julius Caesar*.

4 James Shapiro, *1599: A Year in the Life of William Shakespeare* (London: Faber, 2005), p. 126.

5 Andrew Gurr, 'The Condition of Theatre in England in 1599', in Jane Milling and Peter Thomson (eds), *The Cambridge History of British Theatre, Volume 1: Origins to 1660* (Cambridge: Cambridge University Press, 2004), pp. 264–81 (273).

6 *Julius Caesar*, ed. Spevack, p. 67. David Daniell, it seems, is alone amongst modern editors in stating that the thunder is imitated 'by metal thunder sheets.' I suspect that the thunder-sheet is, in fact, a device that postdates Shakespeare by at least several decades, although confirmation is hard to come by. The *OED*'s first usage of the term is dated 1913.

7 See, e.g. *Julius Caesar*, ed. Humphreys, p. 119.

8 Ibid.

9 Given that by the time of *Every Man In His Humour*'s publication in quarto, this fondness would have manifested itself only in *Julius Caesar* and the much earlier histories, but by 1616 would have accounted for every one of Shakespeare's major storms, this is not too far-fetched. Jonson, by report, was certainly comfortable enough mocking the dialogue of *Julius Caesar*.

10 Anon. (J. C.) *A Pleasant Comedie Called The Two Merry Milke-Maids or The Best Words Weare the Garland* (London: Bernard Alsop for Lawrence Chapman, 1620), sig. A2v.

11 Modern replicas of thunder-runs are relatively common (there is one, for example, in the Victoria and Albert Museum, London). The noise of the reproductions is both convincing and impressively loud. When the acoustic qualities of a playhouse – rather than the museum isolation in which these replicas are found – are taken into account, it is not difficult to imagine the imposing sound which would result from its use at the Globe. Those acoustic qualities were capitalised upon in the reconstructed Globe, when, in the 1999 production of *Julius Caesar*, the thunder was created by the offstage cast and backstage crew rattling and dragging chairs around the heavens.

12 See above, p. 28 and below, pp. 51–2.

13 John Bate, *The Mysteres of Natvre and Art: The Second Booke, Teaching Most Plainly, and Withal most Exactly, the Composing of all Manner of Fire-works for Triumph and Recreation* (London: Ralph Mab, 1634), fols. 76–7. Bate's work is the earliest entry for Swevel in the *OED*: I use the term as a matter of convenience to distinguish from those rockets and squibs that are not run along lines.

14 See Butterworth, *Theatre of Fire*, pp. 99–129.

15 The London Midsummer pageants of 1535, for example, required rockets. See Martin Wiggins (ed.), *British Drama 1533–1642 A Catalogue* (Oxford: Oxford University Press, 2012), vol. 1, p. 26.

16 Quoted by Butterworth, *Theatre of Fire*, p. 44.

17 Ibid., p. 44.

18 Ibid., p. 44.

19 *The Roaring Girl*, sig. K2r.
20 Thomas Dekker, *If it Be not Good, the Devil is in it* (London, 1612), sig. E2r. This play, acted by Queen Anne's company at the Red Bull, provides one example of what the Company of Revels later attempted to 'reform'. The identity of those charged with lighting the rockets is uncertain – only Melton describes them as 'hirelings' (which simply means 'hired actors' i.e. not belonging to the core of the company).
21 See, for example Serlio, above, and John Melton's hirelings (see below, p. 36) who are 'in their Heavens'.
22 Dekker, *If it Be not Good, the Devil is in it*, sig. E2r. If the lines which follow this extract are taken literally, then these swevels were ignited from below the stage: 'KING: from whence flew they? BRISCO: Hell, I thinke.'
23 John Melton, *The Astrologaster, or, the Figure-caster* (London: Barnard Alsop for Edward Blackmore, 1620), fol. 31.
24 I am grateful to Julian Bowsher for pointing this out to me. As Bowsher catalogues the find: 'Stone cannon ball ... Diam 6in (150mm), weight 10lb (4.53kg). Almost certainly a 16th-century cannon ball, probably to be fired from a perier or a culverin ... Its presence on the playhouse site is puzzling.' Julian Bowsher and Pat Miller, *The Rose and the Globe – Playhouses of Shakespeare's Bankside, Southwark. Excavations 1988–90* (London: Museum of London, 2009), p. 218.
25 See Butterworth, *Theatre of Fire*, p. 152 n25.
26 See Bernard Hewitt (ed.), *The Renaissance Stage: Documents of Serlio, Sabbattini and Furttenbach*, trans. Allarryce Nicoll, John H. McDowell and George R. Kernodle (Miami: University of Miami Press, 1958), p. 172. The stepped thunder-run is described by Sabbattini, whose work was published in Ravenna in 1638. It is unclear when the technique was known in England, although several of the techniques described by Sabbattini were used by Inigo Jones, if not before.
27 See Keith Thomas, *Religion and the Decline of Magic* (London: Weidenfeld and Nicolson, 1971), pp. 15–17 and *passim*.
28 Marlowe's plays might have continued to play at the Rose until the Admiral's Men moved to the Fortune. In addition to *Doctor Faustus*, there is a storm in *Dido* (3.4). I can, however, find no evidence of thunder and lightning in the extant plays that seem to have been new at around the same time as *Julius Caesar*. The Red Bull playhouse, eventually the pinnacle of spectacle, was not yet constructed.
29 I am grateful to Claire Van Kampen, former musical director of Shakespeare's Globe, for clarifying this for me. For further elucidation see Bruce Smith, *The Acoustic World of Early Modern England* (Chicago: University of Chicago Press, 1999), p. 219.
30 See *Edward III*, ed. Giorgio Melchiori (Cambridge: Cambridge University Press, 1998), pp. 52–3.
31 *Hamlet*'s usage and stage direction date to the Second Quarto (1604–5).

32 See for example, R[obert] A[rmin], *The Valiant Welshman*: 'a Trumpet within' (2.1.48 and 4.1.52); Dekker, *If it Be not Good, the Devil is in it*: 'Drommes afar off marching', 'Alarums afar off' and 'A march afar' (TLN 2039, 2145, 2321); John Marston, *The Wonder of Women or The Tragedie of Sophonisba* (London: John Windet, 1606), Act 5: 'A march far off is heard' (5.1.sd), 'Cornets a march far off' (5.2.sd) and 'The Cornets a far off sounding a charge; (5.3.sd).

33 Anne Barton, *Shakespeare and the Idea of the Play* (London: Chatto & Windus, 1962), p. 139. Cassius's lines are hardly the play's sole indicator of the metadramatic, nor do they exhaust the device's possibilities. Richard Wilson, for example, contends that 'The opening words of *Julius Caesar* seem to know themselves ... as a declaration of company policy towards the theatre audience' (Wilson, 'Is this a Holiday?', p. 32).

34 Caesar had long been represented in the public pageantry in England. See Clifford Ronan, *'Antike Roman': Power Symbology and the Roman Play in Early Modern England, 1585–1635* (Athens: University of Georgia Press, 1995), p. 47.

35 T. J. B. Spencer (ed.), *Shakespeare's Plutarch* (London: Penguin, 1964).

36 Perhaps the effect of Shakespeare's storm is too powerful on some, who contend that Plutarch does report lightning here. The Oxford editors, for example, write 'As for the portents preluding Caesar's murder (in 1.3 and 2.2) most are in Plutarch – thunder and lightning, fire-charged tempest ...', p. 28 (although they later gloss to the contrary (1.3.9–28n)). The closest I can find to confirming this is the report of thunder and lightning (along with earthquakes and other 'wonders') as portents of murder in Plutarch's *Cicero*, but this has nothing to do with Caesar.

37 Perhaps the closest the play comes to mentioning rain is towards the very end, as Titinius mourns the loss of Cassius: 'Our day is gone: | Clouds, dews and dangers come' (5.3.61). There is no mention of precipitation during the storm and the word 'rain' does not appear in the play. This is quite unlike the rest of Shakespeare's staged storms.

38 Thomas May, trans., *Virgil's Georgicks Englished* (London: [Humphrey Lownes] for Tho. Walkley, 1628), fol. 24.

39 A language of 'preemptive strike', as Christopher Pelling has put it. See Maria Wyke (ed.), *Julius Caesar in Western Culture* (Oxford: Blackwell 2006), p. 4.

40 Many critics have drawn on the parallels of Essex's biography and Shakespeare's *Julius Caesar*, and have attempted to pair that play with *Henry V* as commenting on the Earl. Whilst this has often proven fruitful ground, it is not my intention here: I wish only to draw attention to the storm and its interpretations. For readings on the play in light of Devereaux, see *Julius Caesar*, ed. Daniell, pp. 22–9; Andrew Hadfield, *Shakespeare and Renaissance Politics* (London: Arden Shakespeare, 2003), pp. 68 and 149. For *Julius Caesar* and *Henry V* as companion pieces, see especially Judith Mossman, 'Henry V and Plutarch's Alexander', *Shakespeare Quarterly* 45 (1994), 57–73. The parallels have been seen to extend to *As You Like It*, which Katherine Duncan-Jones reads as concerned with the Essex rebel-

lion. *Ungentle Shakespeare: Scenes From His Life* (London: Arden Shakespeare, 2001), pp. 123–6.

41 John Stow, *Annales* (London: [Peter Short and Felix Kingston for] Ralfe Newbery, 1601), fol. 1304.

42 Ibid., fol. 1149.

43 Stow certainly relates far more damaging storms in his *Annales*. The comparison here is purely to judge the author's tone with regards to harmless, but notable weather.

44 Digges, *A Prognostication Everlasting of Right Good Effectt* (London: Felix Kyngston, 1605), fol. 7. Incidentally, 27 March 1599 (using the Julian calendar) was a Tuesday, one of the two days not to bring death. The Ides of March, 44 B.C. would have been a Wednesday, not, as I'll admit I hoped, a Friday. Not even Shakespeare's Cassius would argue Caesar's case as a harlot. Even so, a connection of thunder and premonitions of murder in early modern superstition here is clear.

45 Thomas Hill, *A Contemplation of Mysteries* (London: Henry Denham, 1574), fol. 52r.

46 Thomas Hill, *The Moste Pleasuante Arte of the Interpretacion of Dreames* (London: Thomas Marsh, 1576), p. 160.

47 See, for example, G. B. Harrison, *The Life and Death of Robert Devereux Earl of Essex* (London: Cassell, 1937), p. 216; R. Lacey, *Robert Earl of Essex: An Elizabethan Icarus* (London: The History Book Club, 1970), p. 190.

48 See Alison Weir, *Elizabeth the Queen* (London: Pimlico, 1998), p. 441.

49 Shapiro, *A Year in the Life of William Shakespeare*, pp. 117–18.

50 Simon Forman (Bod. Ashmole. MS 219/31r) I am indebted to James Shapiro for supplying a transcription of this part of the text. Shapiro acknowledges Robyn Adams for locating the text and deciphering Forman's hand.

51 *Daily Mail*, 13 June 2006.

52 Hadfield, *Shakespeare and Renaissance Politics*, p. 148.

3 Lightning

1 Simon Harward, *A Discourse of the Severall Kinds and Causes of Lightnings* (London: J. Windet, 1607), sig. A1r.

2 Ibid., sig. B1v.

3 Ibid.

4 Ibid., sig. C3r.

5 Ibid.

6 Christopher Marlowe, *Tamburlaine Part I*, ed. David Fuller (Oxford: Clarendon, 1998), 4.2.51–4. Experience of such phenomena does not always result in poetry. On 4 March 2012, the Kielder Observatory in Northumberland 'reported the sighting of a "huge fireball" travelling southwards at 9.41pm. In a tweet, the observatory added: "Of 30 years observing the sky #fireball best thing I have

ever seen period."' (www.guardian.co.uk/science/2012/mar/04/meteor-fireball-night-sky-uk).

7 See *OED*, *Apparition*, n.8: 'That which appears: an appearance, especially of a remarkable or unexpected kind; a phenomenon.' For other examples of what might constitute a 'fire from heaven', see Heninger, *A Handbook of Renaissance Meteorology*, pp. 91–101.

8 George Wilkins, *The Painfull Adventures of Pericles Prince of Tyre*, ed. K. Muir (London: T. P. for Nat Butler, 1608), sig. D3r.

9 John Gower, *Confessio Amantis*, in *The Complete Works of John Gower*, ed. G. C. Macauly (Oxford: Clarendon Press, 1899), Vol. 3. Book II, 998–1001.

10 Laurence Twyne, *The Pattern of Painefull Adventures* (London: Valentine Simmes for the Widow Newman, 1594), sig. E3r.

11 Naseeb Shaheen, *Biblical References in Shakespeare's Plays* (Newark: University of Delaware Press, 1999), p. 689.

12 II Maccabees 9:5; 9:9.

13 Wilkins, *The Painfull Adventures of Pericles Prince of Tyre*, sig. D3r.

14 Fulke, *A Goodly Gallery*, fols. 26–8. Not every commentator uses the same system of classifications as Fulke, nor distinguishes by the same features of lightning. I have chosen Fulke's system to highlight here because it represents an advancement on classical writers such as Pliny, Seneca and Aristotle, and is the most descriptive and exact in its categorisation.

15 Fulke, *A Goodly Gallery*, fol. 26r.

16 Ibid., fol. 27v.

17 Ibid.

18 Ibid.

19 Ibid., fol. 28v.

20 Anglicus Bartholomaeus, *Batman uppon Bartholome his Booke De Proprietatibus Rerum, Newly Corrected, Enlarged and Amended*, trans. Stephen Batman (London: Thomas East, 1582), fol. 164r. To thirl is to 'pierce, to run through ... to perforate' (*OED*, *thirl* v1), and also 'to enslave' (v2) and 'to hurl' (v3).

21 Hill, *A Contemplation of Mysteries*, fol. 54v.

22 For a discussion of thunder-stones, see Matthew R. Goodrum, 'Questioning Thunderstones and Arrowheads: The Problem of Recognising and Interpreting Stone Artefacts in the Seventeenth Century', *Early Science and Medicine* 13 (2008), 482–508. Goodrum traces the scepticism of thunder-stones and the process by which the stones were recognised as human artefacts.

23 Hill, *A Contemplation of Mysteries*, fols. 54r–55v. Gower also includes a description of thunder-stones, although they don't appear to be nearly as dangerous. VIII.337–41.

24 Pliny, *Natural History*, 2.52. For Pliny, this is the third and final variety of thunderbolt, after those 'that come with a dry flash [and] do not cause a fire but an explosion [and those that] do not burn but blacken.'

25 Heninger, *A Handbook of Renaissance Meteorology*, p. 78.

26 Bartholomaeus, *Batman uppon Bartholome*, fol. 165v.

27 Hill, *A Contemplation of Mysteries*, fols. 57r–58v.

28 Harward, *A Discourse*, sig. B2v. The long s and f are extremely similar in the type used in the Harward text (see, e.g. 'should shake iron fetters', sig. B3r.) and 'slayeth' could conceivably be intended 'flayeth'.

29 Quoted by Heninger, *A Handbook of Renaissance Meteorology*, p. 79.

30 Bartholomaeus, *Batman uppon Bartholome*, fol. 164r.

31 Pliny the Elder, *The History of World Commonly called, the Naturall Historie of C. Plinius Secundus*, trans. Philemon Holland (London: Adam Islip, 1601), sig. D1r.

32 According to the Oxford text, at least. The phrase 'both … jewels' is inserted from *Painful Adventures* into line 9.

33 Wilkins, *The Painfull Adventures of Pericles Prince of Tyre*, sig D3r.

34 II Maccabees 9:7.

35 Ibid., 9:7.

36 Ibid., 9:10.

37 Ibid., 9:12.

38 My conclusion here is possibly troubled by the stage direction in Philip Massinger's *The Unnatural Combat* (c. 1624–25, first published 1639), which instructs that Malefort is 'killed with a flash of lightning' (5.2.306). However, this is more practical than poetic: it is likely that a pyrotechnic effect is called for here. It seems, indeed, that Massinger's lightning can also be classified as fulmen: Malefort's corpse is commented on by witnesses, who note both its smell and altered appearance (338–40).

39 See, for example, Daniell (ed.), *Julius Caesar* 2.1.44n, RSC, 2.1.44n and Norton, 2.1.44n

40 Fulke, *A Goodly Gallery*, fol. 8r.

41 Pliny, *Natural History*, 2:43 p. 00.

4 *King Lear*: storm and the event

1 All references to *King Lear* are taken from R. A. Foakes's 1997 text, reprinted as the Arden 3rd Series (London: Arden, 2007), unless otherwise noted, and are included in the text. I have also made use of the Oxford edition, based on the Quarto text, ed. Stanley Wells (Oxford: Oxford University Press, 2001) and Kenneth Muir's 2nd Series Arden text (Methuen, 1952).

2 Thomson, 'The Meaning of *Thunder and Lightning*', 11–24 (14).

3 *OED*, *Event* n., 1a.

4 *OED*, *Event* n., 4.

5 Quoted by Nicholas Royle, in 'Derrida's Event', in Simon Glendinning and Robert Eaglestone (eds), *Derrida's Legacies: Literature and Philosophy* (Abingdon: Routledge, 2008), pp. 36–44 (38).

6 Ibid., p. 39.

7 Perhaps an alignment brought out as Cornwall blinds Gloucester: 'Lest it see more, *prevent* it' (3.7.82; emphasis added).

8 *OED, Event* v2.

9 See for example, George W. Williams, 'The Poetry of the Storm in King Lear', *Shakespeare Quarterly* 2:1 (1951), 57–71; E. Catherine Dunn, 'The Storm in King Lear', *Shakespeare Quarterly* 3:4 (1952), 329–33; Josephine Waters Bennett, 'The Storm Within: The Madness of Lear', *Shakespeare Quarterly* 13:2 (1962), 137–55.

10 I am thinking of positions such as that held by Terence Hawkes, who has expressed his view that there is 'no such thing as the "real" or the "right" version of the play: not even 'Shakespeare's' version could make that claim.' See Terence Hawkes, *William Shakespeare*: King Lear (Plymouth: Northcote House, 1995), p. 62.

11 Ibid., p. 62.

12 James Ogden, 'Lear's Blasted Heath', in James Ogden and Arthur H. Scouten, eds. *Lear from Study to Stage: Essays in Criticism* (London: Associated University Presses, 1997), pp. 135–46; Henry S. Turner, 'King Lear Without: The Heath', *Renaissance Drama* 28 (1997), 161–93.

13 Jonathan Dollimore. *Radical Tragedy: Religion, Ideology and Power in the Drama of Shakespeare and His Contemporaries* (Basingstoke: Palgrave Macmillan, 3rd edn, 2004), p. 186.

14 Hugh Grady, 'On the Need for a Differentiated Theory of (Early) Modern Subjects', in John J. Joughin (ed.), *Philosophical Shakespeares* (London; Routledge, 2000), pp. 34–50 (47).

15 Arthur Kirsch, 'The Emotional Landscape of King Lear', *Shakespeare Quarterly* 39:2 (1988), 154–70 (160).

16 Ian W. O. House, '"I know thee well enough": The Two Plots of *King Lear*', *English* 170:41 (1992), 97–112 (110).

17 See, for example, Estok, *Ecocriticism and Shakespeare*, p. 24.

18 Stephen Greenblatt, *Will in the World: How Shakespeare Became Shakespeare* (New York: Norton, 2004), p. 358.

19 Banishment itself being subject to a strange logic of displacement from an early point in the text: 'Freedom lives hence and banishment is here' (1.1.182).

20 Greenblatt also mentions the heath in his introduction to the play text in *The Norton Shakespeare* (New York; London: Norton, 1997), the so-called 'International Student Edition', p. 2311.

21 See Turner, 'King Lear Without', p. 176.

22 Ibid., p. 176.

23 Admittedly, this evaluation is based on what, in our twenty-first-century apprehension, are currently called tragedies. To those plays, the First Folio adds *Cymbeline* and *Troilus and Cressida*. The latter two characters both have soliloquies, but Cymbeline does not.

24 See *Hamlet* 4.5.16–75 and 160–93 and *Macbeth* 5.1.36–71.

25 See 3.4.45–179 and 3.6 *passim*.

26 See 3.1, 3.2 and 3.4 *passim*. The night is another event in *King Lear* which might justifiably be seen, like the storm, as an organising principle of the play. The two are often juxtaposed ('what i'th'storm, i'th'night, | Let pity not be believed!' 4.3.29–30), but each has various subtle idiosyncrasies. It is notable, moreover, that, although the night is virtually as insistent in the storm scenes as the storm itself (the stage effects excepted) the work of the night in the play is underestimated by critics. Shameful though the irony is of confining this statement to a note, there is not sufficient space in this chapter to give the night the attention it merits.

27 It is hard not to think of Hamlet's speeches here, which are imbued with his particular sense of place: 'HORATIO: Where, my Lord? HAMLET: In my mind's eye, Horatio' (1.2.183–4).

28 I have departed from Foakes here in calling the character 'Gentleman'. As used in both the Quarto and Folio texts, it makes more sense to me than Foakes's substitution of 'Knight'.

29 There are ten such cases: 3.1.32; 3.6.88; 3.7.18, 50–4, 93; 4.1.45, 58.

30 A. C. Bradley, *Shakespearean Tragedy* (Basingstoke: Macmillan, 1985), pp. 213–14.

31 Ibid., pp. 214, 212, 213.

32 Alan C. Dessen, *Elizabethan Stage Conventions and Modern Interpreters* (Cambridge: Cambridge University Press, 1984), p. 84.

33 Ogden, 'Lear's Blasted Heath', p. 137.

34 Ibid., p. 137.

35 Ibid., pp. 138–44.

36 To quote the credit: 'Cover design: interbrand Newell and Sorrell. Cover illustration: The Douglas Brothers.'

37 Matthew 4:1–11; Mark 1:12–13; Luke 4:1–13.

38 Genesis 7:4. Also, Moses remains on Sinai for the same length of time (Exodus 24:18), after '*God appeareth unto Moses upon the mount in thunder and lightening*' (Exodus 19: argument). Forty days is also the time allotted to Pericles by Antiochus, during which the first storm of the play occurs.

39 *OED*, *Heath*. By 'the Christian readings', I mean, chiefly, works which figure the play as illustrative of the power of redemption through suffering as thereby related to the teaching of Christ. Such works are too numerous to list fully, but an illustrative roll might include G. Wilson Knight's *Principles of Shakespearean Production with Especial Reference to Tragedies* (New York: Macmillan, 1937), in which each Shakespearean tragic hero is viewed as 'a miniature Christ'; J. Dover Wilson, *Six Tragedies of Shakespeare: An Introduction for the Plain Man* (London: Longmans, 1929), pp. 32–46; J. F. Danby, 'King Lear and Christian Patience', *Cambridge Journal* 1 (1948), 305–20; Robert G. Hunter, *Shakespeare and the Mystery of God's Judgements* (Athens: University of Georgia Press, 1976), pp. 183–96; Herbert R. Coursen, *Christian Ritual and the World of Shakespeare's*

Tragedies (Lewisburg, PA: Bucknell University Press, 1976), pp. 237–313.

40 Jeremiah 17:5–6.

41 Greg Garrard, *Ecocriticism: The New Critical Idiom* (London: Routledge, 2004), p. 59.

42 Ibid., p. 59.

43 Dollimore, *Radical Tragedy*, pp. 189–203.

44 Garrard, *Ecocriticism*, p. 59.

45 See Morton, *Ecology Without Nature*.

46 Steve Mentz, 'Strange Weather in *King Lear*', *Shakespeare* 6:2 (2010), 139–52 (140).

47 Williams, 'The Poetry of the Storm in King Lear', p. 65.

48 Dunn, 'The Storm in King Lear', p. 331.

49 Martin Rosenberg, *The Masks of King Lear* (Berkeley: University of California Press, 1972), p. 188, my emphasis.

50 Stephen Booth, *King Lear, Macbeth, Indefinition and Tragedy* (New Haven, CT: Yale University Press, 1983), p. 18.

51 To read, as Kenneth Muir did, *outscorn* as *outstorm* is tantalisingly helpful in thinking about the performative quality of Lear in the storm: the notion that Lear attempts to become greater than that which he is implicit in creating, *by creating it*, is a fascinating one. It must be said, though, that *outscorn* makes perfect sense, and the editorial substitution is superfluous, but for the fact that it highlights an attractive response to our reading of Lear's character.

52 It is not possible to know if a unique effect is called for here, but the stage direction 'storm and tempest' can be read as implying two types of sound at once. Certainly the direction is unique in Shakespeare's works, and there is no other instance of it in the extant plays dating 1580–1642. See also Thomson, who notes that 'eight plays [from the period] have a signal for *storm*.' See p. 23 n14.

53 Any interval posited after the end of Act 2 severs this continuity. Foakes, for example has written 'an interval may be inserted here to allow Lear a respite before his rages in the storm scenes' ('Performance and Text: King Lear', *Medieval and Renaissance Drama in England* 17 (2005), 86–98 (86)). The very point, I propose, is no respite at all.

54 Lear uses 'bid' again later, albeit somewhat fallaciously, 'when the thunder would not peace at my bidding' (4.6.101–2).

55 See Williams, 'The Poetry of the Storm in King Lear', p. 65. Whether they believed in these powers or simply saw their potential in their image-making is debateable.

56 Hill, *A Contemplation of Mysteries*, fols. 57r–58v. See also above, p. 55.

57 Janet Adelman, *Suffocating Mothers: Fantasies of Maternal Origin in Shakespeare's Plays*, Hamlet to The Tempest (London: Routledge, 1992), p. 110. See also Rosenberg, *The Masks of King Lear*, pp. 191–2.

58 William R. Elton, *King Lear and the Gods* (Lexington, KY: University Press of Kentucky, 1966).

59 Adelman, *Suffocating Mothers*, p. 112.

60 In G. Bullough, *Narrative and Dramatic Sources of Shakespeare* (London: Rout-
    ledge and Kegan Paul, 1973), Vol. 7, pp. 337–402. *Leir* was probably revived around
    the time of its publication, having been performed at least as early as 1594.

61 Elton, *King Lear and the Gods*, p. 67.

62 Psalms 83:14–16.

63 See above, p. 23.

64 Elton, *King Lear and the Gods*, p. 203.

65 Ibid., p. 262.

66 The complex relation of storm and the Christian god is explored in Chapter 8.

67 This instance is only in the Quarto text. The Folio (and Foakes) has 'Never
    afflict yourself to know more of it.'

68 Stanley Wells, Gary Taylor, John Jowett and William Montgomery (eds), *William
    Shakespeare: The Complete Works* (Oxford: Oxford University Press, 2nd edn,
    2005), p. 194.

69 Compare, for example, 'is this the promised end?' (5.3.261).

70 Dollimore, *Radical Tragedy*, p. 186.

5 Wind

1 Aristotle, *Meteorologica*, 349a.

2 For a discussion of various attributes of winds, and literary uses, see Heninger
   A Handbook of Renaissance Meteorology, pp. 109–28.

3 *OED*, Storm n1.

4 The most familiar of these scales are the Beaufort scale, which ranges from
   completely still (0) to hurricane (12) and the Saffir-Simpson, which categorises
   hurricanes from minimal (1) to catastrophic (5). Several other scales are in use,
   especially outside of the Atlantic and East Pacific, the areas covered by the
   Saffir-Simpson.

5 As Pliny puts it, 'wind is understood to be nothing else than a wave of air and in
   more ways as well', *Natural History*, 2:44.

6 Aristotle, 360a–b.

7 Pliny, *Natural History*, 2:44. Philemon Holland translated the passage in question
   as 'there be certaine caves and holes which breed winds continually without
   end'. Holland, trans. (London, 1601).

8 Pliny, *Natural History*, 2:44.

9 Fulke, *A Goodly Gallery*, fol. 18r.

10 Ibid., fol. 18v.

11 Ibid.

12 Ibid.

13 Ibid., fols. 18r–18v.

14 Fulke, *A Goodly Gallery*, fol. 31.

15 Ibid.

16 See above, p. 51.

17 See Heninger, *A Handbook of Renaissance Meteorology*, pp. 109–10.

18 Ibid., p. 110.

19 Peter Holland, 'Coasting in the Mediterranean: The Journeyings of *Pericles*', in Neils B. Hansen and Sos Haugaard (eds), *Angles on the English-Speaking World* (Copenhagen: Museum Tusculanum Press, 2005), pp. 11–31 (15). Holland understandably wishes to ignore the possibility that Marina is mistaken in her assertion (see p. 28 n9). Happily, Marina is not the only character to note the direction of the wind, as Gower prefaces the scene of Marina's birth with 'the grizzled north | Disgorges such a tempest forth'.

20 *Pericles*, ed. Doreen DelVecchio and Antony Hammond, 4.1.50n.

21 The other examples given by DelVecchio and Hammond are from *Troilus and Cressida* (5.1.18), *Coriolanus* (1.4.30) and *Cymbeline* (2.3.131; 4.2.349). These examples are ambiguous: the first two seem more readily to stem from the notion in early modern England that Italy and especially Naples was rife with venereal disease (these could possibly be spread by wind, but wind is hardly the emphasis in these instances). The second example of Cymbeline sees the South itself as 'spongy', but without the connotation of disease or storm and, again, without characterising the wind, merely the area. If the South carries the negative associations the Cambridge editors' claim in *Pericles*, then it is arguably more to do with connotations of venereal disease (given Marina is soon to be forced into a brothel) than the wind.

22 *Pericles*, ed. Warren, 3.0.47n.

23 Barnabe Barnes, *Parthenophil and Parthenophe* (London: J. Wolfe, 1593), Sonnet LXXXV.

24 Richard Hakluyt (ed.), *Principal Navigations* (London: George Bishop, 1599–1600), p. 189.

25 Ecclesiasticus 43:17.

26 Nicholas de Nicolay, *The Navigations, Peregrinations and Voyages, made into Turkie*, trans. T. Washington (London: Thomas Dawson, 1585), p. 123.

27 William Webbe, *A Discourse of English Poetrie* (London: John Charlewood for Robert Walley, 1586), sig. E3v.

28 Zechariah 9:14. See also Job 37:9: 'The whirle winde cometh out of the South, and the colde from the North winde.' The marginal note glossing this passage reads 'in Ebrewe it [the South] is called ye scattering winde, because it driveth away the cloudes and purgeth the ayre.' Examples of other winds being stormy are also available in the Bible, such as: 'Terrours shal take him as waters, and a tempest shall carie him away by night. The East wind shal take him away, and he shal departe: and it shal hurlle him out of his place' Job 27:20–1.

29 Simon Harward, *Harward's Phlebotomy: or, A Treatise of Letting of Bloud* (London: F. Kingston for Simon Waterson, 1601), p. 97. See also Nicholas Gyer, *The English*

Phlebotomy (London: William Hoskins and John Danter for Andrew Mansell, 1592), p. 84.

30 Pliny, *The History of World* 16:34 (trans. Holland, p. 471).

31 *Exodus* 10:19; 10:13. See, for example, William Charke, *An Answere to a Seditious Pamphlet* (London: Christopher Barker, 1580), sig. D8r. Thomas Adams, *The Devills Banket* (London: Thomas Snodham for Ralph Mab 1614), p. 70; Thomas Granger, *Pauls Crowne of Rejoycing* (London: T. S for Thomas Pauier, 1616), p. 36.

32 *Homer's Odysses. Translated according to ye Greeke by. Geo: Chapman* (London: Rich Field for Nathaniell Butter, 1615), p. 57. Heninger locates a separate Greek and Latin tradition, owing to the mountains in the west of Greece (p. 113).

33 Thomas Dekker, *1603, The Wonderfull Yeare* (London: N. L. and Thomas Creede, 1603), sig. B1v.

34 Luke 12:54. *Shower*, here, is sometimes translated as *storm* or a variant (see, for example, John Prideaux, *Certaine Sermons* (Oxford: Leonard Lichfield, 1636), sig. AA4r).

35 William Philip (trans), *The Description of a Voyage Made by Certaine Ships of Holland into the East Indies* (London: John Wolfe, 1598), sig. L4r.

36 Thomas Hill, *The Profitable Arte of Gardening* (London: Henry Bynneman, 1574), p. 49.

37 John Deacon, *Dialogicall Discourses* (London: George Bishop, 1601), p. 160 (emphasis in original).

38 For an overview, see Heninger, *A Handbook of Renaissance Meteorology*, pp. 107–28.

39 Bartholomaeus, quoted by Heninger, ibid., p. 114.

40 Proverbs 25:23. For use in sermons, etc. see, for example, William Burton's eighth sermon in *Ten Sermons* (London: Richard Field for Thomas Man, 1602), p. 216; Robert Bolton, *Some Generall Directions for a Comfortable Walking with God* (London: Felix Kyngston for Edmund Weaver, 1626); John Robinson, *Obervations Divine and Morall* ([Amsterdam]: [successors of Giles Thorp], 1625); Thomas Taylor, *Christs Combate* (Cambridge: Cantrell Legge, 1618). The verse in Proverbs is not entirely about weather: 'As the Northwind driveth away raine, so doeth an angrie countenance ye sclandering tongue.'

41 Barnabe Barnes, *A Divine Centurie of Spirituall Sonnets* (London: John Windet, 1595), Sonnet LXXXXV.

42 *Julius Caesar* (1.3.1–84 & 2.2.1–38) are clear examples of the same interest in practice.

6 *Macbeth*: supernatural storms, equivocal earthquakes

1 From 'De la littérature considéré dans ses rapports avec les institutions sociales', in Jonathan Bate (ed.), *The Romantics on Shakespeare* (London: Penguin, 1992), pp. 80–1. All quotations from *Macbeth*, unless stated otherwise, are from A. R. Braunmuller's edition (Cambridge University Press, 1998).

2 William Haughton's *Grim the Collier of Croydon* or *The Devil an His Dame* (acted by the Admiral's Men, *c*.1600) stages thunder and lightning very soon after the opening of the play, in a dream of Dunstan's. *The Devil's Charter*, by Barnabe Barnes, which dates from just after *Macbeth* also has thunder and lightning just a few lines in, and in its dumb show before the play. See above, pp. 11–12.

3 Ronald Watkins and Jeremy Lemon, *In Shakespeare's Playhouse: Macbeth* (London: David & Charles, 1974), p. 35.

4 Especially since, as we have seen, drums were used as part of the thunder effects. See above, pp. 33–6.

5 See Taylor et al. (eds), *Thomas Middleton: The Collected Works*, pp. 1165–201. It is perhaps simply a coincidence that the two plays of Shakespeare in which witches accompany thunder and lightning (the other being *2 Henry VI*) are two of that group which have obvious multiple authorial hands.

6 Of Shakespeare's characters who speak in couplets of trochaic tetrameter, only the Duke in *Measure for Measure* has no affinity with magic or the supernatural (4.1.254–75). I am discounting fools' songs in this assessment, but including Edgar as Poor Tom, whose use of verse forms is part of the linguistic disguise which also sees him allude to the foul fiend and witches (see e.g. *Lear* 3.4.113; 121) and claim a familiar (137).

7 James Stuart, *Daemonologie in Forme of a Dialogue* (Edinburgh: Robert Walde, 1597), p. 46.

8 William Perkins, *A Discourse of the Damned Art of Witchcraft* (Cambridge: Cantrel Legge, 1608), pp. 173–4.

9 Alexander Roberts, *A Treatise of Witchcraft* (London: Nicholas Oakes for Samuel Man, 1616), sigs. D2r–D2v.

10 Reginald Scot, *Discoverie of Witchcraft* (London: William Brome, 1584), p. 2. Also found, without the chapter title, in H. R. Williamson's edition (Arundel: Centaur Press, 1964).

11 Ryan Curtis Friesen, *Supernatural Fiction in Early Modern Drama and Culture* (Eastbourne: Sussex Academic Press, 2010), p. 147.

12 We might think of Gothic fiction, here, or indeed horror films, in which the storm is often indicative of the workings of the supernatural. The connection is not confined to the clumsy symbolism of Hammer horror, but can be found in more complex and effective works, such as Stanley Kubrick's *The Shining* (1980).

13 See, for example, Bradley, *Shakespearean Tragedy*, pp. 281–3.

14 It may seem that this division ignores Christian belief. However, the meteorological texts which explicate the 'natural' causes of weather never fail to make it clear that God is responsible for each of those processes. Thus, when weather is 'supernaturally' caused, it is an interruption or invasion of God's power.

15 Stuart, *Daemonologie*, p. 46.

16 We have already seen, for example, the storm which offered a backdrop for the Earl of Essex's departure to Ireland; p. 42.

17 Greenblatt, *Will in the World*, p. 346. Halloween 1590 postdates James's storm-struck return – the 'witches' were apparently gathering for another purpose – but the use of the sieves is still significant.

18 Further credence to the argument that Shakespeare was alive to contemporary reference for this scene is lent by the name of the ship, the Tiger. See M. A. Taylor, 'He That did the Tiger Board', *Shakespeare Quarterly* 15 (Winter, 1964), 110–13; H. N. Paul, *The Royal Play of Macbeth* (London: Macmillan, 1950), pp. 302–3.

19 See, for example, Alan Sinfield, '*Macbeth:* History, Ideology and Intellectuals', *Critical Quarterly* 28:1 (1986), 63–77.

20 I have departed from Braunmuller's text here, and have followed Gary Taylor in inserting 'strike' (instead of 'break') where the Folio text seems to be missing a word. See Taylor (ed.), p. 693. Braunmuller does not depart from the Folio, and takes line 27's 'come' to be understood as applying to 'thunders'. I think a violent verb is more likely, for the reasons outlined above, pp. 28–30.

21 See *OED, Reflection* 4.c (which cites the Captain's use): 'The action of turning back from some point; return, retrogression'.

22 Pliny, *Natural History*, 2:45.

23 Greenblatt, *Will in the World*, p. 349.

24 Bradley, *Shakespearean Tragedy*, p. 281. For other instances, see H. Hawkins, *Strange Attractors: Literature, Culture and Chaos Theory* (Hertfordshire: Prentice Hall, 1995), p. 80.

25 Abraham Fleming, *A Bright Burning Beacon* (London: Henry Denham, 1580), sig. E1v.

26 See R. Mallet, *Catalogue of Earthquakes from 1606 B.C. to 1755* (London: John Murray, 1853), p. 61 which lists other, more localised English earthquakes. It is possible also that Shakespeare would have been in London for the earthquake which struck the city on Christmas Eve, 1601. Fleming lists eight other writers who published 'reportes' of the 'Easter Earthquake', some of which are now lost. Furthermore, it is likely that many others wrote about the phenomenon after Fleming had printed his work, as he published it in 1580, when contemporary reports might not have reached him, or not yet been completed.

27 See, for example, Naseeb Shaheen, 'Shakespeare's Knowledge of the Bible – How Acquired', *Shakespeare Studies* 20 (1988), 201–14.

28 Matthew 27:50–2.

29 Fleming, *A Bright Burning Beacon*, sig. E1v.

30 Revelations 6:12

31 Joel 2:1–2.

32 See *Macbeth*, Arden 2nd Series, ed. Kenneth Muir (London: Methuen, 1959), p. 72, n.7.

33 Quoted in Bullough, *Narrative and Dramatic Sources of Shakespeare*, Vol. 7, pp. 483–4.

34 For an investigation of telepathy in Shakespeare, see Nicholas Royle, *Telepathy*

and Literature: Essays on the Reading Mind (Oxford: Blackwell, 1991), in which Royle offers 'the irresistible hypothesis: Shakespeare is telepathy' (p. 158). See also Royle's 'The Poet: Julius Caesar and the Democracy to Come', Oxford Literary Review 25 (2003), 39–62.

35 Joel 2:10. Published in 1580, The Order of Prayer was ordered by Elizabeth I and the Privy Council. In addition to Joel, it is comprised of Isaiah 58, two prayers, a 'godlie admonition for the time present' and several psalms (including Psalm 46: 'Therefore wil not we not fear, though the earth be moved, and thogh the mountains fall into the middes of the sea; Thogh the waters thereof rage and be troubled, and the mountains shake at the surges of the same' (2–3). It also contains Arthur Golding's report of the earthquake, but does not print Golding's name.

36 Fleming, A Bright Burning Beacon, sig. E3r. Cf. Joel 2:30–1.

37 Ibid., sig. B3v.

38 A. Golding, A Discourse upon the Earthquake (London: Henry Bynneman, 1580), sig. B1v.

39 Pliny 2:81, The History of World (trans. Holland, p. 37).

40 Harward, A Discours, sig. C3r.

41 The Fairie Queen 1.8.76–9; Thomas Dekker A Strange Horse-Race (London: Joseph Hunt, 1613), sig B1v.

42 Harold Bloom, Shakespeare: The Invention of the Human (New York: Riverhead, 1998), p. 525.

43 Booth, King Lear, Macbeth, Indefinition and Tragedy, p. 93.

44 Furthermore Macbeth is responsible for the death of two of the other characters who invoke God: Banquo and Lady Macduff: see 2.3.126 and 4.2.59. The other incidences are Malcolm, the Doctor, the Gentlewoman and Siward.

45 Booth, King Lear, Macbeth, Indefinition and Tragedy, p. 97.

46 Heninger, A Handbook of Renaissance Meteorology, pp. 128–9. Heninger cites Seneca's Naturall Questions as a source for this fear.

47 It may also remind us that Macbeth is divided into clean and filthy air, just as it is split into natural and supernatural weather.

48 Golding, Discourse, sigs. B2r–B2v.

49 Fleming, A Bright Burning Beacon, sig. B3v.

50 Kinki Abenezrah, An Everlasting Prognostication of the Change of Weather (London: M. Sparke, 1625), sig. A4r.

51 Aristotle, Meteorologica, 366a. See also Pliny, Natural History, 2:81. Aristotle does allow for earthquakes that occur 'when a wind is blowing', but (eds). that they 'are less violent'. His description would seem to exclude winds of the force mentioned by Lennox.

52 For an account of Macbeth's violence and its relation to the state, see Sinfield, 'Macbeth: History, Ideology and Intellectuals', passim.

53 See Greenblatt (ed.), The Norton Shakespeare 2.1.59n.

54 Macbeth, ed. Braunmuller, 2.1.59n.

55 See, for example, Frank L. Huntley, 'Macbeth and the Background of Jesuitical Equivocation', *PMLA* 79:4 (Sept. 1964), 390–400; William O. Scott, 'Macbeth's – And Our – Self-Equivocations', *Shakespeare Quarterly* 37:2 (Summer, 1986), 160–74.

56 See Huntley, 'Macbeth and the Background of Jesuitical Equivocation', p. 390.

57 For notes on the uncommonness of speaking stones, see *Macbeth*, ed. Braunmuller, p. 141 n.58.

58 II Esdras 6:14.

7 Rain

1 Shakespeare has no stage directions for rain, but three plays from the period do. It is unclear what sort of effect was called for in such instances. See Dessen and Thomson, *A Dictionary of Stage Directions*, p. 175.

2 Fulke, *A Goodly Gallery*, p. 49.

3 Ibid.

4 Bartholomaeus, *Batman Uppon Bartholome*, fol. 159.

5 Aristotle, *Meteorologica*, 347a.6 William Shakespeare, *The Tragicall Historie of Hamlet, Prince of Denmarke* (London: I.R., 1604), sig. C1r.

8 *Pericles*: storm and scripture

1 I am operating on the necessarily simplistic assumption that George Wilkins is responsible for all of the first two acts and the Chorus to the third, with Shakespeare responsible for the rest. Whilst this conforms with critical consensus it does not take into account the minutiae of the collaborative process – whether one author amended the other's sections, and so forth – which will forever remain the subject of speculation. As we shall see, the use of the storm is clearly different in each section, and operates according to two distinct aesthetics, and I am content with conclusions based on this, if nothing else. DelVecchio and Hammond's edition is an exception to the consensus I have noted. For a comprehensive study of the authorial hands in the play, see MacD. P. Jackson, *Defining Shakespeare:* Pericles *as Test Case* (Oxford: Oxford University Press, 2003).

2 See above, pp. 52–6.

3 G. Wilson Knight, *The Shakespearian Tempest* (London: Methuen, 1953), p. 218.

4 Bradin Cormack, 'Marginal Waters: *Pericles* and the Idea of Jurisdiction', in Andrew Gordon and Bernhard Klein (eds), *Literature, Mapping, and the Politics of Space in Early Modern Britain* (Cambridge: Cambridge University Press, 2001), pp. 155–80 (157).

5 To avoid confusion, I will refer to the poet himself as John Gower throughout, using 'Gower' to refer to the character in *Pericles*.

6 Exodus 9:19; 23.

7 Exodus 9:14.

8 John Gower, l. 999.

9 Shaheen, *Biblical References in Shakespeare's Plays*, p. 690.

10 One of the occurrences listed by Shaheen in Ibid. – Luke 9:54 – is an allusion to this episode, and not itself an instance of lightning.

11 II Kings 1:10.

12 For 'consumed' or 'cosumed', see the Miles Coverdale 1535, Great Bible 1540, Thomas Matthew 1549 and Bishops' Bible 1568. The Thomas Matthew and Bishops' versions both also use 'burnt up' in verse 14.

13 II Kings 1:2.

14 II Kings 1:13–14.

15 T. G. Bishop, for example, notes a 'coded hint of just the kind of violent and incestuous rape that has occurred'. *Shakespeare and the Theatre of Wonder* (Cambridge: Cambridge University Press, 1996), p. 96.

16 *Pericles*, Arden 3rd Series, ed. Suzanne Gossett (London: Thomson Learning, 2004), p. 177 n8.

17 See above, p. 55.

18 Richard Huloet, *Huloets Dictionarie Newelye Corrected* (London: Thomas Marshil, 1572), fol. 203v.

19 I have altered Gossett's text slightly here, removing her full stop after 'see clear', and replacing with the Quarto's colon. See below, pp. 115–16.

20 See, for example, C. Relihan, 'Liminal Geography: *Pericles* and the Politics of Place', *Philological Quarterly* 71:3 (1992), 281–99; Cormack, 'Marginal Waters: *Pericles* and the Idea of Jurisdiction'; Holland. 'Coasting in the Mediterranean: The Journeyings of *Pericles*', pp. 11–31.

21 The conflation of sexual violence and storm is by no means unique to *Pericles*. Of course, the figure of Jove, and Zeus before him, is testament itself to this. George Sandys's 1628 translation of Ovid's *Metamorphoses* makes the link explicit:

> A Virgin, for a Virgins rape, let fall
> Her Vengeance, to *Oileus* due, on all.
> Scattered on faithlesse Seas with furious stormes,
> We, wretched *Graecians*, suffer'd all the formes
> Of horror: lightning, night, showres, wrath of skies,
> Of Seas, and dire *Capharean* cruelties. (p. 401).

22 *Pericles*, ed. Warren, p. 42.

23 *Pericles*, ed. Gossett, 3.1.1–14n; Raphael Lyne, *Shakespeare's Late Work* (Oxford: Oxford University Press, 2007), p. 58.

24 Similarly, in the storm in *The Tempest*, Gonzago says 'I would fain die a dry death' (1.1.67).

25 Ruth Nevo, *Shakespeare's Other Language* (New York: Methuen, 1987), p. 45.

26 Gossett opts for Edmond Malone's emendation: Q's 'left my breath' altered to 'left me breath' and offers a sound argument (2.1.6n).

27 Dent, *Shakespeare's Proverbial Language*, B641.1.

28 As in *King Lear*, 'Lend me a looking glass | If that her breath will mist or stain the stone, | Why then she lives' (5.3.259–61).

29 See above, p. 105.

30 *Pericles*, ed. Gossett, p. 222 n6. The word is used seven times.

31 George Wilkins, *The Miseries of Inforst Mariage* (London: [William Jaggard] for George Vincent, 1607), sig. G2v.

32 *Pericles*, ed. Gossett, p. 14 and 3.1.1–14n.

33 Lyne, *Shakespeare's Late Work*, p. 58.

34 Aside from this juxtaposition, Gossett notes that the verse contains several 'characteristic Shakespearean indicators, absent or infrequent earlier in the play, [which] include enjambments, doubled modifiers (*deafening dreadful, nimble sulphurous*), a complexly directed soliloquy, invocations of the gods alternating with calls to the offstage character' (*Pericles*, ed. Gossett, p. 14). Clearly, the signature of Shakespeare does not inhere in simplicity.

35 Luke 8.24. See *Pericles*, ed. Gossett, 3.1.1n; Shaheen, *Biblical References in Shakespeare's Plays*, p. 686.

36 Psalms 104: 6–7. See *Pericles*, ed. Gossett, 3.1.1n.

37 This was first noted by Norman Nathan. '*Pericles* and *Jonah*', *Notes & Queries* (Jan. 1956), 10–11.

38 Jonah 1:11–12.

39 Jonah 1:13.

40 Jonah 1:4: 'the Lord sent out a great winde into the sea, and there was a mightie tempest in the sea, so that the ship was like to be broken.'

41 Jonah 1:5; 10; 16.

42 In the margins of Jonah 1:5, Jonah is described, 'As one that wolde have cast off this care and solicitude, by seking rest and quietnes'. When his past is made clearer to the mariners, his temper apparently remains even in the face of peril: 'And he said unto them, Take me, and cast me into the sea: so shal the sea be calme unto you: for I knowe that for my sake this great tempest *is* upon you' (1:12).

43 Jonah 1:5.

44 Jonah 1:10. cf. *The Tempest*. See below, p. 131.

45 Jonah 2.1.n.

46 See Heninger, *A Handbook of Renaissance Meteorology*, p. 221.

47 Richard Halpern, *Shakespeare Among the Moderns* (Ithaca, NY: Cornell University Press, 1997), pp. 144–5.

48 See above, pp. 82–5.

49 Holland, 'Coasting in the Mediterranean: The Journeyings of *Pericles*', p. 12.

50 There is no occurrence of 'wolt out' in 3.1, for example, nor a whistle.

9 *The Tempest* and theatrical reality

1 1.1.35–6; 21. All quotations from *The Tempest* unless otherwise noted are taken from the Arden 3rd Series, ed. Virginia Mason Vaughan and Alden T. Vaughan (London: Cengage Learning, 1999). I have also made use of the Oxford edition, ed. Stephen Orgel (Oxford: Oxford University Press, 1998) and the New Cambridge text, ed. David Lindley (Cambridge: Cambridge University Press, 2002).

2 Watson, *Back To Nature*, p. 33.

3 Ibid.

4 Morton, *Ecology Without Nature*, p. 35.

5 Ibid., pp. 31–4. Morton writes, 'There are six main elements: *rendering*, the *medial*, the *timbral*, the *Aeolian*, *tone*, and, most fundamentally, the *re-mark*. These terms overlap, and are somewhat arbitrary and vague' (p. 34).

6 See Michel Chion, *Audio-vision: Sound on Screen*, ed. and trans. Claudia Gorbman (New York: Columbia University Press, 1994), pp. 109–12.

7 Ibid., p. 109.

8 Ibid., p. 224.

9 Morton, *Ecology Without Nature*, p. 35.

10 Ibid.

11 This leaves room for an acknowledgment of the irony of the Boatswain's phrase for an audience member who sees the play twice: 'if you can command these elements' has very different meanings depending on audience expectations.

12 Andrew Gurr, '*The Tempest*'s Tempest at Blackfriars', *Shakespeare Survey* 41 (1989), 91–102.

13 Ibid., p. 102.

14 Sarah Dustagheer, 'Repertory and the Production of Theatre Space at the Globe and the Blackfriars, 1599–1613' (Unpublished PhD thesis, University of London, 2012), p. 181.

15 See *The Tempest*, ed. Vaughan and Vaughan, pp. 126–30.

16 Ibid., p. 130.

17 John Jowett, 'New Created Creatures: Ralph Crane and the Stage Directions in *The Tempest*', *Shakespeare Survey* 36 (1983), 107–20.

18 Gurr, '*The Tempest*'s Tempest at Blackfriars', p. 95.

19 Ioris Staell, *Strange Newes from Antwarpe*, trans. I. F. (London: Ralph Blower, 1612), p. 4; John Foxe, *Actes and Monuments* (London: John Daye, 1583), p. 279; Leo Africanus, *A Geographical historie of Africa*, ed. and trans. John Pory (London: [Printed by Eliot's Court Press] impensis Georg. Bishop, 1600), p. 43.

20 As such, the phrase allows for visible thunder, just as it does audible lightning: 'where they sawe the thunder and lightning'. Such usage would indicate that the stage direction requires 'noise' and 'heard' to specify it as an auditory effect. Lloyd Lodowick, *The First Part of the Diall of Daies* (London: Printed for Roger Ward, 1590), fol. 164.

21 A. F. Falconer, *Shakespeare and the Sea* (London: Constable, 1964), p. 39. Falconer, himself a naval officer, also provides a detailed appraisal of the validity of the emergency procedures which the play's crew attempt.

22 I have not been able to find any similar examples in extant plays of the period. It remains, of course, possible that texts that have not survived provided the same level of authentic nautical detail.

23 The most famous anatopism is in *The Winter's Tale* ('our ship hath touched upon the deserts of Bohemia', 3.3.1–2) although *The Two Gentlemen of Verona* seems fancifully to suggest a naval route between Verona and Milan (1.1.71). And in *The Tempest* itself, Prospero's Milanese bark that 'Bore us some leagues to the sea' (1.2.145), should be listed his greatest magical feat, though also the most injudicious. Shakespeare is careless with geography as he is accurate with naval manoeuvres.

24 Falconer, *Shakespeare and the Sea*, p. 39. There has been no discovery of the types of texts Falconer mentions since *Shakespeare and the Sea* was published.

25 See Ibid., pp. 36–40.

26 Quoted in Ibid., p. xii.

27 Morton, *Ecology Without Nature*, p. 35.

28 John Fletcher, *The Sea Voyage* in *Comedies and tragedies written by Francis Beaumont and John Fletcher* (London: printed for Humphrey Robinson, 1647), fol. Aaaaa.

29 Gurr, '*The Tempest*'s Tempest at Blackfriars', p. 100.

30 Christopher Cobb, 'Storm versus Story: Form and Affective Power in Shakespeare's Romances', in Stephen Cohen (ed.), *Shakespeare and Historical Formalism* (Aldershot: Ashgrave, 2007), pp. 95–124 (103).

31 See above, pp. 2–4.

32 See above, pp. 88–9.

33 See above, pp. 11ff. Thunder and lightning do, of course, provide a backdrop for the ascent of Asnath in *2 Henry VI*, and it is possible that the Witches in *Macbeth* entered from beneath the stage, thus perhaps providing a neat contrast to Edgar as Poor Tom in *Lear*.

34 Thomson, 'The Meaning of *Thunder and Lightning*', 11–24 (14).

35 Ibid., 20–1.

36 As chronology is uncertain, it is possible that *The Winter's Tale*, *Pericles* or both may postdate *The Tempest*. However, the important factor is that both of those plays embody a particular dramatic tradition: they use the present tense, and employ extensive imagery and pathetic fallacy. This is the tradition that Miranda's speech fits into, and which is avoided in the first scene. I have quoted from plays which, like *The Tempest*, date from towards the end of Shakespeare's career, but other examples abound. See, for example, *Julius Caesar* 1.3.4–14; *King Lear* 3.1.8–15 and *Othello* 2.1.1–17.

37 The relevant sections of Strachey's work are reprinted in *The Tempest*, ed.

Vaughan and Vaughan, pp. 287–302. I quote here from page 290. For the most recent account of the evidence for Shakespeare's reading of Strachey, see Alden T. Vaughan, 'William Strachey's "True Repertory" and Shakespeare: A Closer Look at the Evidence', *Shakespeare Quarterly* 59 (Fall 2008), 245–73. As well as presenting a clear challenge to doubts over Shakespeare's use of Strachey, Vaughan provides a thorough history of the debate.

38 Ovid, *The XV Bookes of P. Ovidius Naso, Entytuled Metamorphosis, Translated oute of Latin into English Meeter, by Arthur Golding Gentleman, a Worke very Pleasaunt and Delectable*, trans. Arthur Golding (London: William Seres, 1567), sig T7r.

39 Ovid, *The Three First Bookes of Ovid de Tristibus translated into English*, trans. Thomas Churchyard (London: Thomas Marsh, 1580), sig. A6r.

40 *The XV Bookes of P. Ovidius Naso, Entytuled Metamorphosis* ed. Golding, sig B5r. It is possible that Shakespeare had this passage in mind when writing this scene as, in preceding these lines in Golding's translation, the South wind is described as having a 'dreadfull face as blacke as pitch'. Along with the juxtaposition of sea and sky – and with their characterisation as Jove and Neptune in Ariel's speech – this may seem only to be a coincidence of clichés. However, nowhere else does Shakespeare use 'pitch' in the description of a storm.

41 Falconer, *Shakespeare and the Sea*, pp. 39 & 105.

42 Egan, *Green Shakespeare*, p. 151. *King Lear* 3.2.4–5.

43 Gurr, '*The Tempest*'s Tempest at Blackfriars', p. 95.

44 Both gunpowder and sulphur alone were used on the stage, depending on the effect required. See Butterworth, *Theatre of Fire*, pp. 230–1.

45 Of the other connotations of 'sulphurous', of course, most prominent is the suggestion of Hell.

46 Robert Egan, 'This Rough Magic: Perspectives of Art and Morality in *The Tempest*', *Shakespeare Quarterly* 23:2 (Spring, 1972), 171–82 (178).

47 I have opted to use 're-imagining' here, as I think it suggests (more than, for example, 're-describing') the process through which the audience is compelled to consider differently what has already been seen.

48 Egan, *Green Shakespeare*, p. 160. It helps Egan's argument here that he quotes the lines from Stephen Orgel's Oxford edition of the play, which moves the direction for thunder to the middle of the third line. In Orgel's words, the Folio text 'has this in parentheses as part of the opening stage direction, but it seems more likely to belong here: Caliban takes the thunder as a threatening response to his curse.' See Orgel (ed.), 2.1.3n. My argument follows the Folio text for two reasons. Firstly, I hope to show that, whilst Orgel's point is intriguing, the alteration of the Folio text is unnecessary, and it is equally illuminating to read Caliban's curses as a response to the sound of thunder, rather than a prelude. Secondly, one of the singular characteristics of *The Tempest* is the detail adhered to in the stage directions: there is no direction in the play which could be moved without impinging on the subtleties of meaning in the lines.

49 Indeed, the curses of Caliban and Lear are very similar, a point often over-looked in current editions of *The Tempest*. See especially, *King Lear* 2.2.358–60: 'Infect her beauty, | You fen-sucked fogs, drawn by the powerful sun | To fall and blister!'

50 See above, pp. 27–8.

51 For a fuller understanding, see Heninger, *A Handbook of Renaissance Meteorology*. Caliban's lines quoted here are not the first example of his meteorological curse. At his first appearance, we have: 'As wicked dew as e'er my mother brushed | With raven's feather from unwholesome fen | Drop on you both. A southwest blow on ye | And blister you all o'er' (1.2.322).

52 Egan, *Green Shakespeare*, pp. 160–1.

53 Thomson, 'The Meaning of *Thunder and Lightning*', p. 21.

54 Kiernan Ryan, *Shakespeare* (Hampshire: Palgrave, 2002), p. 149.

55 *The Tempest*, ed. Orgel, p. 49.

56 Compare, for example, Ryan's utopian stance with Orgel's more sinister take.

57 For the long history of critical approaches which relate the figure of Prospero and his magic to the art of the dramatist, see Vaughan and Vaughan (eds), pp. 62–73 and Lindley (ed.), pp. 45–53.

58 See Vaughan and Vaughan (eds), pp. 98–108 and Lindley (ed.), pp. 33–5. Both editions also explicate the varying trends of theatrical productions to bring out colonial elements in the text, via the portrayal of Caliban.

59 See Egan, *Green Shakespeare*, pp. 148–71. For a lengthier exploration of the relationship between empire and deforestation, see Robert Pogue Harrison, *Forests: The Shadow of Civilisation* (Chicago: University of Chicago Press, 1993).

60 See also Prospero's later speech: 'to the dread-rattling thunder | Have I given fire and rifted Jove's stout oak | With his own bolt' (5.1.44–6).

61 Concerning the 'catalogue of tricks' in Act 5, Scene 1, Gabriel Egan contends that 'there seems little possibility that an audience will take it seriously' (Egan, *Green Shakespeare*, p. 167). However, in figuring Ariel both as lightning and as imprisonable by oak, the play establishes a range of lightning power.

62 The power of Prospero is apparently reflected by animals in his similar lines to Caliban: 'I'll rack thee with old cramps, | Fill all thy bones with aches, make thee roar, | That beasts tremble at thy din' (1.2.370–2). The natural, it seems, is subject to the supernatural at every level.

63 Watson, *Back to Nature*, p. 90.

64 Ibid., p. 104.

65 Ibid., p. 106.

66 It is remarkable that, despite all of *The Tempest*'s magic, and the characterisation of Caliban as a 'thing' or a 'monster', this is the play's only instance of 'unnatural', possibly suggesting that the word has been saved for the very irony I have pointed out.

67 Watson, *Back to Nature*, p. 324.

68 Gabriel Egan addresses this issue from a different angle, pointing to the archae-
    ological discovery of a thermoscope in Jacobean Jamestown, remarking that
    'somebody there was experimenting with devices that were used to measure
    and predict the weather, and which certain showmen claimed could be used to
    control the weather', *Green Shakespeare*, p. 153. See also B. J. Sokol, *A Brave New
    World of Knowledge: Shakespeare's* The Tempest *and Early Modern Epistemology*
    (Madison NJ: Farleigh Dickinson University Press, 2003), pp. 97–124.
69 *The Tempest*, ed. Vaughan and Vaughan, p. 285n.
70 See above, p. 88.
71 *The Tempest*, ed. Orgel, p. 204n.
72 Egan, 'This Rough Magic', p. 172.
73 *The Tempest*, ed. Orgel, p. 204n.
74 A parallel may be found in *The Taming of the Shrew*, as Petruchio, detailing to the
    audience his extreme plans for Katherina, demands: 'He that knows better how
    to tame a shrew, | Now let him speak: 'tis charity to show' (4.1.198–9). These lines,
    the closing ones of the soliloquy, are often said with an inviting or soliciting
    tone by actors in modern productions, who then linger in the inevitable silence.
    The 2006–7 Propeller production, dir. Edward Hall and the 2008–9 RSC produc-
    tion, dir. Conall Morrison are two recent examples.

Conclusion

1 See, for example, Thomas M. Lindsay, *Luther and the German Reformation*
   (Edinburgh: T&T Clark, 1913), p. 30.
2 Robert Parsons, *A Defence of the Censure* (London: R. Parsons, 1582), p. 45.
   Parsons goes on to question the validity of this version of events, citing the
   writers Charke, who disagrees with it, and Lyndan and Prateolus, who do not.
   Prateolus, it seems, included in his account the death, by lightning, of Luther's
   companion: see p. 49.
3 Ibid. 'It is not I' is the more common account of Luther's exclamation. See, for
   example, E. H. Erikson, *Young Man Luther: A Study in Psychoanalysis and History*
   (New York: Norton, 1958), p. 23.
4 Nathaniel Pallone and James Hennessy, 'Luther's Call and Nitrogen Narcosis',
   Current Psychology 13:4 (Winter, 1994–95), 371–4 (372).
5 Ibid.
6 John Boys, *An Exposition of the Festiuall Epistles* (London: Edward Griffin for
   William Aspley, 1615), fol. 1328; John Fisher, *The Sermon of Joh[a]n the Bysshop
   of Rochester made Agayn the P[er]nicious Doctryn of Martin Luther* (London:
   Wynkyn de Worde, [1527?]), p. 3.
7 For example, Knight in *The Shakespearian Tempest*, passim, and Ted Hughes in
   Shakespeare and the Goddess of Complete Being (London: Faber and Faber, 1992),
   pp. 382–417.

Select bibliography

Abenezrah, Kinki. *An Everlasting Prognostication of the Change of Weather* (London: M. Sparke, 1625).

Adelman, Janet. *Suffocating Mothers: Fantasies of Maternal Origin in Shakespeare's Plays*, Hamlet *to* The Tempest (London: Routledge, 1992).

Anglo, John. *Spectacle, Pageantry, and Early Tudor Policy* (Oxford: Clarendon Press, 1969).

Anon. *The First Part of the Reign of King Richard the Second, or Thomas of Woodstock*, ed. Wilhelmina P. Frijlinck (Malone Society Reprint, 1929).

Anon., I. F. (trans.). *Perpetuall and Naturall Prognostications of the Change of Weather* (London: J. Wolfe, 1591).

Anon. (J. C.). *A Pleasant Comedie Called The Two Merry Milke-Maids or The Best Words Weare the Garland* (London: Bernard Alsop for Lawrence Chapman, 1620).

Aristotle. *Meteorologica*, trans. H. D. P. Lee (Portsmouth, NH: Heinemann, 1952).

A[rmin], R[obert]. *The Valiant Welshman, or, The True Chronicle History of the Life and Valiant Deeds of Caradoc the Great, King of Cambria* (London: George Purslowe for Robert Lownes, 1615).

Astington, John H. 'Macbeth and the Rowe Illustrations', *Shakespeare Quarterly* 49 (Spring 1998), 83–6.

—— *English Court Theatre, 1558–1642* (Cambridge: Cambridge University Press, 1999).

Babington, John. *Pyrotechnia Or, A Discourse Of Artificiall Fire-Works...* (London: Thomas Harper for Ralph Mab, 1635).

Barnes, Barnabe. *Parthenophil and Parthenophe* (London: J. Wolfe, 1593).

—— *A Divine Centurie of Spirituall Sonnets* (London: John Windet, 1595).

—— *The Divils Charter a Tragedie* (London: G. E. for John Wright, 1607).

Bartholomaeus, Anglicus. *Batman uppon Bartholome his Booke De Proprietatibus Rerum, Newly Corrected, Enlarged and Amended*, trans. Stephen Batman (London: Thomas East, 1582).

Barton, Anne. *Shakespeare and the Idea of the Play* (London: Chatto & Windus, 1962).

Bate, John. *The Mysteres of Natvre and Art: The Second Booke, Teaching Most Plainly, and Withal most Exactly, the Composing of all Manner of Fire-works for Triumph and Recreation* (London: Ralph Mab, 1634).

Bate, Jonathan. *Romantic Ecology: Wordsworth and the Environmental Tradition* (London: Routledge, 1991).

Bate, Jonathan and Eric Rasmussen (eds). *The RSC Shakespeare: The Complete Works* (Basingstoke: Macmillan, 2007).

Batman, Stephen. *The Doome Warining all Men to the Judgement* (London: R. Newberry, 1581).

Bennett, Josephine Waters. 'The Storm Within: The Madness of Lear', *Shakespeare Quarterly* 13:2 (1962), 137–55.

Bentley, Gerald Eades. *The Jacobean and Caroline Stage*, 7 vols (Oxford: Clarendon Press, 1941–68).

Bergeron, David M. *English Civic Pageantry, 1558–1642* (Columbia: University of South Carolina Press, 1971).

Bevington, David, Lars Engle, Katherine Eisman Maus and Eric Rasmussen (eds). *English Renaissance Drama: A Norton Anthology* (New York: Norton, 2002).

Bishop, T. G. *Shakespeare and the Theatre of Wonder* (Cambridge: Cambridge University Press, 1996).

Bloom, Harold. *Shakespeare: The Invention of the Human* (New York: Riverhead, 1998).

Blumenberg, Hans. *Shipwreck With Spectator*, trans. Steven Rendall (Cambridge, MA: MIT Press, 1997).

Bohun, Ralph. *A Discourse Concerning the Origine and Properties of the Winde* (Oxford: W. Hall, 1671).

Bolton, Robert. *Some Generall Directions for a Comfortable Walking with God* (London: Felix Kyngston for Edmund Weaver, 1626).

Booth, Stephen. *King Lear, Macbeth, Indefinition and Tragedy* (New Haven, CT: Yale University Press, 1983).

Bowsher, Julian and Pat Miller. *The Rose and the Globe – Playhouses of Shakespeare's Bankside, Southwark. Excavations 1988–90* (London: Museum of London, 2009).

Boys, John. *An Exposition of the Festivall Epistles* (London: Edward Griffin for William Aspley, 1615).

Bradley, A. C. *Shakespearean Tragedy* (Basingstoke: Macmillan, 1985).

Bruckner, Lynne and Dan Brayton (eds). *Ecocritical Shakespeare* (Farnham: Ashgate, 2011).

Buell, Lawrence. *The Environmental Imagination: Thoreau, Nature Writing, and the Formation of American Culture* (Cambridge, MA: Harvard University Press, 1995).

Bullough, G. (ed.). *Narrative and Dramatic Sources of Shakespeare*, 8 vols (London: Routledge and Kegan Paul, 1973).

Burton, William. *Ten Sermons* (London: Richard Field for Thomas Man, 1602).

Butterworth, Philip. *Theatre of Fire: Special Effects in Early English and Scottish Theatre* (London: Society for Theatre Research, 1998).

Bruckner, Lynne and Dan Brayton (eds). *Ecocritical Shakespeare* (Farnham: Ashgate, 2011).

Chambers, E. K. *The Elizabethan Stage*, 4 vols (Oxford: Clarendon, 1923).

Chion, Michel. *Audio-vision: Sound on Screen*, ed. and trans. Claudia Gorbman (New York: Columbia University Press, 1994).

Church of England. *The Order of Prayer, and other Exercises, upon Wednesdayes and Frydayes, to Avert and Turne Gods wrath from us, Threatned by the Late Terrible Earthquake: to be used in all parish churches and housholdes throughout the realme* (London: Christopher Barker, 1580).

Clark, Stuart. *Thinking with Demons: The Idea of Witchcraft in Early Modern Europe* (Oxford: Clarendon, 1997).

Clark, Timothy. 'Towards a Deconstructive Environmental Criticism', *Oxford Literary Review* 30:1 (2008), 44–68.

Cobb, Christopher. 'Storm versus Story: Form and Affective Power in Shakespeare's Romances', in Stephen Cohen (ed.), *Shakespeare and Historical Formalism* (Aldershot: Ashgrave, 2007), pp. 95–124.

Cormack, Bradin. 'Marginal Waters: *Pericles* and the Idea of Jurisdiction', in Andrew Gordon and Bernhard Klein (eds), *Literature, Mapping, and the Politics of Space in Early Modern Britain* (Cambridge: Cambridge University Press, 2001), pp. 155–80.

Cortes, Martin. *The Arte of Navigation*, trans. Richard Eden (London: R. Jugge, 1561).

Coupe, Laurence (ed.). *The Green Studies Reader: From Romanticism to Ecocriticism* (London: Routledge, 2000).

Coursen, Herbert R. *Christian Ritual and the World of Shakespeare's Tragedies* (Lewisburg, PA.: Bucknell University Press, 1976).

Cunningham, William. *The Cosmographical Glasse* (London: J. Day, 1559).

Dawson, Antony B. and Paul Yachnin. *The Culture of Playgoing in Shakespeare's England: A Collaborative Debate* (Cambridge: Cambridge University Press, 2001).

Deacon, John. *Dialogicall Discourses* (London: George Bishop, 1601).

Dekker, Thomas. *If it Be not Good, the Devil is in it* (London: Thomas Creede for John Trundle, 1612).

——*A Strange Horse-Race* (London: Joseph Hunt, 1613).

Dent, R. W. *Shakespeare's Proverbial Language: An Index* (Berkeley, CA: University of California Press, 1981).

Dessen, Alan C. *Elizabethan Stage Conventions and Modern Interpreters* (Cambridge: Cambridge University Press, 1984).

Dessen, Alan C. and Leslie Thomson. *A Dictionary of Stage Directions in English Drama 1580–1642* (Cambridge: Cambridge University Press, 1999).

Dollimore, Jonathan. *Radical Tragedy: Religion, Ideology and Power in the Drama of Shakespeare and His Contemporaries* (Basingstoke: Palgrave Macmillan, 3rd edn, 2004).

Dollimore, Jonathan and Alan Sinfield (eds). *Political Shakespeare: Essays in Cultural Materialism* (Manchester: Manchester University Press, 2nd edn, 1994).

Duncan-Jones, Katherine. *Ungentle Shakespeare: Scenes From His Life* (London: Arden Shakespeare, 2001).

Dunn, E. Catherine. 'The Storm in King Lear', *Shakespeare Quarterly* 3:4 (1952), 329–33.

Dustagheer, Sarah. 'Repertory and the Production of Theatre Space at the Globe and the Blackfriars, 1599–1613' (Unpublished PhD thesis, University of London, 2012).

Dutton, Richard (ed.). *Jacobean Civil Pageants* (Keele: Keele University Press, 1995).

Eamon, William. 'Technology as Magic in the Late Middle Ages and the Renaissance', *Janus* 70 (1983), 171–212.

Egan, Gabriel. *Green Shakespeare: From Ecopolitics to Ecocriticism* (Abingdon: Routledge, 2006).

Egan, Robert. 'This Rough Magic: Perspectives of Art and Morality in *The Tempest*', *Shakespeare Quarterly* 23:2 (Spring, 1972), 171–82.

Elton, William R. *King Lear and the Gods* (Lexington, KY: University Press of Kentucky, 1966).

Erikson, E. H. *Young Man Luther: A Study in Psychoanalysis and History* (New York: Norton, 1958).

Estok, Simon C. *Ecocriticism and Shakespeare: Reading Ecophobia* (New York: Palgrave Macmillan, 2011).

Estok, Simon C. 'Afterword: Ecocriticism on the Lip of a Lion', in Lynne Bruckner and Dan Brayton (eds), *Ecocritical Shakespeare* (Farnham: Ashgate, 2011), pp. 239–46.

Evett, David. *Literature and the Visual Arts in Tudor England* (Athens, GA: University of Georgia Press, 1990).

Falconer, A. F. *Shakespeare and the Sea* (London: Constable, 1964).

Farmer, Norman K. *Poets and the Visual Arts in Renaissance England* (Austin: University of Texas Press, 1984).

Fenton, Edward. *Certaine Secrete Wonders of Nature* (London: Henry Bynneman, 1569).

Fisher, John. *The Sermon of Joh[a]n the Bysshop of Rochester made Agayn the P[er]nicious Doctryn of Martin Luther* (London: Wynkyn de Worde, [1527?] 1527).

Fleming, Abraham. *A Bright Burning Beacon* (London: Henry Denham, 1580).

Fletcher, John. *Comedies and Tragedies Written by Francis Beaumont and John Fletcher ... Never Printed Before* (London: Humphrey Robinson, 1647).

Floyd-Wilson, Mary and Garrett A. Sullivan, Jr. *Environment and Embodiment in Early Modern England* (Basingstoke: Palgrave Macmillan, 2007).

Foakes, R. A. *Illustrations of the English Stage, 1580–1642* (Stanford, CA: University of California Press, 1985).

—— *Shakespeare and Violence* (Cambridge: Cambridge University Press, 2003).

—— 'Performance and Text: King Lear', *Medieval and Renaissance Drama in England* 17 (2005), 86–98.

Foakes, R. A. and R. T. Rickert (eds). *Henslowe's Diary* (Cambridge: Cambridge University Press, 1961).

Freehafer, John. 'Leonard Digges, Ben Johnson, and the Beginning of Shakespeare Idolatry', *Shakespeare Quarterly* 21:1 (Winter, 1970), 63–75.

Friesen, Ryan Curtis. *Supernatural Fiction in Early Modern Drama and Culture* (Eastbourne: Sussex Academic Press, 2010).

Frye, Northrop. *The Great Code: The Bible and Literature* (New York: Harcourt Brace Jovanovich, 1982).

Fulke, William. *A Goodly Gallery with a most Pleasant Prospect* (London: William Griffith, 1563).

Garrard, Greg. *Ecocriticism: The New Critical Idiom* (London: Routledge, 2004).

Godfridus. *The Booke of Knowledge of things Unknowne Apperteynynge to Astronomye* (London: R. Wyer, [1530?]).

Golding, Arthur. *A Discourse upon the Earthquake* (London: Henry Bynneman, 1580).

Goodrum, Matthew R. 'Questioning Thunderstones and Arrowheads: The Problem of Recognising and Interpreting Stone Artefacts in the Seventeenth Century', *Early Science and Medicine* 13 (2008), 482–508.

Gower, John. *Confessio Amantis* in *The English Works of John Gower*, ed. G. C. Macaulay, 2 vols (Oxford: Clarendon Press, 1901–02).

Grady, Hugh. 'On the Need for a Differentiated Theory of (Early) Modern Subjects', in John J. Joughin (ed.), *Philosophical Shakespeares* (London: Routledge, 2000), pp. 34–50.

Greg, W. W. (ed.). *Dramatic Documents from the Elizabethan Playhouses: Stage Plots, Actors' Parts, Prompt Books*, 2 vols (Oxford: Clarendon Press, 1931, 1969).

Green, Janet M. 'Earthy Doom and Heavenly Thunder: Judgement in King Lear', *The University of Dayton Review* 23 (Spring 1995), 63–73.

Greenblatt, Stephen. *Will in the World: How Shakespeare Became Shakespeare* (New York: Norton, 2004).

Greenblatt, Stephen, Walter Cohen, Jean E. Howard and Katherine Eisaman Maus (eds), *The Norton Shakespeare*, (New York: Norton, 2nd edn, 2008).

Gurr, Andrew. *Playgoing in Shakespeare's London* (Cambridge: Cambridge University Press, 1987).

—— 'The *Tempest*'s Tempest at Blackfriars', *Shakespeare Survey* 41 (1989), 91–102.

—— *The Shakespearean Playing Companies* (Oxford: Clarendon Press, 1996).

—— 'The Condition of Theatre in England in 1599', in Jane Milling and Peter Thomson (eds), *The Cambridge History of British Theatre, Volume 1: Origins to 1660* (Cambridge: Cambridge University Press, 2004), pp. 264–81.

Gurr, Andrew and Mariko Ichikawa. *Staging in Shakespeare's Theatres* (Oxford: Oxford University Press, 2000).

Hadfield, Andrew. *Shakespeare and Renaissance Politics* (London: Arden Shakespeare, 2003).

Hakluyt, Richard (ed.). *Principal Navigations* (London: George Bishop, 1599–1600).

Halpern, Richard. *Shakespeare Among the Moderns* (Ithaca, NY: Cornell University Press, 1997).

Hamilton, Jennifer Mae, "'What is the Cause of Thunder?" A Study of the Storm in *King Lear*' (Unpublished PhD thesis, University of New South Wales, 2012).

Harbage, Alfred. *Shakespeare's Audience* (New York: Columbia University Press, 1941).

Harrison, G. B. *The Life and Death of Robert Devereux Earl of Essex* (London: Cassell., 1937).

Harrison, Robert Pogue. *Forests: The Shadow of Civilisation* (Chicago: University of Chicago Press, 1993).

Harward, Simon. *A Discourse of the Severall Kinds and Causes of Lightnings* (London: J. Windet, 1607).

Hattaway, Michael. *Elizabethan Popular Theatre: Plays in Performance* (London: Routledge, 1982).

Hawkes, Terence. *William Shakespeare*: King Lear (Plymouth: Northcote House, 1995).

Hawkins, H. *Strange Attractors: Literature, Culture and Chaos Theory* (Hertfordshire: Prentice Hall, 1995).

Heninger, S. K. *A Handbook of Renaissance Meteorology, with Particular Reference to Elizabethan and Jacobean Literature* (New York: Greenwood Press, 1968).

Hewitt, Bernard (ed.). *The Renaissance Stage: Documents of Serlio, Sabbattini and Furttenbach*, trans. Allarryce Nicoll, John H. McDowell and George R. Kernodle (Miami: University of Miami Press, 1958).

Heywood, Thomas. *The Second Part of, If you Know not Me, you Know no Bodie* (London: Nathaniel Butler, 1606).

—— *The Golden Age. Or The Lives of Jupiter and Saturne, with the Defining of the Heathen Gods* (London: William Barrenger, 1611).

—— *The Silver Age, Including The Love of Jupiter to Alcmena: The Birth of Hercules. And The Rape of Proserpine* (London: Nicholas Okes, 1613).

—— *The Brazen Age* (London: Nicholas Okes, 1613).

—— *The Iron Age* (London: Nicholas Okes, 1632).

—— *The Second Part of the Iron Age* (London: Nicholas Okes, 1632).

—— *Loves Mistresse: or The Queenes Masque* (London: John Raworth, 1640).

Hill, Thomas. *A Contemplation of Mysteries* (London: Henry Denham, 1574).

—— *The Profitable Arte of Gardening* (London: Henry Bynneman, 1574).

—— *The Moste Pleasuante Arte of the Interpretacion of Dreames* (London: Thomas Marsh, 1576).

Holinshed, Raphael. *Holinshed's Chronicles of England, Scotland, and Ireland* (London: Henry Denham, 1586).

Holland, Henry. *A Treatise against Witchcraft: or A Dialogue, wherein the Greatest Doubts Concerning that Sinne, are Briefly Answered* (Cambridge: John Legatt, 1590).

Holland, Peter. 'Coasting in the Mediterranean: The Journeyings of *Pericles*', in Neils B. Hansen and Sos Haugaard (eds), *Angles on the English-Speaking World* (Copenhagen: Museum Tusculanum Press, 2005), pp. 11–31.

Hooke, Robert. 'A Method for Making a History of the Weather', in Thomas Sprat (ed.), *The History of the Royal-Society* (London: J. Martyn, 1667).

House, Ian W. O. '"I know thee well enough": The Two Plots of *King Lear*', *English* 170:41 (1992), 97–112.

Hughes, Ted. *Shakespeare and the Goddess of Complete Being* (London: Faber and Faber, 1992).

Huloet, Richard. *Huloets Dictionarie Newelye Corrected* (London: Thomas Marshil, 1572).

Hunter, Robert G. *Shakespeare and the Mystery of God's Judgements* (Athens, GA: University of Georgia Press, 1976).

Huntley, Frank L. 'Macbeth and the Background of Jesuitical Equivocation', *PMLA* 79:4 (Sept. 1964), 390–400.

Huxley, H. H. 'Storm and Shipwreck in Roman Literature', *Greece and Rome* 21:63 (1952), 117–24.

Johnson, Richard. *The Second Part of the Famous History of the Seaven Champions of Christendome* (London: Cuthbert Burbie, 1597).

Jonson, Ben. *The Complete Plays in Two Volumes*, ed. Felix E. Schelling (London: J. M. Dent & Sons, 1960).

Jowett, John. 'New Created Creatures: Ralph Crane and the Stage Directions in *The Tempest*', *Shakespeare Survey* 36 (1983), 107–20.

Kermode, Frank. *The Sense of an Ending* (London: Oxford University Press, 1967).

Kiefer, Frederick. *Shakespeare's Visual Theatre: Staging the Personified Characters* (Cambridge: Cambridge University Press, 2003).

Killigrew, Thomas. *The Prisoners in The Prisoners And Claracilla. Two Tragæ-Comedies* (London: T. Cotes, 1641).

Kirsch, Arthur. 'The Emotional Landscape of *King Lear*', *Shakespeare Quarterly* 39:2 (Summer, 1988), 154–70.

Knight, G. Wilson. *Principles of Shakespearean Production with Especial Reference to Tragedies* (New York: Macmillan, 1937).

—— *The Shakespearian Tempest* (London: Methuen, 1953).

Lacey, R. *Robert Earl of Essex: An Elizabethan Icarus* (London: The History Book Club, 1970).

Lindley, David. *Shakespeare and Music* (London: Cengage, 2006).

Lucretius. *On the Nature of the Universe*, trans. R. E. Latham (London: Penguin, 1951).

Lyne, Raphael. *Shakespeare's Late Work* (Oxford: Oxford University Press, 2007).

Macfarlane, Alan. *Witchcraft in Tudor and Stuart England* (London: Routledge, 2nd edn, 1999).

Mallet, R. *Catalogue of Earthquakes from 1606 B.C. to 1755* (London: John Murray, 1853).

Maplet, John. *The Diall of Destiny* (London: Thomas Marsh, 1581).

Marlowe, Christopher. *The Complete Works of Christopher Marlowe*, ed. Fredson Bowers, 2 vols (Cambridge: Cambridge University Press, 1981).

—— *Tamburlaine Part I*, ed. David Fuller (Oxford: Clarendon, 1998).

Marston, John. *The Wonder of Women or The Tragedie of Sophonisba* (London: John Windet, 1606).

Martin, Craig. *Renaissance Meteorology: Pomponazzi to Descartes* (Baltimore: Johns Hopkins University Press, 2011).

Marx, Steven. *Shakespeare and the Bible* (Oxford: Oxford University Press, 2000).

Massinger, Philip. *The Unnatural Combat* (London: John Waterson, 1639).

Melton, John. *The Astrologaster, or, the Figure-caster* (London: Barnard Alsop for Edward Blackmore, 1620).

Mentz, Steve. 'Strange Weather in *King Lear*', *Shakespeare* 6:2 (2010), 139–52.

Meredith, Peter. 'Stage Directions and the Editing of Early English Drama', in *Editing Early English Drama: Special Problems and New Directions* (New York: AMS Press, 1987), pp. 66–94.

Middleton, Thomas. *Thomas Middleton: The Collected Works*, ed. Gary Taylor et al. (Oxford: Oxford University Press, 2007).

Monardes, Nicolas. *The Booke Which Treateth of the Snow*, in John Frampton (ed. and trans.), *Joyfull Newes out of the New-found Worlde* (London: William Norton, 1596).

Montaigne, Miguel de. *Essays done into English, according to the last French Edition, by John Florio* (London: Melch. Bradwood for Edward Blount and William Barret, 1613).

Morton, Timothy. *Ecology Without Nature: Rethinking Environmental Aesthetics* (Cambridge, MA: Harvard University Press, 2007).

—— *The Ecological Thought* (Cambridge, MA: Harvard University Press, 2010).

Mossman, Judith. 'Henry V and Plutarch's Alexander', *Shakespeare Quarterly* 45 (1994), 57–73.

Nathan, Norman. '*Pericles* and Jonah', *Notes & Queries* (Jan. 1956), 10–11.

Nausea, Frederick. *A Treatise of Blazing Starres in Generall*, trans. Abraham Fleming (London: B. Alsop, 1618).

Nevo, Ruth. *Shakespeare's Other Language* (New York: Methuen, 1987).

Nicholl, Allardyce. *Stuart Masques and the Renaissance Stage* (New York: Benjamin Blom, Inc., 1968).

Nicolay, Nicholas de. *The Navigations, Peregrinations and Voyages, Made into Turkie*, trans. T. Washington (London: Thomas Dawson, 1585).

Ogden, James. 'Lear's Blasted Heath', in James Ogden and Arthur H. Scouten (eds), *Lear from Study to Stage: Essays in Criticism* (London: Associated University Presses, 1997), pp. 135–46.

Ovid. *The XV Bookes of P. Ovidius Naso, Entytuled Metamorphosis, Translated oute of Latin into English Meeter, by Arthur Golding Gentleman, a Worke very Pleasaunt and Delectable*, trans. Arthur Golding (London: William Seres, 1567).

—— *The Three First Bookes of Ovid de Tristibus translated into English*, trans. Thomas Churchyard (London: Thomas Marsh, 1580).

—— *Ovid's Metamorphosis Englished*, trans. George Sandys (London: Robert Young, 1628).

Pallone, Nathaniel and James Hennessy. 'Luther's Call and Nitrogen Narcosis', *Current Psychology* 13:4 (Winter, 1994–95), 371–4.

Parsons, Robert. *A Defence of the Censure* (Rouen: R. Parsons, 1582).

Paul, H. N. *The Royal Play of Macbeth* (London: Macmillan, 1950).

Peele, George. *The Battell of Alacazar* (London: Edward Allde, 1594).

Perkins, William. *A Discourse of the Damned Art of Witchcraft* (Cambridge: Cantrel Legge, 1608).

Phillips, Bill. 'The Rape of Mother Earth in Seventeenth Century English Poetry: An Ecofeminist Interpretation', *Atlantis: Revista de la Asociacion Espanola de Estudios Anglo-Norteamericanos* 26 (2004), 49–60.

Pliny the Elder. *The History of World Commonly called, the Naturall Historie of C. Plinius Secundus*, trans. Philemon Holland (London: Adam Islip, 1601).

—— *Natural History*, trans. H. Rackham (Bury St Edmunds: Loeb, 1997).

Proudfoot, Richard, Ann Thompson and David Scott Kastan (eds). *The Arden Shakespeare Complete Works* (London: Arden Shakespeare, 2001).

Relihan, C. 'Liminal Geography: *Pericles* and the Politics of Place', *Philological Quarterly* 71:3 (1992), 281–99.

Roberts, Alexander. *A Treatise of Witchcraft* (London: Nicholas Oakes for Samuel Man, 1616).

Robinson, John. *Observations Divine and Morall* ([Amsterdam]: [successors of Giles Thorp], 1625).

Ronan, Clifford. *'Antike Roman': Power Symbology and the Roman Play in Early Modern England, 1585–1635* (Athens, GA: University of Georgia Press, 1995).

Rosenberg, Martin. *The Masks of King Lear* (Berkeley: University of California Press, 1972).

Royle, Nicholas. *Telepathy and Literature: Essays on the Reading Mind* (Oxford: Blackwell, 1991).

—— 'The Poet: *Julius Caesar* and the Democracy to Come', *Oxford Literary Review* 25 (2003), 39–62.

—— 'Derrida's Event', in Simon Glendinning and Robert Eaglestone (eds), *Derrida's Legacies: Literature and Philosophy* (Abingdon: Routledge, 2008), pp. 36–44.

Rutter, Carol Chillington (ed.). *Documents of the Rose Playhouse* (Manchester: Manchester University Press, 1999).

Ryan, Kiernan (ed.). *New Historicism and Cultural Materialism: A Reader* (London: Arnold, 1996).

—— *Shakespeare* (Hampshire: Palgrave, 2002).

Saluste du Bartas, Guilaume de. *Bartas His Devine Weekes & Workes*, trans. Joshua Sylvester (London: H. Lownes, 1605).

Scot, Reginald. *Discoverie of Witchcraft* (London: William Brome, 1584).

Scott, William O. 'Macbeth's – And Our – Self-Equivocations', *Shakespeare Quarterly* 37:2 (Summer, 1986), 160–74.

Seneca, Lucius Aannaeus. *The Workes. Both Morrall and Natural*, trans. Thomas Lodge (London: William Stansby, 1614).

Serlio, Sebastiano. *The Five Books of Architecture: An Unabridged Reprint of the English Edition of 1611* (New York: Dover Publications, 1982).

Shaheen, Naseeb. 'Shakespeare's Knowledge of the Bible – How Acquired', *Shakespeare Studies* 20 (1988), 201–14.

—— *Biblical References in Shakespeare's Plays* (Newark: University of Delaware Press, 1999).

Shakelton, Francis. *A Blazyng Starre or Burnyng Beacon, Seene the 10 of October Laste* (London: John Kingston, 1580).

Shakespeare, William. *Henry VI, Part 1*, Arden 3rd Series, ed. Edward Burns (London: Thomson Learning, 2001).

—— *Julius Caesar*, Arden 3rd Series, ed. David Daniell (London: Thomson Learning, 2005).

—— *Julius Caesar*, Oxford Shakespeare, ed. A. Humphreys (Oxford: Oxford University Press, 1984).

—— *Julius Caesar*, New Cambridge Shakespeare, ed. Martin Spevack (Cambridge: Cambridge University Press, 2003).

—— *King Lear*, Arden 2nd Series, ed. Kenneth Muir (London: Methuen, 1952).

—— *King Lear*, Arden 3rd Series, ed. R. A. Foakes (London: Arden, 2007).

—— *King Lear*, Oxford Shakespeare, ed. Stanley Wells (Oxford: Oxford University Press, 2001).

—— *Macbeth*, Arden 2nd Series, ed. Kenneth Muir (London: Methuen, 1959).

—— *Macbeth*, New Cambridge Shakespeare, ed. A. R. Braunmuller (Cambridge: Cambridge University Press, 1998).

—— *Pericles*, Arden 2nd Series, ed. F. D. Hoeniger (London: Methuen, 1963).

—— *Pericles*, Arden 3rd Series, ed. Suzanne Gossett (London: Thomson Learning, 2004).

—— *Pericles*, Oxford Shakespeare, ed. Roger Warren (Oxford: Oxford University Press, 2003).

—— *Pericles*, ed. Doreen DelVecchio and Antony Hammond (Cambridge: Cambridge University Press, 1998).

—— *The Tempest*, Arden 3rd Series, ed. Virginia Mason Vaughan and Alden T. Vaughan (London: Cengage Learning, 1999).

—— *The Tempest*, Oxford Shakespeare, ed. Stephen Orgel (Oxford: Oxford University Press, 1998).

—— *The Tempest*, New Cambridge Shakespeare, ed. David Lindley (Cambridge: Cambridge University Press, 2002).

Shapiro, James. *1599: A Year in the Life of William Shakespeare* (London: Faber and Faber, 2005).

Shirley, Frances Ann. *Shakespeare's Use of Off-Stage Sounds* (Lincoln, NE: University of Nebraska Press, 1963).

Sinfield, Alan. 'Macbeth: History, Ideology and Intellectuals', Critical Quarterly 28:1 (1986), 63–77.

Smith, Bruce. The Acoustic World of Early Modern England (Chicago: University of Chicago Press, 1999).

Sohmer, Steve. Shakespeare's Mystery Play: The Opening of the Globe Theatre 1599 (Manchester: Manchester University Press, 1999).

Sokol, B. J. A Brave New World of Knowledge: Shakespeare's The Tempest and Early Modern Epistemology (Madison, NJ: Farleigh Dickinson University Press, 2003).

Southern, Richard. 'The Stage Groove and the Thunder Run', Architectural Review 95 (May 1944), 135–6.

Spencer, T. J. B. (ed.). Shakespeare's Plutarch: The Lives of Julius Caesar, Brutus, Marcus Antonius, and Coriolanus in the translation of Sir Thomas North (London: Penguin, 1964).

Spenser, Edmund. The Faerie Queen; and, The Shepheards's Calendar: together with other works of England's Arch-poet (London: Humphrey Lownes, 1611).

Stallybrass, Peter. 'Macbeth and Witchcraft', in J. R. Brown (ed.), Focus on Macbeth, (London: Routledge, 1982), pp. 189–210.

Stuart, James. Daemonologie, in Forme of a Dialogue (Edinburgh: Robert Walde, 1597).

Taylor, M. A. 'He that did the Tiger Board', Shakespeare Quarterly 15 (Winter, 1964), 110–13.

Taylor, Thomas. Christs Combate (Cambridge: Cantrell Legge, 1618).

Thomas, Keith. Religion and the Decline of Magic (London: Weidenfeld and Nicolson, 1971).

Thomson, Leslie. 'The Meaning of Thunder and Lightning: Stage Directions and Audience Expectations', Early Theatre 2 (1999), 11–24.

Turner, Henry S. 'King Lear Without: The Heath', Renaissance Drama 28 (1997), 161–93.

Twyne, Laurence. The Pattern of Painefull Adventures (London: Valentine Simmes for the Widow Newman, 1594).

Twyne, Thomas. A View of Certain Wonderful Effects, of Late Dayes come to Passe (London: John Charlewood, 1578).

—— A Shorte and Pithie Discourse, Concerning the Engendring, Tokens, and Effects of all Earthquakes (London: John Charlewood, 1580).

Vaughan, Alden T. 'William Strachey's "True Repertory" and Shakespeare: A Closer Look at the Evidence', Shakespeare Quarterly 59:3 (Fall 2008), 245–73.

Viguers, Susan. 'The Storm in King Lear', College Language Association Journal 43 (March 2000), 338–66.

Virgil. Virgil's Georgicks Englished, trans. Thomas May (London: Humphrey Lownes, 1628).

Watkins, Ronald and Jeremy Lemon. In Shakespeare's Playhouse: Macbeth (London: David & Charles, 1974).

Watson, Robert N. Back to Nature: The Green and the Real in the Late Renaissance (Philadelphia: University of Pennsylvania Press 2006).

Webbe, William. *A Discourse of English Poetrie* (London: John Charlewood for Robert Walley 1586).

Weir, Alison. *Elizabeth the Queen* (London: Pimlico, 1998).

Wells, Stanley, Gary Taylor, John Jowett and William Montgomery (eds), *William Shakespeare: The Complete Works* (Oxford: Oxford University Press, 2nd edn, 2005).

Williams, George W. 'The Poetry of the Storm in King Lear', *Shakespeare Quarterly* 2:1 (1951), 57–71.

Williams, Harriet. 'Sizzling Skies', *New Scientist* 2272 (6 Jan. 2001), 14–19.

Wilkins, George. *The Miseries of Inforst Mariage* (London: [William Jaggard] for George Vincent, 1607).

—— *The Painfull Adventures of Pericles Prince of Tyre*, ed. K. Muir (Liverpool: University of Liverpool, 1953).

Wilson, J. Dover. *Six Tragedies of Shakespeare: An Introduction for the Plain Man* (London: Longmans, 1929).

Wilson, Richard. '"Is this a Holiday?" Shakespeare's Roman Carnival', *English Literary History* 54 (1987), 31–44.

—— (ed.). *New Historicism and Renaissance Drama* (London: Longman, 1992).

—— *Will Power: Essays on Shakespearean Authority* (Hemel Hempstead: Harvester Wheatsheaf, 1993).

Wilson, Richard and Richard Dutton (eds). *New Historicism and Renaissance Drama* (London: Longman, 1992).

'W. S.' *The Puritaine or The Widdow of Watling-Streete* (London: G. Eld, 1607).

Wyke, Maria (ed.). *Julius Caesar in Western Culture* (Oxford: Blackwell 2006).

Index

Lightning Source UK Ltd.
Milton Keynes UK
UKOW06n0452200816

281123UK00017B/452/P